GLORY to GRAVE

THE NOT SO ORDINARY LIVES OF NINE CIVIL WAR NOTABLES

Bill Kolasinski

William Kolasinski

ISBN-13: 978-1530544721
ISBN-10: 1530544726

DEDICATION

For my daughters, Kate and Krista,
my grandchildren Anna and Will
and any grandchildren yet to come.
I hope you never grow too old to dream.

CONTENTS

ACKNOWLEDGEMENTS

As a sophomore in high school I read an abridged version of the Life Of Abraham Lincoln by Carl Sandburg. His beautiful prose dazzled me, and started me on a lifelong study of the history of America in the 19th century. Many years later, two of my oldest friends published books of their own. Ron Levitsky wrote a series of thee books chronicling the cases of Nate Rosen, a fictional Jewish lawyer. Gary Koca wrote a book on Forgotten Movie Stars of the 1940's and 50's, and another on Great Cub Players Since 1876. Their works inspired me to contribute something of my own to the books of the Civil War era. When I finally began to write, Gary was a much needed mentor I relied on for advice.

Three years of research and writing led me to complete Glory to Grave, The Not So Ordinary Lives of Nine Civil War Notables. The title was a suggestion from my creative and intelligent grand-daughter, Anna Doane. The cover art is designed by my artist/daughter Kate Doane. Kate and Scott Doane provided much needed help with formatting. I am forever grateful to my wife for the patience she displayed while I spent more time working on this book than I did on household duties. Her confidence that I could get it done kept me on task, and her computer skills helped me through countless "oops" moments as I typed out the manuscript.

Thanks also to my proof readers, Mary Lynn Fontaine, Mike Harper and Gary Koca, for helping minimize the damage I did to the King's English.

This book is for all those people young and old, just beginning to explore the countless fascinating stories about Civil War times. You have years of thrilling reading ahead of you!

William Kolasinski

1

THE SUPERB SOLDIER

Winfield Scott Hancock

A lone horseman, sitting tall and erect in the saddle, calmly picked his way through the bodies and wreckage strewn all along the crest of the hill. Screams of wounded and frightened horses mixed with the deafening explosion of rebel artillery shells bursting overhead, raining down a lethal shower of shrapnel that tore apart men and equipment alike. Winfield Scott Hancock, commander of the Second Corps, Army of the Potomac, was doing his job this afternoon in July 1863, as the general in charge of defending the center of the Union line at Gettysburg. The greatest artillery barrage in the history of North America was just ending, and Hancock knew the rebel infantry would be coming soon to attack their position. His troops were still hugging the ground, thankful for these few extra minutes of life. They marveled at his display of fearlessness as he rode among them, the most conspicuous target on Cemetery Hill. The soldiers' reaction soon changed into frantic concern for his safety as they shouted out to him to move to the rear, where he could command them from a safe distance. He would have none of that. "There are times," he told those who could hear," when the life of a corps commander just isn't that important." He rode on calling on the men to stand and take positions to repel the massive assault now heading directly at them from across a mile of farm field. He could clearly see the rebel bayonets gleaming in the midday sun, row upon row of them moving toward his men like a huge silver wave about to crash against their lines. As he busied himself coolly aligning his men to meet the 15,000 Confederate infantrymen moving toward them he felt a sharp pain in his groin, and a powerful blow like a boxer's punch. The bullet that struck him spun him in his saddle and knocked him to the ground. The wound was serious, and though he would survive it, it would keep him out of the war for a full year, and remind him painfully for the rest of his life, of his awful, glory filled moments in Pennsylvania.

***

Winfield Scott Hancock was born on February 15, 1824 in Montgomery, Pennsylvania to Benjamin Franklin Hancock and Elizabeth Hoxworth Hancock. Elizabeth also gave birth that day to Winfield's identical twin brother, Hilary Baker Hancock. Winfield was named after a hero of the War of 1812, Major General Winfield Scott.

Winfield's father Benjamin was a school teacher who began studying law when Winfield was only a few years old. He was admitted to the bar in 1828 and moved the family to Norristown, Pennsylvania, where he established a practice, became a deacon of the local church and became active in local Democratic Party politics. Winfield was taught reverence for the law, due process and Democratic Party principles from an early age.

Winfield and his brother Hilary attended Norristown Academy together, and were seen by others to be inseparable and indistinguishable, participating in the usual hijinks of boys their age. But they were also studious and respectful. Eliphalet Roberts, Winfield's teacher said of him "I never found a knife mark on his section of the long, old fashioned white pine desk, nor was I ever obliged to speak to him about its condition."

By age 13 Winfield was recognized in his community as one of the town's brightest and best youngsters when he was selected to read the Declaration of Independence at the Fourth of July celebration. One year later the local Congressman, a relative of his father, wrote to the Secretary of War requesting that Winfield receive an appointment to the United Sates Military Academy at West Point. On March 31, 1840 Winfield accepted the appointment, beginning his lifelong career in the army.

In 1844, after completing four years of training and earning mediocre grades in academics, Winfield graduated in the bottom third of his class. This insured that he would receive a posting in the least prestigious of the army's branches. The best and brightest went to the Corps of Engineers, then to topographical engineers, ordnance, artillery and dragoons. The rest received commissions in the infantry. Winfield received a commission as a second lieutenant in the Sixth Infantry Regiment.

***

Two years later the United States entered into a war with Mexico. Each side claimed the other was responsible for beginning the conflict, but neither was willing to back off once the shooting started on the Rio Grande River.

Hancock served in the Mexican War, then the Third Seminole War, the plains conflicts in Kansas and the Mormon rebellion in Utah. Throughout all these assignments his reputation and rank rose, reaching its high point with his command of the Second Corps of the Army of the Potomac as it defended the center of the Union line at the battle of Gettysburg. After he received a serious wound, his

Second Corps fought on desperately and repulsed Pickett's Charge. Hancock's coolness under fire won the admiration of the nation. After months in recovery he went on to command the Second Corps of infantry in the Army of the Potomac until 1865, when Robert E. Lee surrendered his Army of Northern Virginia to U.S. Grant, signaling the beginning of the end the end of the Civil War.

At this time in his life, at age 41, Winfield Hancock was an imposing figure. Frank Haskell, a young officer who served under him at Gettysburg described him thus: "Hancock is the tallest, and most shapely, and in many respects is the best looking officer of them all. His hair is light brown, straight and moist, and always looks, well-his beard is of the same color, of which he wears the moustache and a turf upon the chin; complexion ruddy, features neither large nor small but well cut with full jaw and chin, compressed mouth, straight nose, full deep blue eyes, and very mobile, emotional countenance." Haskell did not mention that Hancock had a reputation in the army for his ability to turn the air around him blue with creative profanities.

***

Within days of Lee's surrender, Hancock was ordered to report to Washington DC. Abraham Lincoln had just been assassinated and the newly sworn in President, Andrew Johnson, was afraid of losing control of the capitol. Mobs were gathering in the streets calling for revenge for the fallen President and spreading fearful rumors of further Confederate plots to cripple the Union government. Johnson called for Hancock to come to Washington to calm the ugly mood of the citizenry. Once Washingtonians learned that Hancock was among them and in control, tempers cooled, fears abated and a sad calm settled on the city.

With Hancock organizing patrols to protect the city and control demonstrations, Secretary of War Edwin Stanton began the biggest manhunt in the history of the country. In two weeks nine of the ten people suspected of conspiring to kill the President were captured or killed. The man believed to be the ringleader of the plot, John Wilkes Booth, was killed before he could be arrested by troops surrounding the barn in which he was hiding. Eight others were arrested and brought to the Old Arsenal Penitentiary in Washington DC. One other suspected conspirator, John H. Surratt, escaped the Capitol before authorities could locate him and would remain on the run for years. President Johnson wanted swift justice, and after conferring with Attorney General James Speed, ordered a military commission convened to try the assassination suspects. On May 9, 1865, the commission, comprised of nine military officers and a Judge Advocate, Joseph Holt, convened. Samuel Arnold, an old Baltimore acquaintance of Booth's, Dr. Samuel Mudd, whose home Booth stopped at the night of the assassination to have his broken ankle splinted, Edward Spangler, a scene shifter at Ford's Theatre, Lewis Payne, a recently paroled Confederate soldier, George Atzerodt, a German carriage painter who smuggled confederate spies across the Potomac, Michael O'Laughlin, a boyhood friend of Booth's from Baltimore, David E. Herold, a young, simple minded pharmacist's assistant, and Mary Surratt, widowed owner of the rooming house where the conspirators frequently met, all stood before the commission to be tried for murder. The entire affair lasted until early June, when the commission found all defendants guilty and issued their sentences. Herold, Payne Atzerodt and Mary Surratt were sentenced to death by hanging, with the remaining defendants receiving from six years to life in prison. The commission also attached a recommendation for clemency to Mary Surratt's sentence.

President Johnson ordered Hancock to oversee the care of the prisoners until such time as the sentences were to be carried out, and for the execution of the sentences. For Hancock there could be no question of legal propriety. He was a soldier following the orders of his superiors. His duties with regard to Mary Surratt were particularly difficult for him to carry out. He was as solicitous of her needs as circumstance would allow. No woman had ever been hung in the United States, and all, including Hancock, expected her to receive Presidential clemency.

On July 6, 1865 Hancock received the warrants for the execution of all four prisoners sentenced to death, including Mary Surratt. He delivered them in person to the prisoners in Old Arsenal Prison. Upon hearing the news that she was to be hung, Mrs. Surratt exclaimed to Hancock "I had no hand in the murder of the President!" and fell to the floor in a faint. Her lawyers began to try all possible legal tactics to save her. On July 7th, the day scheduled for the executions, Anna Surratt, Mary's daughter, went to General Hancock to plead for her mother's life. She asked what more she could do to help her mother's cause. Hancock suggested that she go directly to President Johnson and beg him for her mother's life. Anna ran directly to the White House and tried to see the President. The stairway to his office on the second floor was blocked by two senators and close friends of the President. They told Anna that the President was ill and could take no visitors. After repeated tearful, then hysterical attempts to get to the President, Anna rushed back to her mother's side. By afternoon Mrs. Surratt's lawyers had caused a writ of habeas corpus to be issued, demanding that Hancock yield up the person of Mary Surratt to the courts. Hancock raced to the courts and explained to the judge that he could not produce Mrs. Surratt because he had an order from the President suspending the writ of habeas corpus in this case, and directing him to carry out the judgement of the military commission. There were no more legal remedies for Mrs. Surratt's dilemma.

Hancock left the court and returned to his offices, expecting other attempts to spare Mary Surratt's life. He posted couriers along the route to the White House to speed the delivery of a message of a reprieve in case Anna Surratt's pleadings to the President were successful. When Mrs. Surratt's attorney, John W. Clampitt, asked Hancock if there was any more reason to hope, Hancock replied "I am afraid not. No, there is not." As the minutes ticked away moving them all closer to the time of the hangings, Hancock spoke again to Clampitt,

" I have been in many a battle and have seen death and mixed with it in disaster and victory. I've been in a living hell of fire and shell and grape-shot and - I'd sooner be there ten thousand times over than to give the order this day for the execution of that poor woman. But I am a soldier, sworn to obey and obey I must." At 1:15pm Hancock ordered the prisoners moved from their cells to the scaffold erected in the Arsenal courtyard. As they moved from the dark of the prison into the glaring sun, the condemned prisoners marched past four graves that had been dug for them the night before, then ascended thirteen steps up to the gallows platform. It was a sweltering afternoon, over 100 degrees, with intense heat made worse by humidity so thick it seemed to cling to all. A lack of breeze added to the solemn stillness. The men on the scaffold, afraid that Mrs. Surratt might faint from the heat, provided an umbrella to hold over head and a chair for her to sit on during the reading of the charges and the sentences. Once the readings were completed, the prisoners had nooses looped around their necks and hoods placed over their heads. A priest read some prayers and at 1:25pm Hancock clapped his hands twice, the second clap being the signal for the trap door to be sprung. All four bodies dropped, with Mrs. Surratt perishing first and David Herold last, after some five minutes of twitching and twisting. At 1:35pm the bodies were examined and pronounced dead. Within two hours they were laid in rough hewn wood coffins and buried on the prison grounds. Secretary of War Stanton, in a last act of revenge, had ordered that their bodies not be released to their families, but buried with no marker to identify their location.

***

Once his duties in Washington DC were finished, Hancock's headquarters for the Middle Military Division were moved to Baltimore Maryland. He spent a quiet year there performing administrative duties. Out west, in the Military Division of the Missouri, General William T. Sherman was busily trying to overcome the numerous challenges in his area. One of his Departments was especially troublesome. The Department of the Missouri included the states of Missouri, Kansas, Colorado and New Mexico. Two of the major routes of westward migration cut across this department, the Santa Fe and Overland Trails. Thousands of pioneers moved west on these trails each year, continually stirring up the Indian tribes who had been living there undisturbed for centuries. Worse, the Kansas Pacific railroad was surveying the area and laying tracks that cut straight across the Department. This railroad activity brought with it hundreds of workmen and their camp followers.

Sherman needed help to manage this growing problem, and he sought it in the person of Winfield Scott Hancock, whose talents he believed were being wasted sitting at a desk back east. Sherman lobbied hard with Ulysses S. Grant, then General of the Army, for Hancock's transfer. In August of 1866 his persistence paid off, as Hancock received a promotion to Major General (after the war Hancock's rank had been lowered to Brigadier General in the newly shrunk peacetime army) and was named commander of the Department of the Missouri, reporting to Sherman.

In assessing his new command Hancock found few problems in sparsely populated and far off New Mexico, and only minor local issues with former Copperheads (pro-Confederates living in Union states)in Missouri. Kansas and Colorado would require the majority of his attention. Most of Hancock's new command was part of the Great Plains, which stretched from eastern Kansas to the foothills of the Rockies. The plains were home to the Sioux, Cheyenne, Kiowa and Arapahoe Indian tribes. The Native American tribes had been pushed west from the Atlantic coast and east from the Pacific coast onto the Great Plains. There was nowhere else for them to go as white civilization squeezed them viselike with continued expansion. They had always been a primarily nomadic, hunter society, living out west wherever the buffalo herds travelled. These purely American animals served as the Indian main source of protein, and the hides and bones of the animals were used to make clothing, tents for living quarters and simple tools. The tribes needed space to follow the herds and that space was shrinking constantly along with the population of the buffalo herds. The buffalo were also being sought by white professional hunters employed by the Kansas Pacific to provide meat for the work crews. The tribes were feeling hemmed in and starved out.

When Hancock took over his new command in the late summer of 1866, the plains were deceptively calm. New forts were being built to protect railroad workers as the Kansas Pacific knifed its way further west while the Indians warily watched the advance.

Government policy placed the welfare of the tribes with the Department of the Interior. The Department issued licenses to white traders which allowed them to do business with the tribes. Among the goods approved for trade with the Indians were guns and ammunition (for use in hunting only), and alcohol. Trouble sprang from the fact that many traders were unscrupulous, anxious to increase their profit by selling poor quality foodstuffs at high prices, and liquor, guns and ammunition to any Indian who had something valuable to trade. At the very time that native Indian anger over white incursions into their ancestral lands was growing, the US government was providing them with arms and ammunition.

By late 1866 General William T. Sherman was writing to his brother, Senator John Sherman of Ohio, "I expect to have two wars on my hands. The Sioux and the Cheyenne... must be exterminated, for they cannot and will not settle down." Sherman's fear of an upcoming war led him to plan for an expedition into Indian lands that Winfield Hancock would command.

On March 8, 1867 Hancock returned to St Louis from the funeral of his father. There he met with Sherman to finalize details of what was to be called the Kansas Expedition. The plan was simple: awe the Indians into peaceable conduct with a massive display of force. Hancock would march the largest military force ever seen on the plains right up to the villages of the major Indian tribes and offer them a choice: either stop raids against the settlers and the railroad or come under immediate attack. A mixed force of 1,400 infantry along with cavalry and artillery was gathered, equipped and trained for the mission. Hancock even planned to take along a portable pontoon bridge to aid them in crossing the numerous creeks and rivers they would have to cross. Later Hancock would come under severe criticism for putting together so ponderous a force to subdue the highly mobile plains Indians, but it was Sherman who conceived and oversaw the preparations. Hancock would rightfully share some of the blame for the outcome of the expedition, but its author should bear the lion's share of fault for its outcome.

On March 26th the Kansas expedition marched out of Fort Riley, Kansas, the far western terminus of the Kansas Pacific railroad. The 7th Cavalry, commanded by Colonel A.J. Smith, led the way. Smith was an administrative officer who did not usually go far from his desk, so heading up the column as its field commander was George Armstrong Custer, famous for his many exploits of daring during the Civil War. Joining the expedition as a correspondent filing dispatches for the St. Louis Democrat and New York Times was Welsh journalist Henry M. Stanley, who would later become world famous for his successful search in remote central Africa for the reclusive Dr. David Livingston. Among the guides and scouts for the column was William Butler (Wild Bill) Hickok. Dressed in a bright red Zouave jacket and buckskin leggings, with his perfumed hair dangling down to his shoulders, Wild Bill looked the part of the legend he was already becoming on the plains. The two large ivory handled pistols strapped to his waist discouraged those who might think of challenging his shooting prowess.

A gathering of Southern Cheyenne chiefs was to meet the column at Fort Larned, 150 miles away. Runners would be dispatched to the chiefs to let them know when the column was close to the fort. Hancock, without incident, skillfully led the massive force across rolling hills, rocky, dry creek beds and vast plains almost totally devoid of trees, reaching Fort Larned on April 10. The chiefs had been notified of the column's presence, and they were to be at the Fort on or about April 10. One day before the scheduled meeting, a strong spring storm dumped eight inches of snow on the area around the Fort. Hancock waited throughout the day of April 10, for the chief's arrival. By April 11 he received word from Edward Wynkoop, government agent for the Cheyenne, Arapahoe and Apaches, that the chiefs were delayed. Just as they were preparing to depart for the meeting with Hancock at Fort Larned, the chiefs had been told of a large herd of buffalo nearby, and tore off in pursuit of the animals with a group of young braves. Hancock, not appreciating this show of disrespect, decided to give the chiefs just one more day to show up, after which time he would order his troops to move against the Indian villages. Just before the trumpeters sounded lights out on April 12, two chiefs, Tall Bull and White Horse, along with a small group of warriors, arrived at the camp. Instead of being greeted with customary speeches and a warm meal, Hancock summoned them to his tent. Council would be held immediately. Unaware of Indian traditions that forbade councils held after sundown, Hancock's summons upset the chiefs before even a word was spoken.

Both sides were angry as talks began, the Indians because their customs were being broken, Hancock because only two chiefs had shown up. Hancock dispensed with the usual formalities and got straight to the point. "I have a great many soldiers, more than all the tribes put together... I intend not only to visit you here, but my troops will remain among you. I have heard that a great many Indians want to fight. Very well; we are here and we came prepared for war. If you are for peace, you know the conditions. If you are for war look out for its consequences. I will await the end of this council to see whether you want war or peace."

Cheyenne chief Tall Bull replied to Hancock.

We never did the white man any harm. We don't intend to. The buffalo are diminishing fast. The antelope are now few. When they shall all die away we shall be hungry; we shall want something to eat and we will be compelled to come in the fort. Your young men must not fire on us. I have said all that I want to say here.

Hancock, displeased with what he heard as evasion, replied "You must go to the white man to be taken care of, and you should cultivate his friendship. That is all I have to say."

The meeting proved less than satisfactory. The chiefs departed for their camp and the next day Hancock's command marched 30 miles from Fort Larned toward the Indian village which was believed to be situated on the Pawnee Fork, a tributary of the Arkansas River. The column was brought to a halt near the village by a force of 300 Indian braves, blocking their path formed in a battle line. For many soldiers this was their first close up view of real plains Indians fully arrayed for battle. The Indians' horses were smaller and faster than government mounts, and able to survive on less feed. Their shields, rifles and beads shone in the afternoon sun. It was an unnerving sight for the mainly immigrant, city born recruits who filled the rolls of Hancock's units. The 7th cavalry was ordered to draw sabers. The artillery was unlimbered. As both sides grew more uneasy, a group of 12 Indians rode out from their band under a white flag. The flag was carried by Roman Nose, a famous Sioux war chief, who was accompanied by Cheyenne and Sioux braves. Hancock met the group and asked Roman Nose whether the Indians wanted war or peace. "We do not want war," Roman Nose replied. Hancock then explained that he would continue his march to the village where he expected to meet with all the chiefs that night.

The Indian force returned to its village to spread the word of white troops coming soon for parley. Hancock's troops followed slowly, giving the Indians time to calm down. After a 10 1/2 mile march they came within sight of the village. The column broke formation and set up camp. At 5pm several chiefs came into Hancock's camp to explain that all of the woman and children, terrified at the presence of so many white soldiers, had fled the village. Hancock angrily told the chiefs to go and bring back their women and children. By 9:30pm that evening the chiefs sent word to Hancock that they had chosen to flee with the women and children. Hancock was shocked at what he considered the chiefs deceit and treachery. He ordered Custer and his cavalry to surround the Indian village and prevent anyone else from leaving. When the cavalry surrounded the village and moved to check on the remaining Indians, they found none. All had escaped. Ironically Hancock had succeeded in doing just what Sherman had asked him. He had marched into Indian country and frightened the tribes with the size of his force. Now Hancock was left with hides, buffalo meat, cooking utensils, blankets, tepees- everything but live Indians to meet with. After discussing the situation with the Indian agent Edward Wynkoop, Hancock decided that he had to take action of some kind to reprimand the Indians. The Indians' conduct, he said, had convinced him that they were in fact guilty of launching raids that had resulted in the deaths of white railroad workers and settlers, and of the destruction of private and government property.

The next day, April 14, after everything in the village had been inventoried and some useful items confiscated, over 250 lodges and

1000 buffalo robes were set afire. Indian hostility to whites spread across Kansas as rapidly as the flames that consumed the village. Within days Indian raids began to be reported all along the Kansas stage and rail routes.

For the next two weeks Hancock marched his force to Fort Dodge, Fort Hays and Fort Harker, looking for Indians to parley with. Other than a single meeting at Fort Dodge with Santana, warrior chief of the Kiowa, he found none to threaten or persuade to pursue peaceful pursuits. Hancock was so pleased with his meeting with Santana that he presented the chief with the uniform and hat of a Major General. Later that summer Santana was seen wearing the outfit while leading an attack on cavalry horses grazing near Fort Dodge.

The Kansas expedition came to a close at Fort Leavenworth on May 9, 1867. In two months Hancock had marched 1400 men over 800 miles, held two unsuccessful parleys with Indian chiefs, burned one empty village and killed two Indians. To say that this expedition was unsuccessful is to give it too generous a review.

One other casualty of the Kansas expedition was George Custer's previously unmarred reputation. He had been given six companies of cavalry and ordered to perform a scout to the south and west in search of hostiles. Custer exhausted his men with forced marches. Desertion increased and Custer answered by issuing orders to shoot deserters. One officer began drinking heavily and killed himself. Finally Custer, without approval from his commanding officer Colonel Smith and without appointing another officer to assume command, left his troops at Fort Wallace and rode over 100 miles to visit his wife Elizabeth.

Hancock ordered Custer arrested and a court martial was convened. Custer was found guilty of desertion and sentenced to one year suspension from the Army without pay. Custer claimed that the whole affair had been Hancock's way of distracting the press from reporting on the failed Kansas Expedition.

***

On August 26th, 1867, by order of President Andrew Johnson, Winfield Hancock was ordered to take command of the 5th Military District, comprised of the states of Louisiana and Texas. He had come to the Kansas plains with white and Indian tempers simmering. He was leaving with Indians raiding up and down the stagecoach and railroad routes he was sent to protect.

Hancock, unlike many of his fellow career Army officers, maintained a wide circle of civilian friends. Congressmen, newspaper publishers, reporters and politicians, were all on his list of regular correspondents. And while he kept himself out of active involvement in politics, he remained very aware of public sentiment regarding issues of the day.

His new assignment brought him out of the wilderness and plunged him into the heart of the debate over national reconstruction. Hancock's new headquarters were located in New Orleans, a flashpoint in the conflict between President Johnson's and the Radical Republican plan for how the nation would be reunited after the war. Hancock was replacing General Phillip Sheridan, who supported Radical Republican policies. The radicals wished to deny any former office holder in the Confederate government or officer of its armed forces from holding public office in the United States. They were also working for full enfranchisement of blacks, whose votes would then ensure Radical Republican ascendancy in the South for years to come. Under Phil Sheridan's rule, carpet baggers (northerners who moved south seeking to gain financial or political advantage from the chaotic conditions there after the war) flooded the 5th Military District and were appointed to local and state government positions.

Hancock was not happy with his new assignment. He was a Democrat who believed in states rights and in limitations on the power of the Federal government. He saw no need to reconstruct the southern states. Like Lincoln he believed that southern states had never legally left the Union (which in their view was not constitutionally possible), but had simply revolted against the government. Now that the revolt was over Hancock believed the southern states should be allowed to assume the same status they had enjoyed within the Union before the rebellion. This was not a philosophy shared by his military superior, U.S. Grant.

Before he left Kansas for his new assignment Hancock was ordered to Washington DC to meet with General Grant, a stalwart of the Radical Republicans, and President Johnson, who at this time was pushing the assassinated President Lincoln's approach to reuniting the country. Both wanted to assure themselves of where Hancock stood on the great issue of southern reconstruction. The Radical Republicans, with a voting majority in the House of Representatives, could overturn any Presidential veto of their actions. They had already revoked the President's power to remove Cabinet appointees and military governors. The only power left for President Johnson to exercise was appointment and removal of Military District commanders. The President hoped that Hancock would prove supportive of his policies. Their interview left Johnson encouraged. Hancock's interview with his immediate military superior left General Grant worried.

Hancock wrote to his wife Allie.

I am expected to exercise extreme military authority over these people. I shall disappoint them. I have not been educated to overthrow the civil authority in times of peace....I may lose my commission, and I shall do so willingly, rather than retain it at the sacrifice of a life-long principle.

Hancock arrived in New Orleans on November 28, 1867 and went straight to his headquarters. The city newspapers were filled with speculation about what direction his leadership would take. The speculation was short lived. On his first full day in command of the 5th military district he issued General Orders Number 40. In it he stated that as the civil war had ended "and the civil authorities are ready and willing to perform their duties, the military powers should cease to lead and civil administration resume its natural and rightful dominion." This put Hancock squarely on the side of the conservative Democrats and President Johnson.

With the issuance of this order Hancock drew the attention of the national Democratic Party, which was already beginning to search its ranks for a suitable candidate for the presidency in the upcoming election of 1868. He came from vote rich Pennsylvania and now had strong southern support. Hancock did not shrink away from light being shone on him.

Soon after his arrival in New Orleans, Hancock became aware of rumors circulating around the state about a black uprising. In response to public pressure he requested a regiment of reinforcements to help maintain peace and calm citizen fears. He specifically requested that the troops sent "must be white; black troops are unsuitable for the performance of this particular service." General Grant responded by sending far less troops than Hancock requested. It is not clear what percentage of those troops were blacks.

Texas presented Hancock with his next challenge. Elisha M. Pease, appointed Governor by Hancock's predecessor General Phillip Sheridan, was a Radical Republican. Once in office Pease began removing from state office any elected official who had previously served in the Confederate government or its armed forces. Hancock stepped in when Pease asked him to convene a military court to try three men for murder who civilian juries would not indict. He told Pease that the state had all the powers necessary to try its citizens properly. Hancock refused to have the federal government intervene.

Trouble flared up in Louisiana next. Benjamin Franklin Sanders, the governor of that state by appointment, requested that Hancock remove members of the police jury of New Orleans, alleging that they had committed some unlawful acts. Hancock refused the governor's request and subsequently issued a general order to clarify his views. "The administration of civil justice appertains to the regular courts." Citizen's rights "are to be adjudged and settled according to the laws," not according to "the views of the generals."

Hancock continued to defy the will of the Radical Republicans. A year before he took over command of the 5th Military district, his predecessor, General Phillip Sheridan had issued specific instructions to registrars as to how a person should be disqualified from registering to vote. He targeted ex-Confederates in particular. Hancock revoked that instruction and asked registrars to simply comply with Louisiana statutory law.

In his view Hancock was being loyal to the Union and its Constitution. He saw no need to reconstruct the late secessionist states.

After another disagreement with his superior, General Grant, over Hancock's removal of officials who ignored his order not to hold elections for the position of City Recorder, Hancock tendered his resignation. It was accepted on March 16, 1868. Hancock was ordered to report to General Grant in Washington, D.C.

***

Despite their serious disagreements over reconstruction policies, Grant appointed Hancock commander of the Division of the Atlantic on March 28, 1868. Now headquartered in New York City, Hancock could stay in touch with the many financial and political power brokers who called this crowded little island home. He settled into his new position just as Republicans and Democrats began in earnest to prepare for their Presidential nominating conventions. General Ulysses Grant was the almost certain nominee of the Republican Party, now solidly controlled by its radical wing. These Radicals had just recently failed by one vote in the US Senate to remove Andrew Johnson from the Presidency by impeachment. With the election of General Grant they saw a means of removing the Democrats from national power for years to come. Democrats were divided over the best way to keep Grant out of the White House. Some thought they should rally around a proven party leader like Horatio Seymour, Governor of New York. Seymour had supported the war, but loudly disagreed with President Lincoln on many other policies. Others thought they should select a nominee who could gain the support of Democrats while enticing liberal Republicans to desert the radical-influenced Grant. Chief Justice of the Supreme Court Salmon P. Chase, who was a Democrat before the war, served in the Lincoln cabinet as a Republican, and was now, conveniently, a Democrat again, was yearning to fill that role. Finally, there was a group of Democrats who thought the only way to defeat a war hero was with another war hero. Winfield Scott Hancock was their man, a native of the North who was very well liked in the South.

The 1868 Democratic convention convened in New York City on the 4th of July. It was a rough and tumble affair stretching over 20 ballots.

President Andrew Johnson was nominated, though no one expected him to gather much support. Favorite sons were nominated to hold key delegations from committing too early to any other candidate without quid pro quo's being struck. Ten men received votes as the balloting proceeded, some holding for only one ballot, some surging and receding in the vote total as the convention struggled toward a 2/3 consensus. Hancock had been among the highest vote getters until the twentieth ballot. Then his supporters began to peel away to seek out another champion. Finally, Horatio Seymour, after feigning no interest in the nomination for most of the balloting, received the necessary 2/3 vote of the convention. Hancock took the defeat well, stating that he never believed himself to be a serious contender.

Horatio Seymour went on to campaign against Ulysses Grant in the general election. He did quite well in the popular vote, losing by a small margin. His defeat in the Electoral College vote was decisive.

***

In March 1869, very soon after being sworn in as the new President, Ulysses Grant sent Hancock off to command the Department of Dakota (Minnesota and the territories of Dakota and Montana). Once again, Hancock headed for Indian country and away from the power brokers of the east. This department contained 25% of all the Indians living in the United States, and sprawled over 1,200 miles. To keep the peace in this huge, sparsely populated, undeveloped land, Hancock had but 1,682 soldiers who were stationed across 15 separate posts.

Hancock had learned from his experiences with Indians during the ill-fated Kansas Expedition. After a thorough tour of his new command he set up a council for July 2nd, 1869 with the chiefs of the Mandan, Arikara and Gros Venture tribes. Then he sat down and listened patiently to what they had to say. They told him their people were suffering from diseases spread by white settlers and from starvation due to the buffalo herds being slaughtered to extinction by professional hunters hired to feed railroad work crews. Hancock did all that he could to alleviate the tribes' plight. Years later a chief at that council described Hancock's efforts as a "rift in the passing clouds in the welfare of my people - a ray of light that did not linger long."

Once the immediate concerns of the tribes had been dealt with, Hancock faced several other challenges. First, he had to protect Fort Buford, which had been built at the confluence of the Missouri and Yellowstone Rivers. The Sioux saw it as an unwelcome intrusion onto their hunting lands and constantly harassed its occupants. Far from any post that could reinforce it, Fort Buford was a flashpoint. Next, Hancock had to protect the surveying parties of the Northern Pacific Railroad, whose members were subject to marauding bands of roamers (Indians who left their reservations to hunt white men and buffalo or simply practice their old lifestyle of wandering the plains). Also there were growing numbers of miners to protect in the far away Gallatin Valley of Montana. Finally, there were groups of white settlers to protect who constantly violated treaty agreements by moving into the Black Hills.

Over the next two years Hancock faced these difficult challenges successfully. Three actions in particular form part of his legacy to the West. In 1872 a serious effort was begun to mount an expedition into the Black Hills for the purpose of looking for gold deposits rumored to be found there. The Black Hills were a sacred area to the plains Indians. They believed that the gods and spirits of their ancestors dwelt there. The US government had ceded them that land by treaty in perpetuity. But gold fever threatened the agreement. Hancock's answer to the request for his soldiers to protect an expedition into the Black Hills was a firm "NO." The faith of the government, he said, was pledged to protect the area from encroachment of, or occupation by, the whites. This action by Hancock kept the peace in the area until his successor; Phillip Sheridan approved an expedition in 1874, led by George Custer. Gold was found, and the area was soon overrun by white miners, beginning the Indian Wars that would continue until the Wounded Knee massacre of 1897.

Also in 1872 Hancock recommended to the US Adjutant General that a report submitted to him by Lieutenant Gustavus C. Doane be published. Doane had conducted an expedition to the upper Yellowstone River area, where he discovered fantastic bubbling mud cauldrons, geyser fields, Sulphur springs and a great canyon and falls. The publication of the report led to Congress establishing Yellowstone as the country's first national park.

Hancock's final legacy to the West came in the form of a report he issued calling for a reservation policy for Indians in which they would be treated humanely, provided good food, education, and weapons suitable only for hunting game. His years of experience dealing with the tribes of the West had matured his thinking. Unfortunately this report went unheeded for many years.

***

With relatively peaceful times on the plains, Hancock had time to reflect on his past foray into Presidential politics. During the 1868 Democratic nominating convention he had allowed himself to be placed in nomination but he had not allowed any organization to be formed to work on his behalf, nor had he made any real effort to gain the nomination. Now he decided to use his spare time to write letters to his supporters North and South, asking them to keep his name alive in the political mix, and to provide him with news of current social, economic and political events.

On November 25, 1872 Winfield Scott Hancock was appointed to command the Division of the Atlantic, headquartered on Governor's Island in New York City. This post was a perfect fit for an organizer like Hancock. Most of the issues to be dealt with related to logistics. There were no warlike tribes, no carpetbaggers stirring up the local population. Hancock toured all the key posts comprising his command, letting his new subordinates get to see him in the flesh. Once the tours were finished he ordered reforms and consolidation, merging what were two departments in his division into one single, cost efficient one.

President Grant was coming to the end of his first term in office. Personally he was still quite popular, and would almost certainly be re-nominated by his party. Grant's friends, many of whom he had rewarded with government jobs, turned out to be his worst enemies. Several were caught in schemes to defraud the public and received prison sentences. Democrats were desperate to find a strategy to beat Grant. Nationally they began to coalesce around the idea of a fusion ticket, merging Democrats with Republicans disenchanted with the corruption of the Grant administration. Hancock sensed that this was not the time for him to run again for President. His letter writing to powerful friends continued, but without urgency or any requests for support.

Democrats went on to endorse Horace Greeley, the nominee of the Liberal Republican party, a short lived organization that had just broken from the regular Republican Party over President Grant's re-nomination. Greeley, a New York newspaper editor best known for coining the phrase "Go West, young man," went on to lead his fusion effort to a sound beating at the polls. Grant easily won re-election to the Presidency in 1872.

Hancock spent the next few years managing the Division of the Atlantic, with little of military or political consequence to disturb the unending routine. Sadly this was not the case with his personal life. His daughter Ada, with whom he was particularly close, died suddenly in 1875 at age 18. Her death drove him into seclusion and depression.

When a movement started in his home state of Pennsylvania to run him for Governor he simply ignored it until it fizzled out.

Slowly Hancock's old vigor and enthusiasm returned, just as President Grant's second term was coming to an end. The well entrenched political tradition of no third term for a US President stood squarely in the way of Grant's desire to be nominated yet again. Try as he might, he could not get his Republican Party to break with that tradition. Several powerful party leaders were already organizing to win the Republican nomination. None of these aspirants had the star power of Grant, and all of them looked beatable to the Democrats.

Hancock voiced interest in the 1876 Democratic nomination as did six or seven other party notables. The leading contender appeared to be Samuel J. Tilden, a corporate lawyer whose recent battles with Tammany Hall had earned him a reputation as a reformer. He was a seasoned politician with strong financial backing, and he wanted the nomination badly. Tilden dispatched his agents into all the doubtful states with cash and convincing talking points. Within weeks what had appeared to be an open convention was all but locked up for Tilden. It was over with the second ballot. Samuel Tilden was the Democratic nominee for President. Winfield Scott Hancock's name had been put before three consecutive Democratic conventions without success.

Rutherford B. Hayes was the compromise candidate of the Republican Party. After a tough campaign Tilden won the popular vote, but failed to gain a majority in the Electoral College, A commission was appointed to award the electoral votes of three southern states whose voting results were in dispute. The commission awarded all three states' votes to the Republican Hayes, who was then declared President elect. Though no solid proof has ever come to light, it was widely believed that the Democrats accepted this outcome in exchange for Hayes agreeing to end Reconstruction by withdrawing all federal troops from the South and returning the last three states under military governance to their prewar positions as sovereign states in the Union. Hayes did just that soon after he was sworn into office.

Some Democrats called for a massive 100,000 citizen march on Washington to protest the election outcome, which they hoped

Hancock would lead, mounted on his coal black charger. Hancock refused to support the march. He said "what the people want is a peaceful determination of this matter, as fair a determination as possible, and a lawful one." There was always another chance to reverse the results in four years.

***

By 1877 Hancock's Division of the Atlantic was expanded to include those states in the South now accepted back into the Union. These newly added states were largely without troops. Once President Hayes declared an official end to Reconstruction the troops garrisoned there were shipped west as reinforcements to help fight the Indian wars firing up on the plains.

A financial panic and economic depression struck the country in 1873, and by 1877 most wages for working men had been slashed. Purchase of retail goods declined, then manufacturing slowed, and a decline in railroad shipments of raw materials used in manufacturing followed. As railroads saw their profits dwindle they cut wages more, and then began a ruinous rate war over the small amount of shipments still needed to be made. Workmen who dared to complain about longer hours and less pay were promptly fired.

Unrest amongst railroad workers spread to coal miners suffering the same harsh treatment. Work stoppages were staged in Pennsylvania and West Virginia. Governors and local officials, unable to control these outbreaks with local police and state militia, called on President Rutherford B. Hayes for support from the Army. Hayes set a precedent when he agreed to have Federal troops sent to help restore peace and restart halted mine and railroad work. He assigned the job to Winfield Scott Hancock, who commanded the District in which these troubles were occurring. Hancock moved soldiers into Pennsylvania and West Virginia, closely monitoring their activities to ensure that there were no violent confrontations or overreaction by his men to provocations. Over the following months this cautious, restrained show of strength succeeded where local and state law enforcement had failed. Hancock's calmness and fair treatment of protesters dispelled the immediate threat of labor upheaval.

For his success in handling what could have been a bloody labor revolution Hancock earned the admiration and respect of ordinary citizens and elected officials all around the nation. With the next Presidential contest approaching, Hancock was looming as the man to beat for the Democratic nomination.

General Hancock next dove into the ongoing debate over what theory should govern the organization of the peacetime army. During the Civil War over a million men were under arms. By 1878 the Army numbered just 25,000 men, scattered over 200 duty posts. Everyone agreed that the Army needed to be kept small, but so configured as to be quickly enlarged. Emory Upton, an instructor and administrator at West Point spoke for those who believed in a "skeleton army" concept. He called for the army to be organized with the framework (company, brigade, division, and corps) of a large force, each component being recruited far under normal strength. When trouble arose and the army needed to be made larger each component could simply recruit additional men to bring it to full strength. Hancock supported a "complete and compact" concept. Under this approach an army was established with a small framework, sufficient for 25,000 men or so, but fully staffed, trained and equipped with all the latest weaponry and technology. When expansion was needed this efficient small army could bring in new recruits and form them into new companies, brigades and divisions as needed, utilizing their own sharply honed, up to date skills.

Hancock's concept was not the one chosen by the Army, but Hancock continued over the years to champion the merits of the "complete and compact" approach.

***

The Presidential election year of 1880 found Hancock's key supporters actively seeking delegate votes for him all across the nation. Hancock would not be a passive candidate at this convention, though as a member of the Army he was sworn not to actively seek office. He chose to campaign covertly through private meetings, letter writing and through the actions of surrogates.

At age 56, Hancock felt he was ready to be President. He had seen Ulysses Grant embarrass himself with his corrupt cabal of friends dipping into public coffers to enrich themselves, and he had observed how Rutherford B. Hayes lost most of his powers of political persuasion by announcing he would serve only one term. Hancock was sure he could do better.

Winfield Scott Hancock looked presidential. Standing over six feet tall, he was now a solid 240 pounds. His wavy dark brown hair had whitened a bit at the temples, but this along with his serious demeanor gave him a look of command.

Against him stood Democrats with solid backgrounds of achievement, but none had the charisma of the Civil War hero and the national notoriety of the pacifier of labor unrest. Senator Allen Thurman was a former Ohio Senator whose home state would give him some support in the early balloting. Stephen J. Field of California was an Associate Justice of the Supreme Court who could count on some vote support from western states. Hancock's strongest opponent was Senator Thomas Bayard of Delaware. A consistent critic of radical republicanism, Bayard enjoyed the support of the New York Herald and many northeastern men of money and influence. What worked against him was the fact that he had publically supported the Electoral Commission of 1877 that selected Republican Hayes over the Democrat Tilden in that confusing election. Also, in 1861 Bayard had given a speech in which he suggested that the southern states should be permitted to secede peacefully from the Union. A stiff and unemotional speaker, Bayard came across as a corporate lawyer and aristocrat, not an easy sell to the general Democratic voter base.

Hancock's career spent in the military also gave him an advantage over his opponents who were lifelong politicians. They were forced to take public positions on most controversial issues of the day. Hancock was forbidden to enter publicly into politics. His views on many subjects were not well known. This gave him a certain freedom to define himself as whatever the undecided Democratic delegate wanted him to be.

The Republican Party was in some disarray as the 1880 Presidential election season got underway. Rutherford Hayes had begun his 1876 campaign for the Presidency by making it clear that he intended to serve only one term in office. Even if he had not made that pledge it is likely that he would not have received his party's support for another term. His ending of Reconstruction had weakened the Republican Party's position in the South and his support for the reformers in his party upset many powerful Republican office holders and government functionaries.

Republican Senators James G. Blaine of Maine, Roscoe Conkling of New York, and John A. Logan of Illinois and former Senator John Sherman of Ohio all thrilled at the prospect of Hayes leaving the White House. They were leading proponents of the "spoils system." Begun under President Andrew Jackson, it had become tradition to fill the hundreds of federal jobs controlled by the President with men loyal to the new administration. "To the victors belong the spoils." The Hayes administration had called for the creation of a Civil Service, in which a non-partisan commission would fill federal positions with workers actually qualified to do their jobs. Two non-reform Republicans, Blaine and Sherman, were already working publicly to get their party's nomination. A third major candidate had just returned to America from a triumphant world tour with his wife.

Ulysses Grant had been out of the country for much of the time since he left office after his two terms as President. While he was away the country had recovered from the economic depression that had begun during his last term in office and the investigations and trials of several members of his administration who had defrauded the public had long since ended. The public viewed him once again as the hero of Appomattox and Savior of the Republic. Many of his friends thought he might just be nominated for a third term.

Winfield Hancock's path to the Democratic nomination remained filled with obstacles. The national party was split between supporters of a soft money economy (one based on a looser silver backed currency) and a hard money economy (one based on the current conservative gold standard). His home state of Pennsylvania was torn by a struggle between Speaker of the US House, Philadelphia

Congressman Samuel J. Randall and Pennsylvania US Senator William Wallace for control of the convention delegation. To add further to the pre-convention confusion Hancock faced, yet another candidate emerged for the nomination, old yet new. Samuel J. Tilden, who lost the 1876 Presidential election to Rutherford B. Hayes through the machinations of the controversial Electoral Commission, began to gather support.

In the months leading up to the Democratic convention Tilden's candidacy continued to gain strength. Despite his age of 67 and his ill health (arthritis and a constitution badly weakened by his bruising election loss in 1876) many felt he deserved a second chance to gain the Presidency. Hancock remained in the background, as was required of an active member of the military. His supporters, meanwhile, crisscrossed the country, hoping the people's deep respect for Hancock could be turned into delegate votes.

The Republican convention opened with a delegate war between the supporters of James G. Blaine and Ulysses Grant. Neither side could gain the 2/3 vote needed for nomination, but neither side was willing to give in to the other. For 35 ballots a stalemate persisted. Delegates, hoarse from shouting for their favorites, parched from the stifling heat and choking on all the cigar smoke swirling about the hall, finally rallied around a dark horse candidate, James A. Garfield, a well-respected Ohio Congressman. Garfield was a brilliant orator, a student of the classics, veteran of the Civil War and member of the reform wing of his party. He sought unity within his party by accepting as his running mate a little known bureaucrat named Chester Arthur, who was the current Collector of the Port of New York and a protégé of New York Senator James Conkling, boss of his state's spoils system.

Democrats, surprised by Garfield's nomination, were heading to Cincinnati, Ohio, where their convention would soon open. Samuel Tilden, Hancock, Thomas Bayard and several others were all contenders for the top prize. Hancock forces remained very low key in their electioneering, attempting to make no enemies while lining up support. Most talk was centered on Samuel Tilden and whether he would allow his name to be entered into nomination. Democrats saw that the 1880 election was winnable, but would require a hard, sustained campaign to secure that victory. As a result, Tilden's health was proving to be a greater issue of concern than first thought. Once the opening gavel was struck the real scramble for delegates began. Tilden dispatched his brother to the head of the New York delegation with a letter he intended the delegation leader to read to the entire convention the next day. Instead, the chairman of the New York delegation insisted on reading it to his members right away, so they could take into account what their favorite son Tilden had to say before the next days balloting. The letter contained a statement by Tilden that he was "renouncing re-nomination." It went on to glowingly recall all the good work Tilden had done for his party and his country. Clearly Tilden had hoped that this message, when read to the entire convention, would inspire them to re-nominate him despite his stated wishes to the contrary. The New York delegation, hearing his wish to be removed from consideration, voted that night to do just that. This ended Samuel J Tilden's attempt to be President.

With Tilden out of the running Hancock went on to easily win the nomination on the second ballot. Hancock had finally taken the prize. He would be the Democratic candidate for President of the United States in 1880.

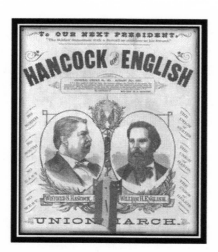

While awaiting the visit of the convention notification committee Hancock remained at his headquarters on Governor's Island in New York harbor. The ferry from the mainland grew very busy bringing boatloads of friends, well-wishers, reporters and family to visit with the General. He stated no public position on major issues of the day to any of them. Harry Heth, a prewar West Point friend and General in the Confederacy's Army of Northern Virginia, came to ask Hancock, in the event of his election to the Presidency, to appoint a friend of his to an ambassadorship. Hancock was not evasive with Heth. While he greatly enjoyed renewing their friendship, he refused to consider Heth's friend for a job.

Tragedy struck on Governor's Island on the very day that the convention notification committee was to officially inform Hancock of his nomination. The General's grandson and namesake, Winfield, suddenly fell ill and died. As the nominating committee officially notified him of his selection as the party's standard bearer, Hancock stood shrouded in gloom rather than joy or satisfaction.

The 1880 election was much more civil than those that had preceded it. Both Garfield and Hancock were well liked, and neither generated the deep emotion, positive or negative, that Ulysses Grant and Samuel Tilden did. The 1880 election was more a duel of parties, with both evenly matched. Democrats had a solid southern base and needed only to secure a few Northern states to carry the election. The fact that Republicans had won the last five Presidential elections helped strengthen the national readiness for a change. Republicans painted Hancock as a good enough soldier, but a candidate who knew little of national economic policy, foreign affairs or the workings of Congress. They also stoked working men's fears of what might happen to American manufacturing jobs if the Democratic Party enacted laws to lower tariffs against competing foreign goods.

The most potent personal attack on Hancock during the campaign came from his old commander, Ulysses Grant. In an October interview that Ulysses Grant claimed was never meant to be made public, Grant made several statements critical of Hancock. He said that Hancock, in assuming command of the 5th Military District after the war, told Grant, "Well, I am opposed to nigger domination." He went on to describe Hancock as "ambitious, vain and weak." He concluded the interview saying that for many years Hancock had been "...crazy to be President." The uneasy truce that had existed between Hancock and his former army superior ended with the publication of these comments.

Grant's comments were quickly countered by two equally famous Civil War Generals usually in agreement with radical republican politics. William T. Sherman was quoted as saying, "If you will sit down and write the best thing that can be put in language about General Hancock as an officer and gentleman, I will sign it without hesitation." And from Phillip Sheridan, "I am not in politics, but General Hancock is a great and good man."

Democrats were not as kind to James A. Garfield. His involvement, however tangential, with the Credit Mobilier scandal during the Grant administration was constantly referenced on the stump by Hancock campaign surrogates. So too was Garfield's alleged complicity in a questionably awarded DeGolyer paving contract in Washington DC.

Republicans continued to wave the " bloody shirt" as they had in past campaigns since the war's end, but with less success. After 15 years this tactic of blaming Democrats for the coming of the war was losing it's effect. The public just could not be brought to believe that "Hancock the Superb" of Gettysburg was in any way allied with Southern ultras wanting to restart the Civil War.

Neither side seemed to be able to find an issue that gave them a clear edge in courting undecided voters.

In September, 1880, Maine held its state elections. All eyes were on the governor's race there. The incumbent, Republican Governor D. F. Davis, was expected to prevail in a close race against a fusion candidate (Democrats in Maine allied with the Greenback Party, a group who favored issuance of paper currency backed by silver rather than gold, this allowing for the printing of more money and easing of credit). In 1876 Rutherford B. Hayes had carried Maine by 16,000 votes. In a shocker, the fusion candidate defeated the incumbent governor by 2,000 votes. Hancock and the Democrats were elated. The Republican margin of 16,000 votes from 1876 had been washed away completely.

What appeared to be a great gift from Maine to the Democratic campaign in 1880 proved not to be in the long run. The loss energized Republicans and prompted them to campaign with a sense of urgency. Republicans also realized that the Maine loss had highlighted an issue. Maine voters had been motivated to choose the winner of their gubernatorial contest based on a discussion of currency policy and how it could affect their lives. Garfield's campaign would now focus on the economy and how their programs could protect and increase the country's prosperity while the Democrats anti-tariff program would lead to job loss and economic decline.

The Democratic/Greenback victory in Maine put the Democrats into a confident mood, a confidence that bred carelessness and lack of focus. They failed for some time to take note of the new Republican campaign strategy, which was a precursor to the mantra of James Carville, one of Bill Clinton's chief strategists in 1992: "It's the economy, stupid."

Indiana's and Ohio's elections came in the second week of October. Indiana looked good for the Democrats. It had a Governor and two US Senators who were Democrats, and had voted Democratic for President in 1876 by a 5,000 vote margin. Also, Hancock's Vice Presidential running mate, William English, was from Indiana. Ohio, on the other hand, was considered Republican ground. Garfield, the Republican Presidential nominee, was a Congressman from Ohio. Ohio had voted in 1876 for Republican Rutherford B. Hayes by a 13,000 vote margin. The best Democrats could hope for in Ohio was to cut into that margin.

Both national campaigns sent surrogates into these states to hammer away for Hancock and Garfield. The Republican effort, now focused on the economy, was led by Roscoe Conkling, Senator from New York. Conkling had been opposed to Garfield's nomination and to Garfield's support for patronage reform through creation of a civil service. At an urgent post-convention meeting Garfield and Conkling somehow buried the hatchet. Rumors circulated that Garfield had given Conkling assurances that as President he would allow Conkling to control all federal patronage jobs in the state of New York. And as a further sign of their new alliance, Garfield had chosen Chester A.

Arthur, a Conkling minion, as his running mate. Once the meeting concluded, Conkling, considered one of the most rousing public speakers of his era, began rallying support for Garfield in the states of Ohio and Indiana.

The Democrats had no one to match Conkling's rhetorical firepower. William English, Hancock's running mate, was expected to work his local connections to build support for Hancock in Indiana and neighboring Ohio. That was a key reason he had been added to the ticket. To Hancock's dismay English proved an ineffective campaigner who grew less, not more popular with each appearance in his home state.

On October 12, 1880 the voters in Ohio and Indiana chose the Republican message of Save Our Economy over the Democrats meessage of change. Ohio went Republican by 20,000 votes and Indiana deserted the Democrats and gave the Republicans a narrow 2,000 vote margin of victory.

While the Republicans celebrated, the Democrats held a post mortem. They concluded that they had lost first because their local candidates were not as attractive as Hancock would be, and second, because of the tariff issue. The party was sure that Hancock would regain lost Democrat support in Indiana and Ohio. But the economic issue needed to be addressed.

The Democrats studied the electoral map of mid-October, and selected their targets for special attention. Indiana was still in play, as was New Jersey, California, Oregon and Nevada. Win these states and the solid south and Hancock would be within reach of the Presidency. But they had to have New York. Lose New York and lose the election.

In 1876, New York, with favorite son Samuel Tilden as one of the candidates, had gone solidly Democratic. But by 1880 the political climate of the state was much different. John J. Kelly and his Tammany Hall machine were fighting with Irwin Hall (the county Democratic organizations outside the city) for control of the state. The Democratic mayor of New York was up for re-election and John Kelly refused to support him. Tammany and Irwin Hall met to pick a candidate that they both could support. The list of men they considered included William Grace. Irwin Hall politicians had placed Grace on the list thinking he would be rejected immediately by Tammany Hall, allowing Irving Hall to the substitute someone else they really preferred at the last second. The politicos of Irving Hall believed that Grace was not electable, given his Irish Catholic background. A Catholic had never been elected city or statewide. Tammany Hall surprised them by agreeing to the choice and ending the meeting before Irving Hall could maneuver for a candidate they really wanted. Grace began his mayoral campaign amid swirling rumors that he was in favor of taking funds earmarked for public education and diverting them to parochial schools. Grace tried his best to explain his position and deny the rumor, but it continued to spread and do damage not only to Grace, but to Hancock. Many non-Catholic Democrats began to consider voting Republican to keep the Pope's influence out of New York schools. With his enemies at Irving Hall strongly supporting Hancock's campaign in New York state, Tammany Hall's John Kelly grew suspicious that a deal had been struck between them and Hancock to give Irving Hall control over state patronage should Hancock be elected President. Despite the Hancock campaign's denial of such a deal existing, Tammany Hall's support for Hancock became perfunctory at best.

Hancock had his hands full trying to defuse the tariff issue that Republicans were using against him to great effect. It had once been thought that Hancock's lack of public statements on major issues of the day would work in his favor. That proved wrong when Republicans were able to paint him as anti-tariff. High tariffs on goods imported from foreign countries had allowed American industry to flourish and make jobs plentiful. Hancock needed the support of Northern working men to win in New York and New Jersey. It was this voting group that was most susceptible to Republican stories of how Hancock's economic positions would spell the end of job growth and their family's financial security. Hancock began to grant interviews to reporters to explain his true position. He said to a reporter for the Patterson Daily Guardian of New Jersey that the position of the two parties was really the same. "They will have just as much protection under a Democratic Administration as under a Republican administration." He concluded the interview with a muddled comment that the tariff question was a local rather than national issue.

This casual description of the tariff being a local question haunted Hancock's final weeks of campaigning. Tariffs were clearly a national issue, regulated by Congress. Hancock had meant that each locality could voice its opinion on tariffs by voting for a particular candidate for Congress whose views they were in agreement with, thereby deciding the tariff question locally. The subtlety of Hancock's remark was lost on the public, who tended to believe the Republican characterization of Hancock's remark as politically naive.

On November 2, 1880 78% of all eligible voters cast their ballots. Hancock remained at his military headquarters on Governor's Island, performing his usual duties, interrupted by occasional updates on vote returns. By mid-afternoon New York City appeared to be going Democratic by as much as 60,000 votes, which would allow Hancock to carry the state by around 25,000. Trends looked good around the country. By 9pm in the evening, feeling cautiously optimistic but exhausted, Hancock announced to his surprised aides that he was going to bed and did not wish to be disturbed with any new results until morning.

Around 5am the next morning, while still in his bed, wife Allie broke him the news that he had been beaten. It was "a complete Waterloo for you," she told him. "That is all right," he replied, "I can stand it." And with that he rolled over and went back to sleep.

The election had been quite close in the popular vote, with Garfield winning by a thin margin of 39,000 votes out of some 9,000,000 cast. In the Electoral College the victory was more solid, with Garfield garnering 214 votes to Hancock's 155. Hancock had succeeded everywhere he needed to except in New York. William Grace had been elected Mayor of New York City, thanks to an untiring effort by John J. Kelly. Hancock lost New York State due in large part to John Kelly ignoring the national ticket to devote more of his campaign worker's time and energy to winning the mayoralty. The Democratic vote for Hancock in New York City was weaker than expected, and was not enough to offset the votes of the Republican strongholds outside the city. New York could have made Hancock President, but that was not to be.

Hancock took the loss well. He felt he had run the best race he could have, and he was perfectly ready to put politics aside for good, and with it all the unpleasant dealings and shady characters that came with it. He was, once again, a soldier serving his country.

***

Everything seemed to move much slower for Winfield Scott Hancock after the election of 1880. He put on considerable weight, and began to suffer from a series of illnesses. Death became a frequent topic at the Hancock home. The General and his wife sparred over their own burial arrangements. Allie wanted them both buried in her family's plot near St. Louis, Missouri. Winfield wanted to be buried with Allie and their daughter Ada (who had died two years before) in a mausoleum he was having built per his daughter's request, in Montgomery County, Pennsylvania near his boyhood family home.

Allie's mother, who had been living with them for several years, died in 1883. Then his chief of staff and old friend William Mitchell passed. In 1884 his 34 year old son Russell died after a brief illness. Both of his and Allie's children were now gone, along with Hancock's beloved namesake grandson. Much of Hancock's former strength and vitality seemed to pass with them.

The General was rarely seen in public during his last years. He continued to perform his duties as commander of the Division of the Atlantic, taking no part in failed attempts to promote him to the ranks of Lieutenant General. Gardening seemed to be his only real passion.

His last taste of national recognition came in 1885. Ulysses Grant had died on July 23 of that year, and President Grover Cleveland ordered Hancock to plan and direct the funeral ceremony, which would take place in New York City. After masterfully orchestrating all preparations, Hancock donned his best uniform, resplendent with gold braid, mounted his coal black charger and led a procession of veterans groups, military organizations, government officials, foreign dignitaries and countless reporters from around the country on an eight mile parade to Grant's temporary burial site. Hancock succeeded in giving Grant a spectacular sendoff. Grant's close friend and wartime aide Adam Badeau, knowing the rough history between the two Generals, gave credit to Hancock for his efforts. "The majestic character of those rites that attracted the attention of the world was greatly due to the tender care and chivalrous punctilio of him who thought the dead chieftain had wounded him."

In November, 1885, Hancock revisited the battlefield of Gettysburg. He went there at the request of area officials who wanted him to clear up confusions over the positioning of troops during the battle. This was a necessary step in determining where future memorials to the fallen troops would be located. Hancock met many old comrades and adversaries on the battlefield that November while walking the "hallowed ground" where he had won hero status 20 years before.

Hancock's physical decline accelerated in January 1886 when he suffered from a painful boil which had formed on the back of his neck. He had a surgeon lance the boil, but seemed considerably weakened by it. An abscess had formed as a result of a leg injury he suffered two years earlier, and that too drained his dwindling reserve of energy. He stubbornly refused his doctors' requests for them to perform a complete physical. They suspected that he was avoiding hearing the bad news that might come. The boil that had been lanced earlier reappeared and grew larger. By February 8th he was unable to turn his head without blinding pain. On the morning on February 9th, as his wife Allie, who had been at his bedside constantly for the past two days, got up to leave the room for a break, Hancock came out of a slumber and said "O, Allie. Allie. Myra! Good....," the last words he would speak.

Later that afternoon he drew a halting last breath and died. It was discovered by his doctors that, like his father, Hancock had severe diabetes, which in the end had caused his death.

Winfield Scott Hancock played a major role in the events of mid and late 19th century America. His exploits during the Civil War were widely reported and admired. Lincoln once said of him:

When I go down in the morning to open my mail, I declare I do it in fear and trembling, lest I may hear that Hancock has been killed or wounded.

His constant presence from 1868-1880 near or at the top of the Democratic Party's list of contenders for their Presidential nomination illustrates the trust he commanded with both politicians and the general public.

He was unique in his day as a public man who drew support from people of both the North and the South. Northerners loved him for his military record, while Southerners loved him for his even handed dealings with them during the reconstruction years.

He was not a creative thinker. He formulated no original concepts, and left no memorable words carved in stone after his passing. He was a man of strong principles who did not bend them to conform with the public mood.

His calmness under pressure, his strong sense of justice, his reverence for the law and the Union might have made him a fine President. His election defeat in 1880 may have been the nation's loss.

He provided a fitting epitaph when he said at the beginning of the Civil War:

My politics are of a practical kind; the integrity of the country, the supremacy of the federal government, an honorable peace or none at all.

THE CLEOPATRA OF SECESSION
Maria Isabella "Belle" Boyd

18 year old Belle Boyd laid down on the floor of a darkened closet in the upstairs room of her Aunt Fanny Seward's Fishback Hotel in Front Royale, Virginia. With her ear pressed to the floor, she listened to the conversation going on in the room directly below her. Union forces had recently occupied her town, and their commander, General James Shields, was holding a council of war there, discussing how Union forces would trap the Confederate army led by Thomas Jonathan (Stonewall) Jackson in the days ahead.

When the meeting broke up around 1 am, Belle slipped out of the hotel and returned to the little cottage nearby that her Aunt had provided for her during her stay in town. After she wrote down all that she had overheard, Belle put on a pair of trousers, a shirt and a cotton kepi cap like the young boys around town wore, and placed her carefully folded notes under the clothing. She then ran to the stables, where she saddled a horse and began a 15 mile night ride to the headquarters of General Jackson, to warn him of what she had learned.

***

Maria Isabella Boyd was born May 9, 1844 to shop keeper and tobacco farmer Benjamin and his wife Mary. The Boyd household would eventually grow to include Belle, her parents, three younger siblings and five slaves. One slave, Eliza, was Belle's personal servant, and had tended to her since her birth. They became inseparable. Belle loved Eliza so much that she broke southern laws by secretly teaching her to read and write. They would share many adventures together.

Benjamin and Mary Boyd discovered quite early that their daughter Belle was not a shy or insecure girl. When her parents refused to allow her to attend a party they were hosting because of her young age, Belle, then 11 years old, turned and left the room without protest. She went directly to the stables, saddled up her horse Fleeter, rode him into the house and stopped him in front of her shocked parents. "Well, "she said to them," my horse is old enough, isn't he?" Her parents told her to stable her horse and head straight to her room, but Belle was saved by an intrigued guest who stopped her parents, saying "Surely so high a spirit should not be thoroughly quelled by severe punishment. Mary, won't you tell me more about your little rebel?" For the rest of the evening Belle was, much to her delight, the center of attention.

Belle attended Mount Washington Female College, receiving an education typical of a daughter of a successful merchant/farmer. She earned a reputation amongst the faculty there as a student with a quick, biting wit and even quicker answers to questions they posed. Those who watched her grow up called her spirited, fearless, outspoken, and opinionated. A female rival of hers in town called her "the fastest girl in Virginia or anywhere else for that matter."

By the beginning of the Civil War Belle was a tall, slender 17 year old who loved to flirt. She seemed blissfully unaware of her average appearance, and was convinced, in fact, that she was quite alluring to the opposite sex. While recruiting her cousin to help her find a suitable mate, Belle described herself:

I am tall. I weigh 106 ½ pounds. My form is beautiful. My eyes are of a dark blue and so expressive. My hair of a rich brown and I think I tie it up nicely. My neck and arms are beautiful and my foot is perfect. Only wear size two and a half shoes. My teeth the same pearly whiteness, I think perhaps a little whiter. Nose quite as large as ever, neither Grecian nor Roman, but beautifully shaped and indeed I am decidedly the most beautiful of all our cousins.

She was not lacking in self-confidence, but was clearly lacking a leavening amount of humility. A diarist of the time described her as having a long, narrow face, a prominent nose and protruding teeth, making her look altogether "too horsy."

***

An incident at their home on July 4th, 1861 started Belle on her career as a Southern patriot and spy. The war, for Southerners, had begun in December, 1860, with the secession of South Carolina from the Union. Martinsburg, Virginia, was occupied soon after Virginia joined South Carolina in secession. The mood in the town grew tense as Union troops began Fourth of July celebrations, with many Union occupiers helping themselves to the locally available supplies of liquor. One such Union soldier stumbled up to the Boyd home and informed Belle's mother Mary that he was going to raise the Union Stars and Stripes over their home, since it was now federal property. Mary objected and the man became belligerent, crudely insulting her. Both Mary and Belle were anxious because they knew there were no men of the family around to defend them, as Benjamin Boyd had departed months before to enlist in the Confederate army. Seeing her mother being manhandled, Belle exploded with anger, grabbed a gun and shot the soldier dead. When the Union officer commanding the town's occupying force reviewed the case, he decided that Belle had acted properly and she was not arrested. Word quickly began to spread in northern Virginia of how this young girl had defied the Yankees, and Belle became a local celebrity and heroine of the cause.

This incident confirmed Belle's hatred of the Yankees, and her determination to do what she could to help defeat them. She soon heard that couriers were needed in nearby Winchester, Virginia (then occupied by Union forces) to pass messages through enemy lines, so she resolved to volunteer for the duty. To pass through Union sentries along the way she secured the unwitting help of Union Lieutenant Abram Hasbrouck, with whom she flirted with frequently. She told him she had to visit friends in Winchester, and that since he had often professed his friendship toward her, would he not prove it by escorting her and her servant Eliza safely to their destination? He agreed.

The journey to Winchester passed uneventfully. Once there the Lieutenant excused himself from Belle to report to headquarters in town. Belle and Eliza headed to the home of a friend in town, where she was to meet her contact. The next morning a rebel colonel disguised in civilian clothes came to her. He gave her a packet of letters, showing her which were the most important, and asked her to deliver them to General Jackson or one of his officers. Belle hid some the important letters in the waistband of Eliza's dress, knowing Yankees would never search a slave. She inscribed the lesser important bundle of letters with the words "Kindness of Lieutenant Hasbrouck," and placed them in plain view in a basket she was carrying. She kept the most important note in her hand, pretending to use it as a fan.

Lieutenant Hasbrouck returned to pick up Belle and Eliza and they left together to return to Front Royal. They were stopped at the picket post on the outskirts of town by detectives working for the Union army, and Belle was told that she was to be placed under arrest. A servant at the home of Belle's friend had seen her receiving the bundles from a strange man and reported her to the Union authorities. When she asked the Union detective why she was being arrested, he told her she was suspected of carrying letters containing secret information. They took the group to a small office nearby and the questioning began, from Colonel Beal, the officer in command. "Do you have any letters?" he asked. In reply Belle pulled the letters out of her basket and gave them to the detective.

The Colonel read the note Belle had scribbled on the packet referencing Lieutenant Hasbrouck. The Lieutenant stood there, confused. Belle spoke up immediately saying the Lieutenant knew nothing about the letters. She wanted to protect him, hoping she could use him again when needed. He noticed that she held a paper in her hand and asked her what it was. "What – this little scrap of paper? It is nothing. You can have it if you wish." She had already decided to swallow it if he did try to grab it from her. Her bluff worked. The Colonel ignored the crumpled note, dismissed Belle and Eliza and turned from them to dress down the young Lieutenant. What became of him is not known.

***

Belle and Eliza headed back to Front Royal as quickly as they could. In her little cottage Belle reviewed the contents of the information she was carrying. It described a concentration of Union troops much greater than was thought to be near her town. Belle realized immediately that if General Jackson was marching on Front Royal, he needed to know that he would be facing more than just the thousand troops garrisoned in the town. Belle knew that her father was among the Rebel troops marching with Jackson, and this made the delivery of the information urgent. She started to make a plan.

The next morning her time ran out. Rifle fire could be heard in the distance. Jackson's troops were nearing town. She ran to her room, gathered up a pair of opera glass binoculars and the notes she had received in Winchester and headed for the hotel balcony. From there she saw a line of Confederate skirmishers no more than three quarters of a mile away. She ran out of the house, wearing a royal blue dress, white bonnet and high laced boots. Her lungs burned from the effort to run in this kind of outfit, but she had no time to change. Through the streets of the town she dashed, and into the fields beyond, waving her white bonnet over her head all the while. Dust began to kick up around her from Minnie balls fired at her by Union pickets. Rebel skirmishers, some of them local boys, saw her running toward them and recognized her. They began to cheer her and then started returning the Union pickets fire. Henry Kidd Douglas, a twenty-one year old aide to General Jackson, recognized her as she drew near and informed the General, who motioned the aide to go to her assistance. "Good God Belle, you here? What is it?" Belle gathered her breath and passed Douglas the information she had, urging him to inform General Jackson immediately. With that, she turned blew him a kiss and made her way back to town. Douglas gave Jackson the information and told him who had delivered it.

Now aware that Union reinforcements were close by, Jackson pushed his attack and forced the Union occupiers of Front Royal to retreat so quickly that they had no chance to await reinforcements. 85 Union soldiers were killed and 700 were taken prisoner.

When Henry Kidd Douglas entered Front Royal after the battle, he found Belle talking with Union troops, now prisoners of the Confederate Army. As he bent down from his horse to greet her she pinned a red rose on his uniform coat. "Remember," she said, "it is blood red, and it is my color."

Later that day a courier came to deliver a note to Belle. It was addressed to Miss Belle Boyd, and it read "I thank you, for myself and for the army, for the immense service that you have rendered your country today." It was signed "Hastily, your friend, T.J. Jackson, C.S.A."

***

Within a month Jackson's forces were called away from Front Royal to assist the new commander of the Army of Northern Virginia, Robert E. Lee, in his effort to push back a Northern army threatening Richmond, Virginia. Once Jackson's forces departed, Federal troops re-occupied Front Royal. Belle's exploits during the battle for the town had created headlines in newspapers North and South. Northern newspapers accused her of being nothing more than a camp follower or prostitute, while southern press created titles for her like "the Cleopatra of Secession," "La Belle Rebelle," and "The Siren of the Shenandoah." That notoriety led to Union forces detaining her as a prisoner in the cottage behind her Aunt's Fishback Hotel. Her status as a prisoner did not lessen her determination to aid in the defeat of the Yankees in any way she could.

Belle's ongoing attempts to gain information were made more difficult by her newfound fame. She knew that she was being watched and followed. A townsman, Eugene Blockley, had been recruited by Union spymaster Allan Pinkerton to trail her. The dispatches he sent Pinkerton about Belle caused the detective to write the following report about her.

She gets around considerably, is very shrewd, <u>and is probably acting as a spy</u>. She is an open, earnest and undisguised secessionist, and talks secession on all practicable occasions…Informant considers her more efficient in carrying news to the rebels of our operations than <u>any three men</u> in the valley.

One day Belle saw a Confederate soldier standing near her cottage under a tree. She approached him and asked for his name. He identified himself as C.W.D. Smitley, a rebel parolee who hoped to soon be able to rejoin Confederate forces. Belle found him to be genial and handsome, and asked him to join her for dinner that night at a neighbor's home. He agreed.

The night's entertainment was a pleasant diversion for Belle, surrounded as she was by loyal Southerners. She played the piano and led Smitley and the dinner guests in a rousing version of the Southern anthem "The Bonnie Blue Flag."

The next day Smitley told Belle that he had received his release papers from Union authorities and was leaving to head south to join rebel forces. She asked him if, on his way south, he would deliver a note for her to General Jackson. He agreed. She then wrote a note containing information about the troop strength and intended movements of an army commanded by Union General John Pope in the Valley area and handed it to Smitley, who promised "by all the hosts of heaven" to deliver it.

Hours later, at yet another party, a Union officer approached her and commented that she was seeing a lot lately of a Confederate officer named Smitley. Belle told him that was none of his business. The Union officer corrected her saying that it was, in fact, his business. Smitley was a spy that he had dispatched to uncover her secret rebel activities. He then hauled her off to her cottage, instructing guards outside to keep her there until further notice.

Two weeks later a group of Union horsemen galloped up to the cottage and ordered Eliza to bring Belle to them. The officer in charge of the group, a Major Sherman, informed her that she was under arrest and showed her his orders.

Sir: You will proceed immediately to Front Royal, Virginia, and arrest, if found there, Miss Belle Boyd, and bring her at once to Washington.

> *I am respectfully,*
> *Your obedient servant,*
> *E.M.Stanton*

Eliza tried but failed to stop the soldiers from taking Belle away. Her neighbors crowded the street to see the ruckus. Not all were sad. A young neighbor woman watched her go, later commenting with bitterness or jealousy:

Belle Boyd was taken prisoner and sent off in a carriage with an escort of fifty cavalrymen today. I hope she has succeeded in making herself proficiently notorious now.

The next day, when she arrived in Washington, Belle was thrilled to hear that she would be placed in Old Capitol Prison, the same jail where the most famous of Southern female spies, Rose O'Neal Greenhow was incarcerated. Finally she was being accorded the recognition her work deserved!

She was introduced to the Superintendent of the facility, who provided her with as comfortable a cell as possible. He also promised to supply her with a maid and whatever else, within reason, she might require. He concluded their meeting by saying "I am glad I have so distinguished a personage for my guest." Belle was insulted by his kindness. How dare he treat her so kindly? She considered herself his enemy, and wanted to be treated as the dangerous spy she felt she was. She resolved to cause whatever trouble necessary to elicit the rougher treatment her exploits had earned her.

She started by demanding that a fire be lit in the fireplace and a rocking chair placed near it. She received both. A detective then entered her cell asked her to sign an oath of allegiance to the United States. When she refused he told her, "Well, if this is your resolution, then you'll have to lay here and die, and serve you right." Prisoners in adjoining cells heard the exchange and cheered her defiance with shouts of "Bravo!"

Belle continued her "resistance" to federal authority in the days that followed by singing rebel songs at the top of her voice and passing notes of encouragement to other prisoners. To make her time in jail more tolerable she began a flirtation with a fellow prisoner. They passed romantic notes back and forth across the next month. Belle felt sure that Lieutenant Clifford McVay, the object of her attentions, was about to propose to her, but he never got the chance. After a little more than one month in prison Belle was informed that she was to be returned to the South as part of a prisoner exchange. She was forbidden to return to the North until the end of the war.

***

In 1863 the northwestern counties of Virginia, which contained more people supportive of the North than the South, held a convention, separated themselves from the state of Virginia and declared their area to be West Virginia, the 35th state in the Union. Belle had been at home in Martinsburg for some time after being released from Old Capitol Prison, and she now found herself living in the North – a violation of her release agreement. She knew she could be arrested, but chose to remain with her family despite that fact. She was helping nurse her 37 year old mother back to health after the birth of Belle's new sister. Within weeks officers showed up at Belle's home and informed her that Secretary of War Edwin Stanton had ordered her returned to Washington, D.C. Her father, still recovering from an injury he received while fighting in Stonewall Jackson's army, was allowed to accompany her on her journey. Outside the gates of Carroll Prison he gave his daughter a kiss goodbye, both fearing that they might never see each other again.

Her stay was much less of an adventure than her previous one. The cell she was provided contained a broken chair, an ancient table, rusty iron bed, broken mirror, washbowl and pitcher. A small amount of light filtered through a tiny window streaked with filth. She was kept under constant watch by the Superintendent's men, in the hopes that she might make incriminating statements while talking with other inmates.

She did manage to engage in some spy craft while at Carroll Prison. Someone identified only as "C.H." began to shoot arrows into her cell from the street outside. The arrows had a rubber ball and note attached. The notes contained information about Union troop movements, apparently gathered in Washington by pro-southern men and women. They had faith that somehow Belle would be able to use her contacts to pass the information to rebel forces outside Washington. She responded to the letters by wrapping the rubber ball in a note of acknowledgment, and tossing it back out the window.

On December 1, 1863 Belle was freed from Carroll Prison in a deal negotiated for her by her father. She was taken by ship to Fort Monroe, Virginia, to await transport by a Confederate prison exchange boat, and then taken to Richmond. She was ordered never to return to Union territory.

***

While in Richmond, Belle learned that her father had died as a result of the wounds he suffered in battle. She had tried to see him after he had obtained her release, while they both were still in Washington D.C., but the Federal government had denied her request. Now he was gone and her bitterness toward her Northern enemies was greater than ever. She wrote to Union officials asking for permission to visit her mother in Martinsburg, but that request was denied.

Unable to return home to Eliza and her mother, and with her father gone, she decided to get as far away from the war as possible by visiting Europe. Belle thought that she might be received well there, among the pro-Southern English people and the many ex-patriot Southerners who had fled there.

***

Belle set sail for England on May 8, 1864, aboard the Greyhound, a fast new steamer driven by three sails and a propeller. She could relax now, safe in the company of ship's captain, George Bier, who had been a friend of her father. She told Bier that she was hiding gold in her skirts, but did not share with him the fact that she was also carrying secret diplomatic dispatches from the Confederate government to be delivered to contacts in England.

The Greyhound left port at night in order to evade Yankee gunboats enforcing a blockade of all Southern shipping. As the morning sun came up everyone onboard breathed a sigh of relief that they had seen no Yankee ships during the tension filled night. But their relief was short lived. Sails appeared on the horizon. It was a ship, a Yankee ship, closing fast. It quickly became clear that the Greyhound could not outrun its pursuer, so the Captain informed his passengers that he would be forced to surrender the ship in a short time. Cannon shots began to land all around the Greyhound as the passengers scattered below decks to gather their things. Belle ran to her cabin, took her dispatches out of their hiding place and burned them.

When Belle came back up on deck she saw a rough looking Yankee officer receiving the ship's surrender from Captain Bier. Union sailors then escorted Belle back to her cabin where she was locked in with guards posted outside. After a brief time Belle's cabin door swung open and she came face to face with another Yankee officer. Lieutenant Samuel Hardinge introduced himself as the man now in charge of the vessel. He had long, dark hair that touched his shoulders, with large, bright eyes that drew her in. "I beg you will consider yourself a passenger, not a prisoner," he told her.

The Greyhound changed course and headed for the port of Boston, and Belle worried what fate awaited her there: jail, or perhaps even hanging as a spy? But fate and love intervened. The ship's commander, Samuel Hardinge, had fallen in love with her. Perhaps the war with its ever present possibilities of death sped love's course, but in a matter of weeks he was proposing to marry her. Even Belle was surprised by her potent powers of seduction. The marriage would have to wait, however. Hardinge was under suspicion of complicity in the escape of Captain Beir from the Greyhound, and would have to answer to a court of inquiry in Boston. Actually it was Belle who had helped Captain Beir to escape, but she did not share that fact with her fiancée.

Once they arrived in Boston, Belle began a letter writing campaign to be set free. Much to her surprise Secretary of the Navy Gideon Welles granted her passage to Canada. She was told to leave within 24 hours and warned that she would be shot if she ever returned to the United States. The lovers parted sadly, with Hardinge promising Belle that he would join her soon in England, where she had told him she was going after landing in Canada. There they would become husband and wife.

***

In August 1864 Belle landed in England and wasted little time contacting Henry Hotze, a southern sympathizer active in passing messages from the Confederate states to the English government. She explained to him what had been contained in the message she had destroyed aboard the Greyhound, for it was her habit to memorize any sensitive information she was asked to deliver, as a backup in case the notes were lost or needed to be destroyed. He then gave her a personal letter he had been holding for her. It was from Lieutenant Hardinge, her intended. In it Hardinge explained that he had been dismissed from the Navy for "neglect of duty" and had travelled to Europe to locate her. He had gotten to England before her, and when he could not find her in London he had travelled to Paris. If he could not find her there he was planning to return to London to continue his search. Belle was overjoyed, and sent him a telegram asking him to return to her as soon as he could. Soon she would be reunited with Samuel, and even better, he was no longer a Yankee soldier! She would see to it that he became a proper rebel.

Their wedding took place at Saint James Church in Piccadilly. Belle dressed in white and carried a bouquet of orange blossoms, usually representing chastity, purity and fertility. That may have been a bit of a stretch in this case.

Belle asked her husband to return to the United States and visit her family home. There he could introduce himself to her family and share stories of their wedding. She, of course, could not join him, per her release agreement from Carroll Prison. While Samuel readied himself for the trip, Belle decided to write a letter to the President of the Confederate States, Jefferson Davis. She wanted to make sure that she and her exploits were not forgotten while she was in exile.

Honorable Jefferson Davis

Dear Sir,
I suppose that the news of my marriage has been rec'd in the Confederacy…My husband will soon be in the South, where I trust he will meet a warm reception… I trust from my marrying a man of Northern birth my Country will not doubt my loyalty…Mr. Hardinge has given up all property and everything. His father…has disinherited him for joining the Southern Cause and marrying a rebel.
Do you think there will be peace soon? England wishes for it and all here sympathize with the South…If at any time I can be of benefit to my country, command me.

Samuel left London and set sail for America. He then travelled overland to Martinsburg, Virginia, and, as Belle wanted, slept in her old room. He met Eliza, but not Belle's mother, who was away visiting friends in another town. The next morning he boarded a train to Baltimore, Maryland. He was stopped by detectives before he got to the city. They asked him where his wife was, and whether he was carrying secret messages. He told them she was not in the United States and that he was not in possession of any messages, but that did not stop them from arresting him for desertion. The charge was false, as Hardinge had been dismissed from the service, but it allowed the detectives to detain Hardinge for more questioning in Washington D.C. Once they transported him to the Capitol he was tossed into Carroll Prison, the same place Belle had been held not so long before.

Back in England Belle was working on a plan to keep her name in the forefront of the news. She was writing a memoir. It was to be entitled "Belle Boyd, in Camp and Prison." It was her story as she wanted it known, full of fanciful encounters, colorful characters, death defying escapes and some actual truths. When the book was nearly completed Belle learned through the London newspapers of her husband's arrest and detention. Never one to back down from a fight, she resolved to free her husband. The urgency of her mission was increased by her recent realization that she was with child. Her pen and her book became her weapons of choice. She wrote a letter to President Lincoln himself.

Honorable Abraham Lincoln
President of the United States

I have heard from good authority that if I suppress the Book I have now ready for publication, you may be induced to consider leniently the case of my husband, S. Wylde Hardinge, now a prisoner…If you will release my husband & set him free …I pledge my word that my Book shall be suppressed. Should my husband not be with me by the 25th of March I shall at once place my Book in the hands of a publisher.

Belle alluded to facts contained in the book that would prove very embarrassing to the Lincoln administration in its efforts to convince England to halt its support of the South in the war. It was a remarkably bold act to threaten the President of the United States, but boldness was something that Belle had in abundance. The war in America was winding down with Union forces everywhere slowly strangling the life out of what was left of the Confederacy, and Lincoln was busy day and night guiding his country to a bloody victory. He never replied to Belle's letter, but on February 3, 1865, 10 days after Belle issued her threat, Samuel Hardinge was released from prison. Within weeks Samuel was back at Belle's side in London.

***

The monies that Belle had been receiving from supporters in the South stopped coming. Perhaps it was because the South was in ruins as the war ended. Belle suspected that Union officials were at fault, intercepting her packages from home. The result was that the Hardinges' were out of funds. They were evicted from their rooms at the fashionable Brunswick Hotel for non-payment, and took up residence in a less than desirable part of London. Belle began to berate her husband for their state of affairs, calling him "the fool that had married her," and he took to drinking to escape her anger, frequently drinking until he passed out.

Her pregnancy was advancing, and Belle knew that she must provide for the child to come. She would have her book published (not including the facts embarrassing to the Lincoln administration, if there ever were any) and then train for her debut on the stage. Once she mastered acting (as she was sure she would), she could commence her career as a lecturer/performer, playing herself in dramatizations of stories from her memoir of life as a female Southern spy.

Belle's sadness at the collapse and surrender of Southern forces in 1865 was lightened by the birth of her daughter Grace. Married life brought Belle no security or domestic peace. Samuel Hardinge spent many evenings away from his wife and baby, preferring the company of Fannie Sinclair, known locally as a "courtesan."

Belle threw herself into preparation for the stage, receiving training from Walter Montgomery, an English Shakespearean actor, and an American actress named Avonia Jones. On June 1, 1866 she appeared in the romantic comedy The Lady of Lyons at the Theatre Royal in Manchester, England. While she was criticized for displaying a surprising timidity onstage for one so famed for braving enemy bullets in war, the reviews were, on the whole, very favorable. She went on to appear in several other productions during the months that followed, convinced that she had now found an exciting and challenging new career to replace her adrenaline inducing exploits as a spy.

In the United States, President Andrew Johnson, who had replaced the assassinated Abraham Lincoln as the Civil War ended, was engaged in a struggle with Congress to shape a reconstruction policy he hoped would bring Southern states peacefully back into the Union. To further that end he issued a proclamation of amnesty to most former rebels. When Belle read about the amnesty in English newspapers, she made a decision. She had for months considered her former savior and husband, Samuel Hardinge, "utterly worthless." She booked passage for herself and Grace on a steamer leaving for the United States.

Once they arrived in the U.S., Belle filed for and was granted a divorce from her husband. She asked for no alimony. Free from him and his name, she began to work on getting bookings to continue her career on the American stage. When anyone inquired about her ex-husband, she simply replied that he had died. Whether he was dead at that time is not known.

Over the next two years Belle travelled across the country, appearing in her show entitled "The Perils of a Spy," and billing herself as Belle Boyd, "The Cleopatra of the Secession." Frequently the show would open with Belle, riding a horse onto the stage, costumed in one of the outfits she wore during her days as a rebel courier.

After a performance in New Orleans in 1869 a man from the audience approached Belle and asked her to dinner. Her admirer was John Swainston Hammond, a handsome 40 year old Englishman and former Union soldier who now made a living as a travelling coffee and tea salesman. The dinner must have gone well, for within a month the two were married. Belle gave up the stage and together with Grace and Hammond moved to California.

Belle was not cut out to be subservient, deferential, or particularly domestic, which was what men expected women of the day to be. She struggled with the role of wife and mother. There were many heated arguments and much heartache. After suffering some sort of mental breakdown Belle checked herself into an insane asylum for treatment. There, in 1870 she gave birth to a son, whom they named Arthur Davis Lee Jackson Hammond, after her heroes of the Confederacy. The baby died months later while she was still under care at the asylum.

In the fall Belle's doctors declared her "recovered," and she went home to her husband. Swainston's job forced them to move repeatedly, never really allowing them to build any lasting friendships or attachments. Belle gave birth to three more children: a boy named

John, and two daughters named Byrd and Maria Isabella, known, like her mother, by the nickname "Belle."

***

If Belle's early life had been unconventional, her middle years became completely bizarre. During 15 years of absence from the stage her name had remained in the news, not through her efforts, but through those of imposters. A woman in Virginia had been lecturing in Masonic lodges around the state as Belle Boyd, the Southern Spy. In Pennsylvania a female scam artist was using the name Belle Boyd to cash fake checks. When the real Belle and her family moved to Texas they learned that someone claiming to be Belle Boyd was making money appearing in small town opera houses telling tales from the real Belle's memoirs.

In 1884 Belle's 19 year old daughter Grace took up with a man, and when she learned of it, Belle confronted him and shot him. Fortunately for Belle, he was only wounded. She then disowned her daughter as "ruined," and "dead to the family." Later that same month, after she discovered that her husband John had another wife, she divorced him. When he subsequently divorced the second wife Belle remarried him. Soon after John accused Belle of having an affair and they both headed to divorce court, each claiming to be the injured party. Grace, despite having been read out of the family not long before, supported her mother in the proceedings. She accused her father of beating and berating her mother. A divorce was granted in November.

John Swainston's accusation of Belle's having an affair was probably justified. Less than six weeks after their divorce was granted, Belle, the apparently incurable romantic, married again. Swainston had been fourteen years older than Belle when they married. This time she was the one marrying a youngster. At age forty she married Nathaniel Rue High, a 24- year- old actor who generally played juvenile roles in small acting companies.

For a time Belle earned extra money for the family by giving elocution lessons, but that amount, together with her husband's wages, was not enough to pay their bills. So, with her husband encouraging her and serving as her business manager, Belle went back to the stage. She began touring with a show she called "The Perils of a Spy," booking engagements in towns big and small. Sometimes she would perform for Confederate veteran's organizations to augment her earnings. When she was with groups like those she would come onstage wearing a plumed hat that she claimed Jeb Stuart, the famed rebel cavalry leader, was wearing when he was shot and killed. Then she would bring her audience to tears with a little speech in which she claimed that her first two husbands had died bravely defending the South. Neither claim was true, but both were crowd pleasers.

For the next fourteen years Belle crisscrossed America appearing before a steadily diminishing crowd of fans. She and her family barely managed to stay a half step ahead of debt collection companies.

On June 12, 1900, while giving a recitation to members of the Methodist Church of Kilbourn (now Wisconsin Dells), Wisconsin, 56-year-old Belle Boyd suffered a heart attack and died. Her family was too destitute to afford a proper burial for her, so the Women's Relief Corps, a branch of the Grand Army of the Republic (predominantly Union veterans) took up a collection to pay her burial expenses. In death Belle's bitter Yankee enemies forgave her and saw her to her grave. Her pall bearers were four veteran Union soldiers.

***

Belle Boyd lived a wholly unconventional life. She was a fearless, self-confident, headstrong, opinionated woman who lived in an age when women were supposed to be seen and not heard. She was on the losing side in war, and more often than not, in love. She was a romantic who never gave up the hope that her next love would be The One. She died poor and surrounded by former enemies, but she died onstage, the center of attention. She would have loved that.

3

FAME IN FAILURE

George Edward Pickett

People who know very little about the Civil War and care even less about history still recognize the name George Pickett. "He's the guy who led that charge, right?" they say. Their knowledge of him, like their recognition of Custer at the Little Big Horn and Crockett at the Alamo is part of the mythic history of America created when what they learned from their teachers is mixed in with what they watch as "history" on television and at the movies. The images these famous names conjure up for us may not be correct, but they are bright, colorful and exciting.

***

The day that wreathed George Pickett's name with glory, July 3, 1863, began for him in predawn darkness as he moved about his camp watching his officers stir their men from a long night's rest. His division, part of James Longstreet's First Corps of the Army of Northern Virginia would have a short march to make, then move into position on the battlefield at Gettysburg, Pennsylvania to play a crucial role in the biggest battle ever fought on the American continent.

The life that peaked that day in brutal violence began very differently. George Pickett was born on January 16, 1825, on his family's plantation on Turkey Island, Henrico County, Virginia. He was the oldest of the eight children of Robert and Mary Pickett. Considered one of the "first families" of Virginia, his family could trace their ancestors back to France some 800 years before.

Most of George's early years were spent hunting and fishing on his family's plantation. His father, Robert Pickett, had inherited it from George's namesake grandfather, who had been a senior partner in a Richmond mercantile firm. George loved the outdoors, but was not what one would consider a hardy outdoors type. He grew to be of less than average height, with a small- boned, delicate frame, small hands and feet. He kept his curly dark brown hair long. He, like his mother, was being prone to nervous disorders and intestinal problems.

In order to establish his independence and stand out, George developed a tendency to disobey orders and defy authority. To help him learn to live within limits, his parents enrolled him in Richmond Academy, a quasi-military school for the landed gentry. While there he engaged in frequent schoolyard fights, winning acceptance from his peers by facing up to bigger schoolmates who tried to bully the younger students.

During these early school days it became apparent that George would not become a scholar. He showed no aptitude for English or Mathematics, though he did excel in his ability to read and speak French. His interests were quite singular. He loved the military drill and tactics taught at the Academy.

The military life was in George's blood. His family was known as "the Fighting Pickett's of Fauquier County." Fifteen of George's relatives served in the Revolutionary War and a goodly number in the War of 1812.

Pickett's preparations for a future in the military seemed certain until his parent's fortunes hit a low point during the financial panic of 1837. They could no longer afford to send George to Richmond Academy. George's mother appealed to her older brother, Andrew Johnston, an established lawyer with a practice in the frontier town of Quincy, Illinois. She asked him to help George by allowing him to study law with Johnston in preparation to join the Bar.

George dutifully moved to Quincy and began to study law under the watchful eye of his uncle. Studying precedents and treatises and writing out wills and deeds was not the exciting challenge that George craved. He soon let his parents and uncle know he needed to steer his life in some other direction. He would not move back in with his parents because he knew they were still struggling to make ends meet. George decided to ask his uncle for help in pursuing his real dream – a life in the military.

Andrew Johnston had good political connections through his active membership in the Whig Party. He sought help for George from one of his close friends, a young Springfield lawyer named Abraham Lincoln. Lincoln had a law partner named John T. Stuart, who was currently serving a term as a US Congressman. As a member of the US House, Stuart had the power to appoint young people to West Point. Johnston, Lincoln and Pickett began a campaign to convince Stuart that Pickett was worthy of such an appointment. On April 19, 1842, that campaign ended in success as George Pickett received his appointment to the US Military Academy at West Point, class of 1846.

***

The traits that caused him difficulty at Richmond Academy manifested themselves again in George's days at West Point. George's need to challenge authority and ignore rules garnered him a near record number of demerits as he neared graduation. William M. Gardner, a faculty member, said of him that he was "a man of ability, but belonging to a cadet set that appeared to have no ambition for class standing and wanted to do only enough to secure their graduation." This he did accomplish - barely. On July 1, 1846 George Pickett graduated last in his class of 59 students. In his defense, nearly 1/3 of those who began studies with him at West Point washed out before ever graduating.

Such low ranking in a graduating class at West Point meant that the newly minted Lieutenant would receive his first posting to the infantry, not the highly preferred Corps of Engineers. And that posting would be to some obscure fort far away from possibilities of fame or rapid advancement. George travelled home to his family's plantation in Virginia to await orders for his new posting. He passed the days, then weeks anxiously waiting for word of where he might be sent. This could have been a miserable time for George had he not been able to spend much of it keeping company with a charming and attractive 17-year -old neighbor, Sally Minge. They grew close in the short time they had together. Despite the pleasure of Sally's company, George was thrilled to finally receive his orders. They were all he could have hoped for.

In the last year of his studies at West Point relations between the US and Mexico had become strained to the breaking point. President James K Polk was determined to obtain land in the Southwest from Mexico. He offered to buy land, but Mexico refused to consider it. He then ordered a small army under the command of General Zachary Taylor to march across Texas to the Rio Grande River and camp on a piece of land whose ownership was in dispute between Mexico and the US. Inevitably a skirmish occurred between Mexican and US forces. Both sides claimed the other was the aggressor. Polk had his justification for war. Claiming Mexican troops had attacked the peaceful army camp on US soil, Polk ordered Taylor's army into Mexico to punish the aggressors.

***

Second Lieutenant George Pickett was ordered to report for duty with the 8th Infantry regiment in General Zachary Taylor's army at its camp in Monterey, Mexico. There would be no quiet, obscure first posting for George Pickett. He was headed to the front lines of a brand new war.

During the following 1½ years he spent in Mexico, Pickett formed some crucial relationships. Two that lasted for the rest of his life and had great influence on the course of it were his friendship with James Longstreet, who went on to become Pickett's mentor and commander in the Civil War, and Ulysses S Grant, who helped Pickett in a time of need after the war. George also won two brevets, or promotions, as a result of his actions in battle at Churubusco and Chapultepec.

***

By July 1848, the US and Mexico ended the war by signing the Treaty of Guadalupe Hidalgo. Soon brevet Captain George Pickett and the 8th Infantry were ordered out of Mexico to their next duty station, Jefferson Barracks, outside Saint Louis, Missouri. This marked the beginning of a 13- year stretch of peacetime duty for the Hero of Chapultepec.

The regiment spent a few months at Jefferson Barracks reorganizing, refitting and recruiting back to full strength. Then they were ordered to Camp Worth, outside San Antonio, Texas. Their main function was to keep the peace between the settlers out on this fringe of the frontier and to police the actions of raiding Kiowa and Comanche Indians. Pickett and his troops had small skirmishes with Indians, but mostly they were quick hit and run affairs. Pickett's days were filled with the monotonous chores of frontier army officer, overseeing forage details, wood cutting parties, repair crews, infantry drill, and occasionally getting away to visit officer friends at neighboring outposts.

In December 1850 Pickett took extended leave to visit Sally Minge, with whom he had been corresponding for nearly two years. When he last visited his family plantation on Turnkey Island, Virginia, he had met and courted her, then continued the courting by mail. Now that long distance romance was concluding with their marriage. George and Sally wed on January 28, 1851, and enjoyed an extended 6- month honeymoon. George's leave was up, so they packed all of Sally's necessaries into a wagon and began the long trek west back to Texas. For Sally this was an especially difficult journey, as she was six months pregnant.

Once the young marrieds arrived in Texas, Sally did her best to set up a home for them on the post. She had moved from the comfort of her family's big home in Virginia to a post full of strangers in the middle of what was then called The Great American Desert. Extreme temperatures, poor housing, food and sanitation, as well as tarantulas, scorpions and poisonous insects of all sorts were the norm.

After less than three months of harsh frontier life, Sally Minge Pickett died during childbirth. Her baby died with her. George, a usually easygoing, happy man, sank into depression. Friends said he never fully regained his old demeanor. He remained prone to fits of moodiness and anger for the rest of his life. More than a year after his wife's passing he wrote, "I am no longer the same person; the buoyancy of youth is past. I look forward to nothing with pleasure. It is sinful to cherish such feelings, still there are many times when I cannot stifle them."

Soon after his wife's death, in an attempt to lessen the anguish he was dealing with, Pickett again took a leave and returned home to Virginia. At his family's plantation George took long walks in the woods. He particularly liked to stroll along the seawall near Fort Monroe, at the tip of the James Peninsula. In the spring of 1853, while resting under a tree during one of these strolls, he met a little four-year-old girl named LaSalle Corbel. She was visiting her grandmother who lived nearby. The little girl sat down next to Pickett and asked him why he was alone and looked so sad. She told him she too was alone and sad because she was away from and missed her family. She had whooping cough and they had sent her to her grandmother so her family would not be exposed to it. She wondered if he had whooping cough too. He smiled, snapped a salute and said no. She was very touched by how sad he seemed – and, according to her diary written years later, by his good looks and splendid uniform. She recalled her first sight of him, "As he lay stretched in the shade, not tall, and rather slender, but very graceful, perfect in manly beauty."

With a child's unknowing insensitivity, LaSalle pressed him about the reason for his sadness, and he finally broke his silence, telling her of how his little family had died and left him so lonely. Moved by the story, she told him that she would be his little girl now and his wife just as soon as she grew up.

He returned her kindness by giving her a ring inscribed with his wife Sally's name. Pickett and little LaSalle met several more times while he was home on leave. He taught her how to write her first two words, Sallie and Soldier.

Pickett returned to Texas when his leave ended. His time with 4 -year-old LaSalle Corbell was a healing balm for his suffering heart, but he did not expect to see her again.

The next two years found Pickett changing posts in Texas several times, all the while leading his company in suppressing Indian raids. In March, 1855, Pickett was ordered to report to and take command of Company D, 9th Infantry, which was at that time recruiting and refitting at Fort Monroe Virginia, where he had met young LaSalle Corbell years before.

By summer, Pickett was drilling his new company, getting them ready for their next duty assignment. In the crowds of locals that came to view the drills were La Salle Corbell and her family. Having heard that Pickett was returning to the area, she had convinced them to come with her to see "Her Soldier." The two had very few chances to rekindle their oddly paired friendship (he was 23 years her senior) in the coming days. Orders had arrived and Pickett was very involved in last minute preparations for moving his company to their next duty station in the Northwest.

La Salle came back to Fort Monroe in November. Pickett had not departed with his company, but had been directed to report to Florida for court martial duty. She waved to him from shore as his ship departed, carrying him South.

His stay in Florida was short, only a few months. He then departed in March of 1856 for the Columbia River Territory, and then on to Fort Steilacoom near Puget Sound in Washington Territory. This area would be his home for the next five years. He survived the loneliness of outpost life here by marrying a Haidu Indian maiden named Morning Mist, reputedly a princess of her tribe. Marriage to local Indian maidens was then a very accepted part of frontier military life. Many times this arrangement was only "common law," but in Pickett's case they legally married. Unfortunately for Pickett this marriage was not to bring lasting happiness. On December 31, 1857 Morning Mist gave birth to a boy, who they named James Tilton Pickett. The boy grew strong and healthy after birth. The mother did not. Complications set in right away for the mother, and in early 1858, with only the most basic medical assistance available to help her, Morning Mist died.

Pickett threw himself into his soldiering without reservation, leaving his son for extended periods of time in the care of good friends in the area. While in the Northwest he earned high praise for his handling of a difficult military and diplomatic situation that developed between the United States and Great Britain. Tensions flared and troops were deployed by both sides in a dispute over ownership of a small island in Puget Sound. Pickett and a small contingent of soldiers built a fort on the island and stood firm against threats of full scale invasion threatened by the British Admiral in the area. Eventually diplomacy replaced sword rattling and the issues were peacefully resolved.

As this incident, referred to in history as The Pig War (it all began over a pig that wandered from American land to British land) came to a slow boil, the United States was descending into the hell of Civil War.

***

By November 1860, Abraham Lincoln, the good friend of George Pickett's uncle (who had helped him get into West Point), was elected President. The election highlighted the growing gulf between northern and southern states. It was the most starkly geographic Presidential vote to date, with Lincoln garnering almost all of his support in the North and doing very badly in the South. By December, South Carolina had seceded and many Southern states, Pickett's Virginia included, were debating whether or not to join South Carolina. US military officers of Southern birth who had sworn an oath to serve the Union were beginning to resign their commissions and return home. Far away, in Washington Territory, Pickett felt a decision being forced on him.

While I love my country, I love my household, my state, more, and I could not be an infidel and lift my sword against my kith and kin, even though I do believe... that the measure of American greatness can be achieved only under one flag.

Events moved quickly. On April 14, 1861, after two days of sustained coastal artillery bombardment, Fort Sumter in Charleston Harbor lowered the flag of the United States and surrendered to South Carolinian militia forces. President Lincoln immediately called on the nation for 75,000 volunteers to serve until the rebellion could be ended. Virginia, which had up to this time been undecided, voted to secede from the Union rather than see its citizens enlist in a war against southern brethren. George Pickett knew that his ultimate loyalty was to his state. He resigned his commission in the US army and headed home to fight a war that would pit him against many of the good friends he had made during his studies at West Point and while fighting in the Mexican War.

George Pickett did not reach his home in Virginia until September of 1861. When he did finally arrive he was met with a less than enthusiastic reception. Neighbors thought it had taken him far too long to respond to his new country's call. Already there had been one great battle fought without him. Bull Run had proven that the South would not be an easy opponent for the North to defeat. Irwin McDowell's Union forces had been soundly defeated and driven back to Washington in a rout. Pickett began to send letters to and visit with influential friends, seeking an officer's commission in the armies of the Confederate States of America. His friend James Longstreet had commanded a brigade at Bull Run, and had performed so well that he earned promotion to Brigadier General. Pickett appealed to Longstreet to speak on his behalf to Richmond military authorities for a commission. On September 23, 1861, Pickett's and Longstreet's efforts were rewarded when George received a commission as a Colonel of infantry, and was ordered to command a mixed group of militia and volunteers defending the area around the lower Rappahannock River.

Pickett performed his duties well in this assignment, but he ran afoul of his commanding officer, Theophelious Holmes, when he publicly questioned some of his soldiers commitment to the cause. He felt that the non-slave holding and poor white soldiers of the army had less at stake than the land holding class, and would not be as reliable as was needed. When he travelled to Richmond to state his case to authorities above his commander's head, Holmes retaliated by stating that the number of troops now in the Rappahannock River area was insufficient to require an officer of Pickett's rank. Surely he was needed more somewhere else. Pickett, a Colonel without assignment, went back to Richmond to again lobby for a position with the premier Confederate army in the field, the Army of Virginia, commanded by Joseph Johnston. Johnston's Virginia family had long been friends with the Picketts, and Johnston had been familiar with Pickett's commendable record in the Mexican War. What finally tipped the scales in Pickett's favor in his endeavor to join Johnston's army involved a tragedy that befell his friend Longstreet. While they were both in Richmond an outbreak of scarlet fever occurred, infecting Longstreet's family. James was untouched, but three of his children contracted the illness and died. George devoted much time in assisting his friend, and Longstreet showed his appreciation by strongly endorsing Pickett to General Johnston for a position. On February 13, 1862, George Pickett received word that he had been promoted to the rank of Brigadier General and was assigned to head a brigade in the division commanded by the newly appointed Major General, James Longstreet. This rapid rise within the army created resentment of Pickett amongst some officers who thought that his connections rather than his qualifications lifted him to his current position.

By the spring of 1862 another of Pickett's Mexican War comrades had risen to prominence. George B. McLellan had been named Commander and Chief of the Union armies, replacing the aged Winfield Scott. A brilliant tactician and organizer, McLellan had taken over command of the Army of the Potomac, shattered by its defeat at Bull Run, and by reorganizing, re-equipping and retraining it, turned it into a confident 100,000 man host ready for new battles. McLellan then showed his tactical genius by surprising Joe Johnston's 50,000 man army with a move both unexpected and quick. He organized a massive flotilla of transports, loaded up his army and all its supplies, and sailed south by water along the Virginia coast to the tip of the James Peninsula near Fort Monroe, where the entire expedition disembarked some 90 miles from Richmond. He had bloodlessly skirted around Joe Johnston's entrenched army and was closer to Richmond than they were. Johnston recovered his poise quickly and marched his troops south to the James Peninsula in time to block McLellan from moving directly to Richmond untouched.

In the next few weeks each general showed his cautious nature. McLellan moved forward slowly, bringing his heavy siege cannon along with him. Johnston retreated in front of this numerically superior force, waiting for McLellan to make a mistake that would allow Johnston to strike a part of the Union army with overwhelming force.

During this retreat George Pickett's brigade took part in a battle at Williamsburg, Virginia, while guarding the rear of the army as it fell back. Union troops attempted to break through Pickett's rearguard and throw the main force of Johnston's army into confusion. Pickett's men fought off this attack, and in his after action report James Longstreet praised Pickett for having employed "his forces with great effect, ability and his usual gallantry."

Johnston's army now occupied a position very close to Pickett's family plantation, and to the home of LaSalle Corbell, the little girl who years ago had befriended Pickett when he was home on leave. Despite his many pressing duties, the two met several times during this campaign, their fondness and admiration for the other growing stronger.

Eventually Johnston ran out of space to fall back, as Richmond was only a handful of miles away. McLellan was near his goal. He wanted to force Johnston into a defensive posture in the massive earthworks surrounding Richmond, then move up his siege guns and pound the Confederate army to pieces and force the surrender of their capital. He finally made the tactical mistake Johnston was hoping for on the evening of May 31st, when the Union army's disposition for the night found it split into two parts. Two corps of McLellan's infantry were entrenched south of the Chickahominy River, with three more corps north of it. The river was running very high and only one old bridge connected the two. A heavy downpour might destroy the bridge and isolate the two wings of McLellan's force. Even without the rain, moving infantry across the creaky old bridge might prove dangerous. Unfortunately for McLellan, it began to rain heavily during the night.

Joe Johnston ordered an attack on the two corps south of the river to commence early in the morning on June 2nd, to be commanded by James Longstreet. Confederate infantry enjoyed success early in the day, nearly overwhelming Union forces south of the river. The attack faltered, then failed when McLellan was able to strengthen his stranded two corps by getting them enough reinforcements over the one bridge that still stood. Pickett and his troops were disappointed that they had missed the day's fighting, but their mood changed that night as they received orders to join Longstreet's main force at Seven Pines, south of the Chickahominy River. McLellan was planning to attack in the morning to regain the ground he had lost the day before, but James Longstreet beat McLellan to the punch and launched an attack on his position first, with Pickett's brigade joining in the fight. After heavy casualties on both sides, with no clear winner or loser, fighting came to end late in the day. The Federal advance toward Richmond had been halted, but they were still entrenched dangerously close to the Confederate capital.

The most important result of the Battle of Seven Pines was the wounding of the Confederate Army commander, Joe Johnston. His serious wounds forced him out of the war for some time, and he was replaced by Jefferson Davis' military advisor, Robert E Lee. Lee's reputation at this time was one of a cautious commander and his nickname said it all – "Granny Lee." Once he took over leadership of the Army of Northern Virginia, Lee began to prove that reputation totally inaccurate. Over the next several weeks Lee launched a series of powerful attacks against the Army of the Potomac which first stunned, then drove them back from the gates of Richmond to a defensive position on the James River far upriver from the rebel capital.

During one of these attacks, at Gaines Mill, George Pickett and his brigade played a key role. They found themselves facing a heavily defended enemy breastwork which had halted the Confederate attack. As the officers debated what to do Pickett's men jumped forward and began scrambling up the sides of the small fort into the face of heavy fire. Pickett, mounted on his black charger, raced up to their front, urging them over the top. He was struck in the right shoulder by a musket ball and knocked off his horse onto the ground. He then struggled to his feet and watched as his men swarmed over the fortification and drove the defenders away. He was carried from the field in considerable pain to begin what would be a three month recuperation.

***

Pickett spent the summer healing at his sister's home in Richmond. There was considerable swelling in his right shoulder and arm, and it took weeks for him to build the strength to sit up in bed. His real recovery began when LaSalle Corbell took leave from her studies at Lynchburg Academy and travelled to Richmond to nurse him. She sang for him, read to him and changed his bandages. He later wrote of how her nursing healed him, "blessing and cheering me. I can feel now the soft touch of your little white hands."

Pickett's wounds caused him to miss the second battle at Bull Run and the Antietam campaign. By October, 1862, he was ready to rejoin the army. Combat casualties had thinned the general officer ranks, so when Pickett rejoined the Army of Northern Virginia, he did so as a Major General, commanding a division in the First Corps, led by Lieutenant General James Longstreet.

Pickett's division was held in reserve during the battle of Fredricksburg in December, 1862. They could do nothing but watch as the new Union army commander, General Ambrose Burnside, ordered his troops to repeatedly charge the strongest point in Lee's defensive line. The defeat Burnside's army suffered was decisive and bloody. For his blundering mismanagement of the campaign, Burnside was relieved of command and replaced by Joe Hooker, whose sobriquet, "Fighting Joe'" was indicative of his command style.

In February of 1863 Pickett's brigade joined the rest of James Longstreet's First Corps as it was detached from the Army of Northern Virginia and ordered to take back the port of Suffolk, Virginia, from Union troops. The First Corps was to also forage about the rich farmlands in the area to gather supplies for Lee's army.

While down in the Suffolk area, Pickett was able to visit with his young love Sallie Corbell. She had been forced to leave her home when it became an active battle zone, moving to her Aunt's home at Barber Crossroads Virginia, just 10 miles from Suffolk. Pickett made the round trip ride from his division headquarters to Barber Crossroads almost every night. His adjutant disapproved of these nightly rendezvous. "I don't think his division benefitted by such carpet-knight doings in the field." Pickett ignored his objections saying "I must go. I must see her. I swear…I will be back before anything can happen." In the end his visits caused no real harm, except to his reputation. Within weeks he and Sallie were engaged. Their marriage was planned to take place that summer after Sallie graduated from Lynchburg Academy.

Before Longstreet could complete his mission of taking Suffolk he and his forces were recalled to the Army of Northern Virginia by Robert E Lee.

Pickett and Longstreet were not able to rejoin Lee's army before it had to fight Joe Hooker and the Army of the Potomac. Even without their forces, Lee was able to soundly outmaneuver and defeat Hooker at Chancellorsville, waging in the process a strategic masterpiece that is studied today as a classic example of boldness and calculated risk.

While Longstreet and Pickett were marching north to rejoin him, Lee sent orders for Pickett to detach two of his brigades for duty in other areas. This reduced his division from 6,000 to 4800 men. Pickett went so far in his anger over this perceived slight as to criticize Lee by letter, saying to him "it is well known that a small division will be expected to do the same amount of hard service as a large one and, as the army is now divided, my division will be the weakest."

After Chancellorsville, Lee conferred with President Jefferson Davis and convinced him that the time was once again right for an invasion of the north. Food would be plentiful there, troops could be recruited from the southern leaning citizens of Maryland and Virginia's citizens could for a brief time enjoy a respite from occupation by northern troops. And if a great battle could be won in the north, perhaps peace talks could begin. Davis was convinced and approved Lee's plan.

In late June of 1863 the Army of Northern Virginia marched north rapidly, with Union troops in Virginia unaware of their departure. Longstreet's Corps and an angry and slighted George Pickett caught up to Lee on the march north.

Once Lee's forces marched through Maryland and into Pennsylvania, Pickett's forces were assigned the duty of guarding the supply and ambulance wagons parked near Chambersburg. Pickett's men settled in, watching Longstreet's corps plus the army's commander, Robert E. Lee, head off down the road toward Cashtown and beyond it to the rail hub at Gettysburg. Days later they watched in dismay as stragglers and wounded soldiers came back up that same road telling them stories of a battle being fought at Gettysburg. The advance troops of Lee's main force had run into advance elements of the Army of the Potomac, now being led by George G. Meade, who had replaced Joe Hooker after the battle at Chancellorsville. The Union army had been searching desperately for Lee's army after it left
Virginia without them being aware. Finally they had found it. Pickett was frustrated. His division was understrength and could not move to help the army until some other troops came to relieve him and he received orders to do so. On July 1st cavalry detachments arrived to take over guarding the wagon train, and on July 2nd Pickett received the order he was waiting for. Longstreet ordered him to join the army at Gettysburg immediately. Pickett called in his officers and told them "We must move at once to Gettysburg. Order the men into line and lead the movement!" After a hard day-long march Pickett's men encamped just outside the town, awaiting orders for thenext day's

action.

Both armies had fought hard on July 2nd, with rebel forces nearly destroying the 3rd corps on the Union left flank and pressing the Union right flank position on Culp's Hill almost to the breaking point. By sunset Union forces were shaken but still in position holding the hills and ridges just east of the town of Gettysburg. In conference that night James Longstreet urged Lee to march around the Union left flank, get between Meade's army and Washington and thereby force Meade to attack Lee's army at a place of Lee's choosing. Lee's naturally aggressive nature would not let him ignore the fact that for two days his army had gotten the best of Meade's troops. He stated his opinion clearly, saying "The enemy is there, and there I will strike him." Orders were drawn up for a three stage attack at the earliest possible time in the morning. Lee believed that the weakest point in the Union line was its center. Troops had been drawn from there to reinforce both flanks of the Union line in the past two days, so it should be lightly held. The first stage of the assault would be a massive artillery barrage directed at the center of the Union position on Cemetery Hill. This would neutralize Union artillery there, stopping them from shelling advancing Confederate infantry. The second stage would be the infantry assault, comprised of parts of the three divisions commanded by George Pickett, Isaac Trimble and Johnston Pettigrew. The largest part of that force would be the 6,500 Virginians of Pickett's command. James Longstreet would be in overall charge of the effort, with Pickett coordinating the attack as it unfolded in the field. The third stage of the assault would be a cavalry attack led by J.E.B. Stuart, on the rear of the Union position on Cemetery Hill as the infantry struck from the front. This should cause panic amongst the hard pressed troops of the Union center, and Lee hoped, would cause their position to collapse and lead to a complete victory.

Once the meeting with Lee was concluded, Longstreet issued the necessary orders to his chief of artillery and to the three division commanders whose men would comprise the infantry assault.

At 3am Pickett woke his men and moved them toward their jump off point on the reverse slope of Seminary Hill. While they rested in the shade of the woods, Pickett rode out of the tree line to scout the ground his men would have to cross in order to strike the Union position. He saw before him almost a mile of treeless farmland, dotted with farmhouses, fences and ditches. At the far end of the fields, a small clump of trees could be seen atop a gentle slope. That was Cemetery Ridge, the target of the attack. He could see how difficult the task would be. It would take at least 15-20 minutes for the infantry to cross the open fields, nearly all of that time in range of Union artillery on Cemetery Ridge. How many of his men reached the Union lines would depend on how effective the opening confederate cannonade was in silencing those guns. When he returned to his men in the tree line he met Richard Garnett, one of his brigade commanders and told him to move as quickly as possible across the fields, "for in my opinion you are going to catch hell."

The heat of the day was stifling as Pickett's men began their final preparations. Ammunition was distributed, knapsacks and cooking gear were discarded, weapons cleaned and checked, final letters to loved ones written and passed to friends not making the assault. Soldiers scribbled their names on pieces of paper and pinned them to their uniforms so they could be identified if struck down. Prayers were whispered, songs were sung with friends.

Then, at 1 pm the quiet was shattered by the opening of the greatest artillery bombardment ever heard on the North American continent. Rumbling was heard as far away as Baltimore, Maryland. Windows were rattled in Washington D.C. After two hours of continuous shelling, Longstreet's chief of artillery, E.P. Alexander, saw movement on Cemetery Hill. The artillery stationed there was pulling out. He reported to Longstreet that now was the time to send the infantry forward. George Pickett, who was standing nearby awaiting the order to launch the attack, asked Longstreet if he should move his men forward. Still believing that a flanking maneuver was a better option than frontal assault, Longstreet merely looked up at Pickett, who took that as an affirmative response. Longstreet later recalled the moment, with Pickett riding "gracefully with his jaunty cap raked well over on his right ear and his long auburn locks, nicely dressed, hanging almost to his shoulders. He seemed rather a holiday soldier than a general at the head of a column which was about to make one of the grandest, most desperate assaults recorded in the annals of war."

Pickett and his staff moved forward with the men, who stretched across almost a half mile of ground, staying behind the leading brigades of Kemper and Garnett and ahead of Lewis Amistead's troops. He continued forward with them until they reached the Emmitsburg Road, about ½ mile from the Union lines. He, like his men, had been under heavy long range fire for most of the advance. The cannon on Cemetery Ridge that were thought to have been driven off had now returned to the crest of the ridge and were causing heavy casualties in the advancing Confederate ranks. Seeing his lines being rapidly thinned, Pickett yelled to his troops, "Give them a cheer boys!" and ordered them to advance at the double quick, hoping to lessen their time exposed to the damaging barrage.

The assaulting columns surged forward at a near run, with Pickett moving off south and to the rear to some higher ground that would allow him a clear view of his entire force as it closed with the Union lines. He would be criticized later by some for not leading the attack from the front, but he believed his main duty during the battle was to manage, not to inspire. He stayed where he could watch and react to unfolding events, maneuvering his advancing troops so that they would all converge at their objective, the clump of trees on Cemetery Ridge.

As his men reached a point some 300 yards from the waiting Union troops they had to deal with a serious obstacle. A wooden fence ran for several hundred yards between them and the base of Cemetery Ridge. Normally this fence would be quickly torn down by the advancing infantry, but this particular border fence was very solidly built and the troops could not tear it down. Instead they had to climb over it, all the while presenting themselves as almost stationary targets for Union rifleman and artillery looking down on them. Unit cohesion was disrupted and heavy casualties were taken. Once over the fence there was another delay while surviving officers attempted to regroup their forces for the final push up the ridge, all the while being raked with rifle fire. As officers shouted orders and Confederates dressed their lines the Union artillerists switched from using solid shot (heavy balls designed to strike the ground just in front of a target and bounce along striking troops) to canister, which turned the cannon into giant shotguns, each muzzle load containing hundreds of small round pellets that would shred and tear men to pieces. The scene around the fence line was hell on earth. The air filled with whistling minie balls and canister, the ground slippery with spilled blood and severed limbs. As the badly depleted ranks of Pickett's infantry charged the last 200 yards up the gentle slope of Cemetery Ridge, thousands of Union infantry leveled their rifles and steadied their aim at the crowd of Confederates now just yards away. Union officers shouted the command to fire and in an instant Pickett's men seemed to melt away. Lewis Armistead's brigade had gotten to this point largely intact. They stood at the clump of trees in the center of the Union line. Another 100 yards and the Union line would be broken. But Armistead's brigade was being shot down by rapidly arriving Union reinforcements.

Back at his vantage point Pickett could see little of what was happening to his division through the heavy cloud of gun smoke that hung over Cemetery Ridge. He saw Armistead's regimental flags move up the slope of the ridge and then disappear into the shroud of smoke. He could also see many Union flags converging on the clump of trees up there. Pickett looked for the brigade of Cadmus Wilcox, who was to advance now to reinforce Pickett's men on the ridge, but he was not where he was supposed to be. Up on Cemetery Ridge, Lewis Armistead's brigade was being forced backward by the tide of Union troops rallying toward the clump of trees. Armistead anxiously looked back over his shoulder for the support troops he had been promised. They weren't there. Wilcox had blundered into the Union lines at the wrong point on the field and had been driven back with heavy losses. Some of Armistead's men, exhausted and bleeding, began to back off the ridge. Others, exhausted or too badly wounded to retreat, dropped their weapons and held up their hands. Armistead himself went down with a bullet through both lungs. Days later he would die in a Union hospital.

George Pickett, staring in disbelief with his field binoculars, saw the remains of his attack force suddenly appear out of the smoke. They were moving slowly back across the field, picking their way between the bodies of their fallen friends as they headed for the Confederate position on Seminary Ridge. Acknowledging the obvious, Pickett ordered a full retreat of all attacking troops who could respond. Up on Cemetery Ridge, Union troops were standing up, waving their flags and guns and taunting the retreating rebels with the chant "Fredricksburg! Fredricksburg!" The horrible losses they had sustained there were now avenged.

Reports began to arrive from his staff informing Pickett of the casualties. It was as bad as he imagined. Of his brigade commanders, Richard Garnett was dead. James Kemper was thought to be mortally wounded (he would survive). Lewis Armistead was badly wounded and captured. Within hours Pickett would know that he had lost 2,700 of the 6,300 men he had sent into combat. His division, as a cohesive fighting unit, had ceased to exist.

Once back on the ridge, Pickett ran into James Longstreet, commander of the assault force. "General," Pickett said, "I am ruined; my division is gone. It is destroyed." Soon General Lee rode up to join them. Anxious to repel any counter attack Meade's forces might mount, he ordered Pickett to regroup his division and prepare to meet the enemy. Pickett stared at him and said "General, I no longer have a division."

George Pickett's enmity toward Robert E. Lee began that day and remained with him the rest of his life. Lee did not reciprocate those feelings, even that day. On the evening of July 3rd Lee said to one of his cavalry officers "I never saw troops behave more magnificently than Pickett's division of Virginians did in that grand charge upon the enemy."

In the after action report Pickett wrote just after the battle, he blamed the failure of the attack on the lack of promised support from Wilcox's brigade. He also laid blame on several other general officers, including Robert E. Lee. Lee returned the report asking Pickett to eliminate the bitter comments of blame. He had a war yet to fight and needed his army's officers battling the enemy, not themselves. Pickett threw the report away without making the requested changes, and submitted nothing else.

Lee recognized that Pickett's division needed a chance to heal, and rebuild its numbers through recruiting. He assigned the division to guard some 4,000 Union prisoners captured at Gettysburg in a march to bring them south for internment. The rest of Lee's army would slowly retreat from Pennsylvania, hoping all the while to lure Meade's army into an attack that could allow Lee to yet turn defeat into victory.

As Pickett and his division marched south across the Potomac River into Virginia, his spirits began to revive. There was a wedding to plan. By the time the Union prisoners were delivered to their cavalry escort at Hanover Junction for the last leg of their journey to prison, George and Sallie had agreed on a wedding date of September 15, in Petersburg, Virginia. The planning would be made easier by the fact that Pickett's new orders called for him to command a district in and around Richmond and Petersburg. There, near to two major Southern cities, Lee felt that Pickett could easily recruit the men necessary to rebuild his division. It also kept him close to his fiancée, who was already busy with wedding details.

***

Pickett's new posting away from the front lines gave George and Sallie time to go ahead with their wedding. On September 15, 1863 Pickett, age 38, married LaSalle Corbell, age 20, "…amidst a salute of guns, hearty cheers and chimes and bands and bugles." Among the guests were the President of the Confederacy, Jefferson Davis, his entire cabinet, friend and commanding officer James Longstreet, and Sallie's father and uncle. The couple honeymooned nearby on the Pickett family plantation.

The honeymoon lasted for several months and was finally interrupted by Pickett's new orders. He was directed to take command of the Department of North Carolina, headquartered out of Petersburg, Virginia. He and his new wife moved into a five story home there. In early January, 1864, he was ordered to mount a campaign to seize New Bern, North Carolina. The campaign, after some early successes, failed. Pickett was blamed for poor co-ordination of troop movements and his reputation suffered. He grew especially angry at North Carolinians loyal to the Union and others in Confederate uniforms, who he felt were not fully committed to the cause of southern independence. During the New Bern campaign 22 men who deserted the Confederate forces and switched sides to fight in Union blue were captured by Pickett's men. When they were brought before him Pickett was heard to say "every god damned man who didn't do his duty, or deserted, ought to be shot or hung." A quickly convened court found all 22 men guilty of desertion and sentenced them to hang.

General Peck, commander of Union forces in the area, appealed to Pickett, saying he hoped that the captured men would be accorded "the same treatment in all respects as you will mete out to other prisoners of war." The two men exchanged heated notes, but Pickett would not alter the verdict of the court. The 22 men were hung. One was a drummer boy 14 years of age. Another was a soldier born with severe physical deformities. Press in the North was outraged.

By May 4th, 1864, Pickett's division had rebuilt its strength, and Lee immediately issued orders for its return from detached service back to the Army of Northern Virginia. An old West Point and Mexican War friend, Ulysses S. Grant, had recently been appointed General in Chief of all Union Armies, and was travelling with Meade's army. Grant was determined to break Lee's army and capture the Confederate capital, Richmond. A brutal campaign lay ahead, unlike any that had been waged before. Grant knew that the North possessed greater manpower and supplies and planned to use that strength to grind down Lee's forces. He was not hesitant to incur heavy casualties, if necessary, to gain victory. Pickett was thrilled to rejoin the main army, but sadness and worry came from having to leave the side of his wife, who was now several months pregnant. His first two wives had died as a result of complications from childbirth, and Sallie was having a difficult time.

The tearful parting never happened. Pickett received a report from his spy network that a large Union force had sailed up the James River and landed troops just nine miles from his headquarters in Petersburg. Frantically Pickett tried to get details of the Union troop strength and intentions while marshalling all local men able to carry arms. Over the next several days, with almost no sleep, he secured reinforcements and moved swiftly and decisively to meet this new Union Army of the James commanded by Benjamin Butler. He managed to trap them on a bottle shaped peninsula by digging entrenchments across a narrow bit of land that corked them up. Pickett had turned the crisis into a standoff, but he paid a price. He suffered some sort of breakdown. Instead of getting credit for bold action, rumors began to circulate that he had collapsed from excessive drinking.

In 10 days Pickett, nursed by his pregnant wife, recovered enough to depart Petersburg and rejoin his division with Lee's army. Grant's big push for Richmond had begun. In a major battle in a heavily wooded area called the Wilderness, Pickett's good friend, James Longstreet, suffered a severe wound, and was lost to the army for several months. To replace Longstreet as commander of the First Corps Lee chose Richard Anderson, a division commander from another corps. Pickett thought the promotion should have gone to him, being the senior division commander in the First Corps. The hard feelings Pickett had for Robert E Lee since Gettysburg grew harder still.

After the battle in the Wilderness, Meade's army (with Grant directing strategy) did what no Union army had done before. Even though they had been defeated, they continued to move south. The next major battle occurred at Cold Harbor as Lee blocked Grant's advance once again. Once again Grant attacked. Pickett's division was part of the defensive line that mauled Union regiments that came against them, wave upon wave. All attacks were repulsed with great Union losses. After two days of attacks Grant moved his army during the night around Lee's right flank and continued to march south.

Grant now showed how willing he was to use all his strength to subdue

Lee's army. As he maneuvered around Lee at Cold Harbor, Ben Butler's Army of the James, bottled up near Petersburg, began to show signs of renewing their advance, perhaps toward Richmond. Grant was applying pressure at as many points as he could, believing that somewhere Southern will or strength would give way. Lee responded by stripping his army of troops it badly needed, sending Pickett's division south to Petersburg, to deal with Butler. Lee then resumed his dance with Grant, heading south to find Grant's army and once again block its advance toward Richmond.

It soon became clear to Robert E Lee that the real target of both Grant and Butler was not Richmond, but Petersburg. The rail line that both Lee's army and the citizens of Richmond counted on to bring in supplies passed through Petersburg. If Grant and Butler could capture Petersburg they would cut his supply line, causing the inevitable surrender of both Richmond and Lee's army.

Lee ordered the construction of a series of entrenchments that protected both Richmond and Petersburg. His army was stretched so thin that he would have to stay on the defensive, preparing to shift troops to the points most threatened. Grant would keep probing all along Lee lines until he found a weak spot. The confrontation settled down to trench warfare.

Grant launched several attempts at breaking through Petersburg's defenses, but was driven back each time. He then decided on a different strategy. He ordered a large force of 31,000 cavalry and infantry under the command of Phillip Sheridan to move south of Petersburg beyond the strong fortifications of the city and attack the South Side Railroad at Five Forks Junction. Cut the line there and Petersburg will fall, then Richmond, then Lee's army. Lee grasped Grant's intentions and quickly dispatched a combined force of 19,000 infantry and cavalry under George Pickett's command to defend Five Forks against Sheridan's attack.

Pickett's performance at Five Forks left much to be desired. Perhaps he had not yet fully recovered from the collapse he suffered weeks earlier. He was outnumbered and was trying to protect a larger area than he could with the men he had at hand. Even so his actions brought him much censure. He failed to have his men build adequate defensive breastworks. The defensive line he did create had a left flank that was anchored by a weak cavalry force.

 His worst decision came when he left his command to attend a shad bake dinner celebration several miles from Five Forks without designating an overall commander in his absence. Just as dinner and drinks were being served by his host, cavalryman T.R.R. Rosser, Union General Phillip Sheridan attacked Five Forks. The main attack struck the weakest part of Pickett's line, where only cavalry defended the ground. When Pickett heard the sounds of gunfire growing louder and louder, he excused himself, leapt on his horse and raced to rejoin his men. He barely evaded capture as he dashed through attacking Union troops. In the confusion caused by his absence the left flank of his troops position had been forced back and it's center was collapsed under the weight of the Union assault. Pickett could see that defeat was inevitable and he made his way back to safety in Petersburg. He had lost his last battle in a most embarrassing fashion. The last rail line servicing Petersburg and the confederate capitol of Richmond had been severed. Lee's army was cut off by Union forces to the south, north and east.

Lee had only one option. He abandoned Richmond and Petersburg and marched the ragged remnants of his army west, toward another distant rail line in Lynchburg, Virginia. Grant was in hot pursuit, with Phillip Sheridan's cavalry leading the chase. If Sheridan could get ahead of Lee's troops and block their move west, the South's largest army would be forced to surrender.

Pickett, having escaped the disaster at Five Forks, joined Lee's retreat just west of Richmond. There he discovered an order from General Lee relieving him of his command and releasing him from the army. There is no historical record of Pickett's reaction, but he must have been shocked. Despite receiving the order Pickett stayed with the rear element of Lee's army as it moved west. At Appomattox Court House. Phil Sheridan's cavalry overtook the Army of Northern Virginia and blocked its way west. Coming up rapidly behind Lee was the bulk of the Union army. There was nothing left to do but ask for terms of peace. On April 9th, 1865 Lee met with Ulysses Grant and negotiated a generous surrender. Confederate soldiers could keep their weapons and horses and return home after signing a pledge never to raise arms against the federal government again. Pickett signed his pledge and returned home to Sallie, now living in Richmond. She greeted her exhausted soldier at their doorway, remembering "the peace and bliss of that moment."

Richmond was a city in ruins. Confederate soldiers had set fire to supply stores in the city to keep them from Union hands, and strong winds had fanned the flames out of control, burning up large areas of factories, homes and shops. Food, clean water and medical supplies were scarce. There were few jobs available for former confederate soldiers, whose families were starving. The Pickett's, with Sallie pregnant with their second child, decided to leave Richmond and move in with Sallie's parents.

George had taken the oath of allegiance to the US government as the terms of the surrender required. He had also petitioned for a pardon, writing to President Andrew Johnson that he was "ready to renew my allegiance as a loyal citizen of the US government, and I have advised and counseled all men belonging to my division to return to their homes and the peaceful pursuits of life." He waited months for a response, all the while hearing that many of his comrades in arms had received their pardons. His did not come.

Radical Republicans who controlled Congress were singling out certain high profile Confederate leaders for investigation of questionable conduct during the war. Former Confederate President Jefferson Davis was already in prison and investigations were under way to consider trying Robert E. Lee and others for treason. George and Sallie were very afraid of what their future held in store. Soon those fears were justified. Complaints had been lodged by the widows of captured former Confederate turned Union troops whom Pickett had executed at New Bern, North Carolina, requesting that federal officials "bring to justice certain wicked and cruel men who deliberately murdered, by public hanging, a number of loyal citizens and soldiers of the US when prisoners during the late rebellion…"

An initial recommendation was made by investigating authorities for the Judge Advocate General of the Army to appoint a commission to try General Pickett. After considering the evidence collected, the Judge Advocate General chose not to convene a commission, but to order further evidence of guilt be gathered before such action should be taken.

Pickett and his wife learned of all this and discussed what they should do to safeguard their family. They discovered through newspaper reports that more evidence and testimony showing the general to be a war criminal was being gathered. They decided that the best course of action open to them was to flee the country immediately.

Pickett made his way north to Montreal, Canada, where there was a large presence of former Confederates already living in exile. With their financial assistance his family could live decently until events in the United States grew more favorable. Sallie and the children soon joined him there. Their stay was short. Only six weeks after arriving in Canada they were headed back to Richmond. Pickett had been led to believe that the Army investigation of his New Bern actions were over. He soon discovered that he had been misled. Looking to secure a peaceful future for his family, Pickett took the risk of travelling to Washington DC. There he appealed to his old West Point and Mexican War friend, Ulysses Grant. Grant was now General of the Armies and a close advisor to President Johnson. Pickett explained to Grant that all he wanted was "a guarantee that I may be permitted to live unmolested in my native state, where I am now trying to make a subsistence for my family (much impoverished by the war) by tilling the land."

Grant took Pickett's plea to the President and personally vouched for his future conduct. As for Pickett's harsh actions at New Bern, Grant excused them as necessary to maintain discipline in times of war. The President ordered that no further government action be taken against George Pickett.

With a future free of government prosecution assured, the Pickett's, along with their two sons George Jr. and Corbell, returned to the family plantation on Turnkey Island, Virginia. The buildings on the plantation had been burned during the war by order of General Benjamin Butler. The family worked hard over the next few years building a new home there and planting crops to feed themselves and rebuild their shattered finances. Unfortunately George was not much of a farmer.

In March of 1870, Pickett went with friends to meet Robert E Lee, who was then visiting Richmond. What Pickett hoped would come of this meeting is unclear. Perhaps he sought to make peace with Lee after their disagreements or to defend his wartime actions before his former commanding officer. Whatever his plan, things did not go well. At Lee's hotel he met John S. Mosby, a confederate cavalry general known during the war as The Gray Ghost, famed for his exploits against his Union counterparts. Mosby was also there to see Lee, and met with the old general first. Upon exiting Mosby told Pickett that the meeting had been excellent and that Lee was in a very good mood. Pickett then went in to see Lee. Pickett steered what began as an exchange of pleasantries to a discussion of the battle at Gettysburg. As the discussion moved in that direction Lee became cold and formal. Pickett took this as an insult and broke off the meeting, leaving the room abruptly. Outside he angrily told Mosby "That old man…had my division massacred at Gettysburg!"

Other opportunities for employment came Pickett's way. He was offered a position as military advisor to the Khedive of Egypt, but turned it down. He did not want to move his young family so far from home. Ulysses Grant considered him for a posting as US Marshal of Virginia, but George turned the offer down, telling the President that while it would help the Pickett family financially, it would hurt Grant politically.

By the early 1870's Pickett finally settled on a job as an agent for the Washington National Life Insurance Company of New York. He supervised the sales efforts of several other agents while personally soliciting key customers, using his name and fame as an effective door opener. He worked long hours and travelled the state of Virginia extensively. He felt the work to be beneath the talents of a former major general, but it provided him with a decent income and was better than anything else he could find. Another old Civil War friend, former Lieutenant General P.G.T. Beauregard, a high official with the Louisiana State Lottery, offered him a position, but George refused it saying "There was not enough money in the world to induce me to

lend my name to it."

The drain of energy and spirit that comes from working a job you dislike gradually took its toll on George Pickett. By 1874 he said of his insurance work, "I'd sooner face a cannon than ask a man to take out a policy with me." By 1875, with his physical health declining from the exertions of his job and the recent unexpected death of his young son Corbell, Pickett grew weak and feverish. Despite not feeling well he felt compelled to do his job and travel to Norfolk, Virginia for meetings. While there he fell more seriously ill. Heart problems had plagued him for decades and now they grew more severe. His wife and her uncle travelled to Norfolk to be with him. It was clear to them that he was waging his last fight. On the evening of July 30, 1875, while lying in his bed, he grasped Sallie's hand tightly and said, "Well, the enemy is too strong for me again…my ammunition is all out." With that he closed his eyes. Hours later George Pickett passed from life, his wife Sallie still holding his hand.

The real George Pickett was a vain man, whose fame exceeded his abilities. He is a good example of business's "Peter Principle." He received promotion after promotion until he began to fail. Then his failures became career ending.

His most lasting success was in love, with his child bride Sallie. To her he was the beau ideal of a soldier. She was drawn to his sad but romantic nature, never deserting him even in his lowest moments.

His career as a soldier suffered a sad end and his peacetime career as an insurance agent was one he tolerated only out of financial necessity.

In the end he managed to achieve the immortality that so many men seek, not by great success, but as the field commander of one of the most epic failures of the Civil War.

4

PETTICOAT PATRIOT

Anna Elizabeth Dickinson

Anna Dickinson never commanded troops in battle, never held elective office, never married a man of wealth or influence, yet she became more famous in her lifetime than most politicians and great men of business. Mark Twain even got second billing when they appeared together onstage. A little Quaker girl in the 1800's was not supposed to be able to do that.

***

Anna Dickinson was born on October 27, 1842 in Philadelphia,

Pennsylvania. She was the youngest of the 5 children of John and Mary Dickinson, Quaker members of the American Anti-Slavery Society. John Dickinson opened his home up to fugitive slaves fleeing north in search of freedom. He died when Anna was two years old, beginning the Dickinson family's struggle to earn enough money to maintain hearth and home.

***

On a Sabbath Sunday in January of 1860, seventeen- year- old Anna Dickinson attended a meeting organized by The Friends of Progress at Clarkson Hall in her hometown of Philadelphia, Pa. It was to be a discussion of "Women's Rights and Wrongs." Local dignitaries were to speak on the subject and exchange ideas for the edification of the audience in attendance. Anna took her seat and listened closely as the first speakers shared their thoughts. Dressed in conservative Quaker fashion, and standing only 4 foot eleven inches tall, she was easily unnoticed amongst the adults in the crowd. As one particular gentleman took his turn speaking onstage Anna felt a most unfamiliar emotion rise within her – anger. The longer the man spoke the more her cheeks flushed, her hands clenching tightly. The gentleman loudly declared that his daughter was the equal of any other man's daughter, and like them, was destined to live a life of quiet domesticity, being unsuited for a career in law, medicine or banking. Suddenly Anna found herself standing up, pointing her finger like a pistol directly at the speaker onstage, and loudly declaring, "In heavens name sir, what else is to be expected of such a father!" She rattled both the audience and the unfortunate speaker with a continuous stream of well phrased invectives. Soon the man fled the stage and the audience, dazed but thoroughly entertained by the oral fireworks of the young Quaker girl, left the hall and began telling their neighbors and friends stories of the fearless and eloquent girl they had encountered that night. Anna Dickinson's career as a platform speaker had begun without her even knowing.

***

For several months Anna made public remarks at similar events in her home town. Her reputation was spreading to neighboring towns as well. She was still more of a novelty than a serious contributor to public discussions. Female speakers were virtually unheard of. It was very much against the social norms of her time for a woman to speak to the public, or enter into public discourse on current events and politics.

The presidential election of 1860 was fast approaching and arguments for and against slavery were declaimed from church pulpits and bar rooms to street corners and lyceum stages. On October 23, 1860 Anna was invited to share speaking time on stage with several nationally known abolitionists at Kennet Square outside Philadelphia. She had quickly graduated from brief remarks spoken from the audience to sharing the stage with better known, established male speakers. She met the challenge confidently and aggressively. While other speakers talked with passion about the evils of slavery, Dickinson struck at it with a well-reasoned, logical argument. She referenced the many laws supporting slavery and pointed out that while slavery is a word that does not appear in the Constitution of the nation, the spirit of it does in the form of the Fugitive Slave Act. She alone of all the speakers that night boldly called for a Constitutional Amendment banning slavery as the necessary goal of the abolition movement. Other speakers at the event disputed her arguments, but the very image of abolitionist sages toiling to rebut the ideas put forth by a diminutive Quaker girl with a head full of curly jet black hair guaranteed that Anna would be the subject of much publicity following the evening's discussions.

Other speaking engagements came, with modest remuneration. Anna left her job teaching in Philadelphia to become a clerk at the US mint in the city, and soon thereafter gave her first major address. In it she spoke against the many institutional barriers society put up to obstruct advancement of gender equality. She spoke for two hours without notes. Her effort earned mixed reviews. The public had not yet embraced the concept of an articulate, aggressive female speaker. The Philadelphia Evening Bulletin, while saying she had given a speech that many public speakers would be proud of, went on to close their coverage of her effort by saying "We were sorry to hear the lady damaging her cause by claiming intellectual equality with men."

Anna found that she had become a local celebrity, receiving numerous invitations to speak at neighboring town gatherings for small fees. This augmented her modest salary as a clerk at the Philadelphia Mint. The income was sorely needed, as Anna attempted to help support her mother, sister and brothers in the difficult times following the death of her father many years earlier.

***

The election of Abraham Lincoln in 1860, and the commencement of civil war, soon after marked a turning point in Anna Dickinson's life. She continued working at the Mint, but quickly decided that her real future lay in public speaking. The issues raised by the war gave her new material to research, write and speak about, and fueled her passion to do so.

By October of 1861 Anna was, by his invitation, sharing the stage with William Lloyd Garrison, nationally known editor of The Liberator, a widely read abolitionist newspaper. This was a notable achievement for the 19 year old girl, and it reinforced her conviction that she had something to say that people found worth hearing. Her performance with Garrison impressed him so much that he promised to help further her speaking career in any way that he could.

Anna's skill at using sarcasm and invective soon caused her to lose her job at the Mint. After calling the commander of the Union Army, George McLellan, treasonous for losing the battle of Ball's Bluff, she was sacked.

Garrison, as he had promised, helped Anna earn a meager living by setting her up with several speaking engagements sponsored by the Massachusetts Anti-Slavery Committee, mostly in small towns near Philadelphia. Garrison also ensured, through his many contacts that Anna receive good reviews printed in local abolitionist newspapers. These small speaking engagements allowed Anna to sharpen her platform skills and hone her message, taking cues from Garrison's many letters to her in which he reviewed her development.

In 1862 both Garrison and Anna felt she was ready for a major speaking engagement before the more discerning audience of a big city. She was to share the stage at the Music Hall in Boston Massachusetts with Wendell Phillips, who, like Garrison, was a major voice in the national abolitionist movement. As the appointed day approached Anna received a letter from Phillips in which he explained that he was too ill to speak, and would she please take his time and place on the stage as the main speaker that night? Both frightened and flattered, Anna readily agreed. The night before the engagement Anna barely slept or ate, but she felt ready.

Of this, her first appearance on stage in a major city as the main speaker, Anna wrote her mother, "Well, I had a great cram - 4 or 5 thousand people …All the literary fragments floated up there –and they all said it was a magnificent success." Wendell Phillips, too sick to speak, came to listen from the audience and said he had never before been so gratified -   and so deeply moved. "Actually my dear Anna brought tears to my eyes." Anna finished her letter to her mother touching on a subject of deep concern to the family, money. "I am making my own way and name now. When I come again next time Mr. Dall (sponsor of the event) says I can demand my own price."

Anna Dickinson, age 20, could now count two of the greatest abolitionists of her time, Wendell Phillips and William Lloyd Garrison, among her growing group of admirers.

By 1863 Anna was crisscrossing the northeast, lecturing on abolition, women's rights and the ongoing struggle of the Lincoln administration to maintain the Union during the Civil War. Anna was at odds with the President's administration over his handling of slavery. She felt his commitment to ending slavery was too weak and indecisive. She sounded a clarion call from the stage for complete abolition.

In March of 1863, after an impassioned address in Hartford Connecticut a reporter covering her wrote an article in which he called Anna America's Joan of Arc. It was a title that she would proudly acknowledge for years to come.

The war was not going well for the Union. By May of 1863 its main army, the Army of the Potomac, had gone through four different commanders while losing battles at Bull Run twice, Fredericksburg, Seven Pines, Gaines Mill and Chancellorsville. Huge northern casualty lists regularly shocked the nation and filled its hospitals with wounded soldiers. There was no end in sight for the war or slavery. The President instituted the first draft(compulsory enlistment into the armed forces) in the country's history and New York was plagued with violent protest riots for days following the declaration. Blacks were mobbed and killed in the streets there.

With these depressing headlines bombarding the people of the North, Republicans looked to the upcoming Congressional and Presidential elections with real concern. Peace Democrats were calling for a negotiated end to the conflict, with restoration of the Union "as it was" as their aim. The South could rejoin the Union with slavery intact. Could the Republicans hold on to a majority in Congress and the Presidency, or would they and Lincoln be swept out of power on a wave of rising anti-war sentiment?

An enterprising local New Hampshire Republican, Benjamin Prescott, having heard Anna Dickinson speak in the town of Concord, decided that she might be effective rallying the citizens to the party's banner. New Hampshire was to hold the first of the Congressional elections preceding the Presidential election of 1864. He convinced his Republican state committee to hire Anna to speak at 20 different town meetings. Only one New Hampshire Republican candidate asked that Anna not speak in his community, telling Prescott "don't send that damned woman down here to defeat my election." When the ballots were cast and counted in New Hampshire it became clear that Republicans had won nearly all the most hotly contested races. The candidate who refused to have Anna speak in his district lost.

With her power as a political campaigner proven in New Hampshire Anna found herself in great demand by Republican candidates for office all across the Northeast. Passions were running high as the November Presidential contest grew closer. During her speech in Middleton Connecticut, Democrats in the audience turned off the gas, leaving her standing onstage in almost complete darkness. She continued speaking in the dark, saying "…there are those here who evidently love darkness better than light, because their deeds are evil." Later, with the gas back on and the stage lights turned up the rowdies continually interrupted her with cries of "Fire!" To that she replied "By God's grace we have kindled a fire which these people by their acts are assisting, that will never go out till naught is left of the principles they profess, or their party, save ashes!" Anna was not easily intimidated.

Gatherings were taking place all over the North to help recruit new soldiers to fill the North's badly depleted ranks. Anna spoke at one such rally, intended to spur enlistment of free black men. She spoke with a passion that belied her youth.

"Anglo-Africans, we need you. You hold the hammer which, upheld or falling, decides your destiny. You have not homes – gain them. You have not liberty, gain it. You have not a flag – gain it. You have not a country – be written down in history as the race who made one for themselves and saved one for another."

With Anna Dickinson's help, 1863 Republican Congressional candidates in the Northeast were able to remain competitive and win more seats than was expected, but anxiety in the party was still high. Lincoln was so pessimistic about his re-election chances that he wrote a memorandum that he sealed and gave to his cabinet, instructing them to open it after the election. It was later revealed that in it he said with his defeat they should do all they could to secure peace on the best possible terms with the South before the new Democratic administration took over. But the tide which had been running steadily against Union forces during the early years of the war was turning. Robert E. Lee's army of Northern Virginia invaded Pennsylvania and by July 3rd, 1863, was defeated. Ulysses Grant and his western army, after many long months of stalemate, captured the key Confederate city of Vicksburg on July 4th, securing free passage of the entire length of the Mississippi River all the way down to the Gulf of Mexico for Union gunboats and troop carriers, thus cutting the Confederacy in two.

Anna Dickinson had been approached many times during the 1864 election and asked to publicly support Lincoln for re-election. She refused to do so because she felt that the President was taking too soft a stance on post war re-admittance of southern states to the Union, while calling for too few protections for freed blacks from their former masters. Despite her unwillingness to actively support Lincoln in 1864, Republicans in Congress, recognizing her yeoman work to secure their governing majority, invited her to speak in the House of Representatives. She would be the youngest person and the first woman ever to do so. On January 16, 1864 Anna Dickinson, now 21 years old, stood before a packed House and delivered a speech entitled The Perils of the Hour. The President, first lady, Vice President and the entire cabinet were in the audience, along with most everyone of high political or social standing in Washington DC. Never one to equivocate, Anna spelled out her disagreements with the President. Despite being called out by the combative Quaker girl on the rostrum, the President took her comments in good humor. Anna closed her remarks by calling on all citizens in this hour of peril to continue their support for the nation's leader. As the President rose to leave, the audience urged him to make some remarks. He elicited laughter from the crowd when he replied that he was too embarrassed to speak.

Newspapers across the North split predictably in their comments on Anna's address in the House chamber. Whitelaw Reid, an influential newsman from the Cincinnati Enquirer, reputedly smitten with her, effusively praised her efforts. Others called it a complete success. But as always, Anna had detractors, mostly chauvinists and Democrats. The New York World's response was typical of the negative press that Anna had received since becoming a public figure. "She attracts crowds when she speaks by appealing to the same love of the marvelous and monstrous which Barnum has made his fortune in exhibiting wooly horses, dwarves, Feegee mermaids and other queer fish. Yet this silly young person was allowed the use of the Hall of Representatives...to make one of her unwomanly displays." The Geneva New York Gazette characterized her speech as "the absurd endeavors of women to usurp the place and execute the male sex. It is a moral and social monstrosity – an inversion...of the laws of nature."

In the spring of 1864, Congressman William Kelly of Pennsylvania arranged for Anna to join him in a private meeting with President Lincoln. Afterword, Congressman Kelly and Anna had very different memories of the encounter. Kelly recalled that Dickinson had little to say as he and Lincoln discussed war developments and reconstruction plans for the state of Louisiana. It is very hard to picture Anna Dickinson ever having little to say. Dickinson, referring to the meeting at future speaking engagements, declared that she had been blunt in opposing the President's reconstruction plans. What happened later might shed light on what really transpired in that meeting. Anna's friendship with Congressman Kelly ended and her criticism of President Lincoln's gentle handling of the South in reconstruction matters grew sharper than ever.

Anna began to hear negative comments from those who were her most steadfast supporters, calling on her to be more demonstrative in backing the Republican Party before the 1864 election vote. In response to this pressure she sent an open letter to the newspapers in which she stated that foremost, she was a patriot, not beholden to a political party. She concluded the letter stating "I shall not work for Abraham Lincoln; I shall work for the salvation of my country's life that stands at stake." Finally, in October, just weeks before the vote, she proclaimed that a patriotic nation must stick with the current administration.

Lincoln went on to win a solid victory in the 1864 election, and Anna began to reshape her speeches to deal with the inevitable battle to come over reconstruction. In her newest platform speech entitled "A Glance at our Future," she called for stern treatment of the rebels and strong protections of the rights of newly freed slaves. She also gave speeches making "A Plea for Labor" and "Women's Work and Wages" her focus. She was working to shape an agenda for post war America.

On April 14, 1865, President Lincoln was assassinated. The national outpouring of grief for the slain President, the first ever killed in office, and his near deification by the press and the people created difficulty for Anna. She felt the need to speak, but given her well known antipathy for the Lincoln administration policies, she was hesitant. Finally, in early May she agreed to speak at New York's Cooper Union. Her topic was "Our Martyred President." She admitted her difference with certain of Lincoln's policies remained constant, but went on to eulogize his memory.

**

During the years of the Civil War, Anna Dickinson had grown from a diminutive Quaker girl who spoke out of turn at local meetings to a woman who was nationally recognized as a powerful speaker for the causes of freedmen's rights, gender equality and fairness in labor laws. She had also grown into an attractive woman who found male suitors wherever she went. Whitelaw Reid, who would go on to become editor of one of the nation's most powerful newspapers, was one of her earliest suitors. In 1863 he wrote the following description of her: "To begin with, this is no scrawny featured, sallow-faced pantalooned female of forty, of the women's rights persuasion, but a girl a few months over twenty… with graceful outlines half concealed by the neatly fitting dress, glossy black hair cut tolerably short and falling in luxuriant profusion about the neck...with ripe lips that curl into a score of expressions in an instant...."

It should come as no surprise after reading that description that Reid sought Anna out and proposed marriage several times over the years. As she would with all future male suitors, she turned him down, while maintaining a friendly relationship. She could not see herself locked into a 19th century marriage which would keep her home bearing and raising children and keeping house. There would always be causes to fight for and who better than Anna to fight them?

With the Civil War over Anna Dickinson faced the pressing problem of how she would continue to make money to support herself and her family. Her brothers tried to help, getting and losing a series of jobs, some gotten through Anna's friends and supporters. Her sister's time and energy was spent caring for their ailing mother. The family always seemed to be calling on Anna for financial help.

Dickinson turned to the growing Lyceum circuit to earn the money to support herself and her family. The Lyceum movement started in New England in the 1830's as a local attempt to provide entertainment and education. Speakers were invited by local townspeople to lecture on scientific, philosophical, religious and cultural topics. By the 1850's the movement had evolved into more of an entertainment venue, featuring artists, authors, and humorists who frequently touched on subjects of current interest. Henry Ward Beecher, Mark Twain and Petroleum V. Nasby were popular speakers at Lyceum events. These main players on the circuit would command from$200 to $1,000 per appearance. The top earner on the circuit, John Gough, earned over $40,000 in one year.

For the next decade, Anna spent eight months a year travelling the country, giving speeches on the circuit. She would typically take a break during the cold days of the Christmas season and conclude with the coming hot days of summer in June. During the 1870-71 seasons she averaged 130-150 speeches, at an average pay of $130-150 per event.

***

After 11 years of speaking at events arranged by Lyceum managers and travelling as they arranged for her to, Anna broke with convention and became her own manager. She booked her own speaking engagements and travel arrangements, trusting no one better than herself to guard her financial and physical health.

One of her most popular lectures dealt with the life of Joan of Arc. Anna clearly identified with the gender defying maiden of France. Anna's take on Joan was more political than religious. She portrayed Joan as motivated not by strange voices "but just as you and I are called to do the appointed work of God by following our conscience." Joan was not a tool of the French or English but "a creature of genius, of power and patriotism." Knowing how closely they linked her to Joan, Anna must have known that many in the audience believed she was describing herself.

She took the stage frequently to speak about women's rights. In "Women's Work and Wages," she was one of the first major public figures to call for women to receive the same pay as men for equal work. In her speech "Idiots and Women" Anna ridiculed the legal system which gave women the same legal status as the mentally ill, both being ineligible to vote.

Mark Twain saw Anna speak in New York during these post war years. He filed a story about her with a California newspaper, beginning with a description of her as she appeared that night.

"She had on a heavy cherry colored silk dress cut very plainly with lace cravat and cuffs. Her thick, straight hair is short-only just touches her collar behind. I cannot possibly guess her age."

He then began to comment on her speaking style.

"She talks fast, uses no notes whatever, never hesitates for a word, always gets the right word in the right place, and has the most perfect confidence in herself." And although she was born in Philadelphia, "she wanders into a brogue frequently that sounds very like Irish."

Twain felt that she was worth the price of a ticket, and did her work well. He found sarcasm to be her best weapon on the stage and opined that "she will make a right venomous old maid someday."

Anna was no longer a lone female speaking out in public. Her success inspired a host of other women who challenged the common perception of a woman's place in American culture. Elizabeth Cady Stanton, Mary Livermore, Susan B. Anthony and several others began appearing on the Lyceum circuit, speaking out in advancement of women's rights, temperance, and fair treatment of freedmen.

As Stanton and Anthony gathered adherents to their banner of women's suffrage they looked to Anna Dickinson for support. Anna had been speaking for years about expanded opportunities for women. She seemed to be a perfect fit to join the movement, yet she did not. Anna always seemed to prefer a separate, solitary path. She argued that women should receive the vote because they had special skills and insights that would be valuable in helping shape the future of the nation. She did not agree with the suffragette position that women, simply by virtue of the fact that they were citizens, should have the right to vote.

***

From the time that she became a nationally known public figure, speculation about Anna's love life became a favorite subject of her friends, admirers and the newspapers. One of the first serious suitors for her hand appears to have been Whitelaw Reid. Reid had wit, intelligence, ambition and good looks. Anna warmed to his attentions and they shared nearly a decade of intimate letters and rendezvous, falling in and out of love with frequency. In January 1871, Reid and Anna met just before she was to leave for a western speaking tour. Reid seems to have pushed Anna too hard to return his affection, for the following day he wrote to her explaining his "mortification at having done the worst to make" her final night "as disagreeable as I would have had it be bright." Their friendship and letter exchanges continued, but their frequency and the level of intimacy in them never resembled what it was before.

***

During this very busy period in her professional life Anna began to suffer from the toll extensive 19th century travel was taking on her small frame. Following a particularly hectic 1872 tour through Ohio, Indiana, Michigan and Illinois, she was confined to bed with "epidemic catarrh" and typhoid symptoms. It was at this time that she began to self- medicate with alcohol, per her doctor's suggestion, and to consume noticeably large quantities in some social situation. Illnesses would plague her for the rest of her life. Her chosen remedy for them would prove as debilitating as the illnesses themselves.

In 1873, Anna rekindled a friendship that had begun during the Civil War. Benjamin Butler was a financier, lawyer and powerful politician 24 years her senior. After the war she helped him in his failed foray into speaking on the Lyceum circuit by providing him with contacts and some engagements. They remained in touch until Anna called on him to represent her in a lawsuit against a Lyceum manager who claimed she had broken her contract with him. Once that concluded she came to him for help in getting her frequently ill brother Edwin a steady job. He secured Edwin a position at the Pension Bureau. The Dickinson family joked about what Butler might have in mind from Anna as a quid pro quo. His wife had been seriously ill for a long time, and his correspondence with Anna included more personal than business references. She never revealed the slightest attraction to him to her friends or family, but continued over the years to come to him for financial and legal aid, sprinkling her letters with sentiments designed to keep the flame he held for her burning, if only weakly.

***

She enjoyed the attention of men and the help they could provide, but her closest and longest lasting relationships were with women. During and just after the Civil War, Lou Brackett and Sarah Logan were two women with whom she shared, in those ladies words, intimacies and kisses. In 1866 she began a relationship with a married woman named Sarah Logan. Logan wrote to Anna "How can I have thee, Queen of my loving heart?" She went on to declare the "wild rebellious wish that I could shelter you from yourself and the world. Can I never be a man?" Logan continued to send Anna such passionate letters for several years. Then began what at first was a mentor/student relationship with Susan B. Anthony, who was 20 years Anna's senior. Over time the relationship morphed into something much more intimate. How much so can only be inferred from correspondence they exchanged. Susan Anthony began calling Anna pet names like "Darling Dicky Dicky," "My Chickadee" and "My Dear Chicky Dick Darling." In several letters to Anna, Anthony refers to a large double bed she hopes they will share. Anthony, like Anna, never married despite having many male suitors. Her relationship with Susan Anthony waned, but was replaced over the years by romantic entanglements with numerous other women.

By the summer of 1874 Anna's relationship with her public began to change. On a vacation with her female friend Lou Brackett in Atlantic City, Anna commented on an incident she had with a black maid, who was "impertinent." She made mention to friends that many hotels were taking on white rather than black servants because the hotel guests "will not endure the manners of blacks." She referred to an incident in which her friend Lou Brackett had been told by a black servant "I reckon I have a right to say what I please-I am as free as you now." All these observations came from the same woman who for years spoke so passionately on behalf of freeing black people from slavery and calling for their just and equal treatment under the law.

***

By 1875 Anna was not enjoying the income she hoped she would from the Lyceum circuit. She was feeling the financial pressure created by a family that constantly looked to her for funds to make ends meet. She wrote to her sister, "It is no use Dickey, I have tried faithfully to stick to the platform, but the platform won't stick to me." She decided she would try her luck at writing a stage play in which she would appear as the lead actress.

Dickinson knew that she wanted to play a strong, independent character, free from the shackles of social conformity in thought and action. She researched history for an appropriate female to be the focus of her new work. She considered, Katherine of Aragon (Henry VIII's first wife), Anne Boleyn (his fourth wife), and Lady Jane Grey. In the end she settled on Anne Boleyn.

Throughout the winter of 1876 Anna worked on drafts of her play, "A Crown of Thorns." She would depart from the current view of that sad lady, showing her to be neither weak nor immoral. Anna's Anne Boleyn was a noble, pure and heroic soul, holding fast to her morals while surrounded by a king's court full of corrupted courtiers.

The play premiered on May 8, 1876, at the newly rebuilt Globe Theatre in Boston, Massachusetts. The audience was packed with notables from the world of reform movements, culture, literature and politics. Longfellow, Emerson, Julia Ward Howe, Mark Twain, and William Dean Howells all sat elbow to elbow, eagerly awaiting Anna Dickinson's first foray into theatre. New England based theatre critics wrote of the opening performance with high praise, though commenting on her lack of technical acting skills as revealed by her uneven accent, poor stage presence and forced gestures. The powerful and influential New York based critics called Dickinson's move from the rostrum to the stage a mistake. The New York Times critic in the audience labelled the play "eminently dull."

Dickinson herself, fueled by the positive response of her home town critics and her own euphoria over finally taking her first steps onto a new career path, considered her opening a success. She wrote to her family that her new work as a playwright and actress "has money in it."

Anna continued to tread the boards at the Globe Theatre, enjoying good ticket sales. As she came near the end of her run at the Globe, she met with the theatre owner to determine how financially successful she had been. It was then that she had a rude awakening to the business end of theatrical productions. The owner pointed out to her that their contract called for the first $850 dollars of ticket sales from each performance to go toward covering the supporting cast salaries, production and theatre management expenses. Her performances rarely had more than $850 dollars in ticket sales. So, despite playing to generally large audiences Anna realized very little money. This experience began Anna's mistrust of theatre managers.

She left Boston and took her play on tour for 6 weeks out West, gaining much experience but little in the way of profits. True to the nature of her play's heroine, Anna fearlessly took her play into the lion's den of her harshest critics in New York City. "A Crown of Thorns" opened there on April 4, 1877 to tepid reviews. By April 9th Anna had had enough of the snobbery she felt from the big city critics. She concluded her play that night by addressing the audience and her critics in it directly. Striding to the center of the stage after the final curtain, Anna, still in full costume and holding a stack of negative reviews in her tightened fist, began to speak. For nearly an hour the author and actress read from the reviews of her harshest New York critics, referring to them as "these little men." She countered the bad reviews with readings from her many supporters' letters, building the case that her work was worthy of her audiences. Sounding occasionally like the put upon maidens she so often defended, but mostly like a crusader against injustice, she finished her unusual scene and left the stage and her somewhat bewildered audience.

She resolved that night to continue her newly chosen career believing that the great mass of people were with her. She also saw no better path to earning the money she needed to support her needy family.

As the New York run of her play neared its end, family tragedy struck. Benjamin Butler, at Anna's request had secured a job with the government for her younger brother Edwin, who had been living with Anna's mother and sister for some time. All had depended on Anna's contacts and financial assistance. She now received word that Edwin, frequently ill, had suddenly died. Her mother was growing frail, her sister was the mother's full time nurse, and Anna remained as the sole breadwinner. The pressure on her to continue earning good money grew.

Anna wrote more plays but failed in her attempts to secure agreements with established actors to financially support and appear in them. The men and women she approached either turned down the plays as unsuited to their talents or demanded to purchase the rights to the scripts, which Anna refused to sell. So, needing steady income, she returned to the lecture circuit with a new subject, "The Platform and the Stage." This provided her with the money she needed for herself and her family while she continued to work on theatre projects. She once again wrote a book, hoping to see greater sales with it than she had before. "A Ragged Register," based on her life on the stage and lecture circuit, sold only 100 copies, forcing her to face the fact that she would never earn a living as an author of books.

***

In October of 1879 Anna met Fanny Davenport, one of the foremost theatrical stars of the period. Fanny asked Anna to write a historical play for the next theatre season that Fanny could star in and produce. This began a partnership that was fragile at best. Two woman with large egos, both stubborn by nature and used to getting their own way, began trying to coordinate the writing and staging of a new play. With only a verbal agreement, Anna agreed to write the play for Fanny Davenport. Anna still needed to continue her lectures to earn money to support her family. The play writing would take place between lectures as she found the time to do it.

Three months passed and Fanny Davenport had still not seen a single sentence of the new play Anna was to write. When Miss Davenport requested that Anna send her a synopsis of what she was planning to write, Anna took offense, replying that she had declared herself willing to write a play, not a synopsis. Fanny backed off in her requests for the moment.

By March, 1880, six months after their first meeting, Anna wrote to Fanny Davenport stating her financial terms for delivery of a completed script. Anna was to receive $1,500 plus $350 a week in royalties once the play began running.

Fanny thought the terms to be too extravagant, but nonetheless agreed, asking Anna to begin writing immediately, sending Fanny whatever part of the script she could as she went along.

After pleading illness for some time as her reason for not providing any written scenes from the promised historical play, Anna instead sent Fanny a comedy she had already written to consider instead. Fanny refused the comedy and insisted that Anna honor their agreement. After more months passed, Anna finally delivered Fanny the finished script of "An American Girl." The play read very much like a biography of Anna's life, with a strong, attractive female overcoming the barriers to her success put up by society while choosing a life on the stage as a means of supporting her suffering family. As the villain of the piece, an evil manipulative businessman continually tries to ruin her reputation and career. Anna also included a heated romance, misunderstandings and some tragedy to flesh out the plot lines.

Fanny Davenport liked the script and proceeded to gather a cast and make necessary plans to stage the production. "An American Girl" opened in New York in September of 1880 to positive but not glowing reviews. The curious combination of American's leading actress and one of America's most famous platform speakers staging a new theatrical entertainment guaranteed good, though not great audience attendance. After Fanny reviewed the play's finances in December she wrote Anna that the play's modest success could not support the large royalties she had agreed to pay her, and that Anna would have to agree to lower the royalty payments or Davenport would have to close the show. Anna threatened to sue Fanny and Davenport responded by closing the show explaining that it was "a pecuniary failure." Anna never followed through with the threatened lawsuit and Fanny Davenport never paid Anna any further monies.

***

Anna Dickinson then tried to tour the country for two other theatrical managers while playing very untraditional stages roles, taking the lead in Hamlet and Macbeth. Both tours failed, with critics complaining that in these usually male acted roles Anna showed too much feminine sentiment.

In 1883 Anna contracted for yet another tour, under the management of J.W. Wentworth, appearing in smaller towns and cities in various plays. She and Wentworth did not get along. Anna believed that Wentworth, ignoring her suggestions, had scheduled the tour poorly, with too many appearances, too much travel, and poor accommodations, all of which exhausted her. She wrote her mother "I believe the man never lived who did not think he could do a thing he knows <u>nothing</u> about a deal better than any woman could suggest or help him." Wentworth quit the company when it reached Detroit, Michigan. Within two weeks the touring company folded leaving Anna and the crew broke and unable to continue. Theatre friends in the Midwest ran a benefit for Anna and collected enough money for her to return home to her family.

Unable to develop a new scheme to earn money for her family and herself, Anna turned to a former male admirer, Ben Butler, whose advances she had rejected years before. She asked Butler for $1000 to finance a trip to England, where she could improve her health and renew her acting career. Butler reluctantly supplied the cash requested along with an additional $1,500. When several months passed without Anna taking the trip, but spending the money he provided, Butler grew exasperated, and wrote her a letter explaining that he would not respond to any additional requests she might make of him, and that there was nothing in their relationship that would indicate he should supply her with any more money.

***

Anna continued to live a modest life, first in Chicago, then New York. She was occasionally sought out by reporters for interviews that dealt with her exciting days as a speaker during and after the Civil War. She made friends with some up and coming young female speakers who found inspiration in Anna's success on the lecture circuit, and some she may have shared romantic interludes with.

In the summer of 1887 Anna suffered severe pains in her side and doctors performed emergency surgery. The exact nature of the illness is not known, but Anna nearly died from it.

Her recovery took months, and the bills began to pile up. With Anna unable to perform and earn money for the family, her sister Susan wrote to Benjamin Butler and appealed to him once again for money. Despite their recent rough parting Butler was sympathetic, sending Anna and her sister $500 even though he also was sick and in some financial difficulty. When an article appeared in the New York Daily Graphic that revealed how Butler had once years before proposed to Anna, with her refusing him, he asked her, for the sake of his wife and daughter to issue a public denial that it ever occurred. Anna angrily refused and Butler once again swore never in the future to come to her assistance.

1888 found the nation once again embroiled in a heated Presidential contest, this time between the incumbent Democratic President seeking re-election, Grover Cleveland, and the Republican Governor of Indiana, Benjamin Harrison. Anna was thrilled when representatives of the Republican National Committee approached her and asked if she would consent to go on a speaking tour of the Middle West and East in support of Benjamin Harrison. She agreed to give 30 speeches for $125 each, with a $1,250 bonus to be paid her if Harrison won. The national committee made plans for her appearances with room and board fully paid and sent her on her way. Once again Anna was rousing audiences, attacking the sitting President with speeches that dripped with partisan sarcasm.

Harrison won the election, barely. He lost the popular vote, but carried a majority of the Electoral College. Anna got into a dispute with the Republican National Committee. She had only been asked to give 17 speeches, even though she contracted for 30 of them. The committee agreed to pay her for 30 speeches at $125. Anna continued to fight them demanding the $1,250 bonus she was promised in the event of a Harrison victory. They refused to answer Anna.

In 1889 Anna's health once again took a turn for the worst. According to her doctor, she suffered a "nervous breakdown" due to "neurasthenia…and liver troubles." She had been drinking a considerable amount of whiskey, at first as a prescribed medicinal, later as a comfort. When told by the doctor that he would no longer prescribe alcohol, she grew angry and argued with him. As she continued to exhibit major mood swings her doctor feared these symptoms might be a precursor to "lunacy."

With Anna in an agitated state of mind and unable to work, her family's mounting debts drove her sister Susan to desperate measures. Susan wrote once again to Benjamin Butler, pleading for money. When he very bluntly refused she wrote him back threatening to reveal to the press letters he had written to Anna as a married man, declaring his affections for her. Butler did not reply.

Within weeks of that correspondence, Anna and Susan's mother died at age 90 after a long illness. Susan took pen in hand to beg for money to help Anna, still suffering from liver problems. This time she appealed to ex-President Rutherford B. Hayes, for whom Anna had effectively campaigned many years before. Hayes never replied.

While Anna was still recovering she assisted her sister Susan in soliciting loans and financial gifts from celebrity friends and politicians to cover their ongoing medical bills. Anna wrote to President Benjamin Harrison, explaining that he and his party still owed her a $1,250 bonus after his successful election campaign. He did not reply to her, but his secretary did, saying that they forwarded her request to the Republican National Committee. It was up to them to take action. They never did.

***

Due to her reduced financial situation Anna was now living in the small town of West Pittston, Pennsylvania with her sister and her sister's maid Martha. Martha had little tolerance for Anna's increasingly erratic behavior, as Anna ranted about various conspiracies against her by old lovers, former stage managers and Presidents. The local wine merchant told of her frequently ordering large quantities of liquor to be delivered to her home. Neighbors testified that she had the strange habit of asking people to pull hard at her fingers or stomp on her feet to distract her from severe headaches and pains in her arms and legs.

Anna began to suspect that her sister and the maid Martha were trying to poison her by placing strange crystals in her coffee, so she locked herself in her room, taking all her meals there and consuming only what she deemed safe after careful inspection. One night when Susan and Martha came to her room to collect all the dishware that had collected there, Anna started a violent argument with them. Afterward, Susan consulted with a doctor and it was decided that Anna needed to be confined to an asylum for the insane. They hoped that there, with proper care and quiet, Anna might get better.

Anna was released after only 5 ½ weeks, but did not return to stay with her sister. She moved in with Salle Ackley, a lady who had been a member of the staff at the asylum, whom she had befriended during her during her brief stay there. Though the lady was married, it seems that the two grew romantically attached.

Anna Dickinson spent her final years living with the Ackley's in Goshen, Indiana. It was a long twilight, lasting some 30 years. Reporters no longer came to interview her; politicians no longer sought her support. Her sister Susan died in 1915. The little Quaker girl that had shot from obscurity to national prominence slowly winked out in the quiet little Midwestern town, passing away on October 22, 1932, just days away from her 90th birthday.

Fittingly, she had the last word. A plaque marking her grave describes her as "America's Civil War Joan of Arc," and concludes with this quote from her

"My head and heart, soul and brain, were all on fire with the words I must speak."

***

In an era when women could not vote, did not enter into political discussions and were expected to abide quietly in the background while men ran things, Anna Dickinson was a warrior in the battle for gender and race equality, and as such, an oddity and frequently an irritant.

She used men throughout her life to obtain money and professional advancement, and in the end paid for her overstepping of societal boundaries by drawing upon herself public scorn and professional failure.

She gained public attention in the turbulent mid-1800's, a star shining brightly for a time, then disappearing completely from view. There is little reference to her in any current histories of the Civil War, few biographies on library shelves. But forgotten as she now is, she did live a unique and colorful life as a woman who would not defer to men, no matter the cost.

ANNA ELIZABETH DICKINSON
1842 - 1932
"AMERICA'S CIVIL WAR JOAN OF ARC"

In January of 1864, President Lincoln invited Anna to address Congress, the Cabinet and the Supreme Court, to rally support for the Union cause and the fight against slavery.

Anna devoted the rest of her life to justice, liberty and basic human rights for all people: male or female, black or white, rich or poor; and contributed to the 15th Amendment, prohibiting the disenfranchisement of any person based on race, sex, color or previous servitude.

Anna Dickinson lived at this site, in the Village of Goshen, for the last forty-one years of her life.

"My head and heart, soul and brain, were all on fire with the words I must speak"

THE KNAVE OF HEARTS

Daniel Sickles

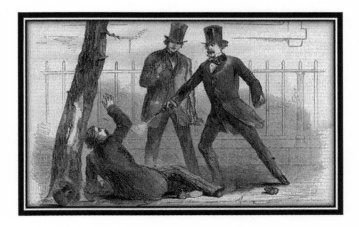

Teresa Sickles lay prostrate on the floor of her room, crying and begging her husband's forgiveness. After getting her to confess the details of her affair, Dan Sickles, her distraught and enraged husband paced around the room considering what to do next. When he looked out the window he saw his wife's lover, Phillip Barton Key, in Lafayette Park, across the street, waving his white handkerchief; a sign Key and Teresa had established to signal the desire for a meeting. Dan threw on a heavy coat, stuffed his pockets with three loaded pistols and ran across the street into the park where Key was waiting for Teresa. Dan drew one pistol and shot Key in the leg just below the groin. Then he drew a second pistol and tried to shoot him in the head, but the gun misfired. He calmly drew a third pistol from his coat and shot Key in the chest. Key died from these wounds soon after.

***

Daniel Edgar Sickles was a man for whom the adjective was invented. Rash, moody, combative, sentimental, gregarious, intelligent, courageous, libidinous, outrageous, scandalous- all these and more could on any given day of his life be applied to him.

Dan Sickles was born in New York City in 1819, the only child of George Garret Sickles and his wife, Susan. George Sickles was a speculator, dealing with cotton merchants from the South whose commodities were being shipped to New York docks for sale to mills along the northern coast and to England. George was loquacious, stubborn and quite charming. Dan's mother was pious, generous and a regular attendant at Trinity Church, one of the wealthiest in the area.

In 1836, when he was barely 17 years old, Dan Sickles gave one of his first speeches, at a rally for the Democratic Presidential candidate Martin Van Buren. A man in the crowd, hearing Dan, asked the rally organizer who the young speaker was, saying "who is that young man God Bless him; if he lives he will be great!"

By 1838 Dan was studying law, preparing for the New York bar at the offices of Benjamin Butler, former law partner of former President Martin Van Buren and former Attorney General and Secretary of War under President Andrew Jackson. Sickles' gregarious nature and sharp intellect were making him powerful friends and supporters, an ability he would use to his advantage throughout his life.

Dan opened a law office in New York City in 1843, in a building that his father owned. While practicing law he made the acquaintance of Isaiah Rynders, who happened to be a leader of the Empire Club, also known as the Dead Rabbits, a gang affiliated with the powerful Democratic organization known as Tammany Hall. Named after a Delaware Indian chief, Tammany Hall grew in power by approaching Irish immigrants on the docks as they came off ships from the old country, recruiting and exploiting them. Confused and desperate to make their way in this new land, these new citizens proved to be an easy mark for Tammany men promising to give them jobs, money and a future.

Dan continued to rise in New York politics, and was elected the youngest member of the general committee that ran Tammany Hall in 1846.

By 1847, with Tammany's support and the aid of a wide circle of powerful and loyal friends, Dan ran for and was elected to the New York State Assembly. While he was serving in Albany he invited a prostitute named Fanny White, with whom he had a long standing arrangement, to travel with him to the capitol and tour the Assembly chambers. Dan's Democratic friends, well aware of his "sporting" nature regarding women and gambling, were not surprised, but opposition Whig party members, seeking to slow his rapid ascent, introduced and passed a motion to censure his conduct. In this era private affairs were considered private, not fodder for public debate, so the motion did nothing to diminish Dan's growing popularity or his affinity for the "sporting" life.

By 1848 he had made enough of a name for himself in party circles to be elected as a delegate to the Democratic Presidential nominating convention. While working the floor at the convention Dan met and impressed August Belmont, the US representative of the House of Rothschild, one of the richest and most powerful families in the world.

Four years later Dan was yet again elected a delegate to the Democratic Presidential nominating convention. He worked for a lesser known candidate, Franklin Pierce, rather than the leading contenders. His instincts were good. The major candidates deadlocked at the convention, and after many frustrating ballots the convention turned to a dark horse, Sickles' friend Senator Franklin Pierce of New Hampshire. Pierce went on to win the Presidency, and now, amongst all his other powerful friends, Dan had one in the White House.

That same year the 33- year- old Dan Sickles married 15- year- old Teresa Baggioli, the daughter of an old friend. Their age difference, while shocking today, was less so then. Teresa was described by friends as beautiful, brilliant, and highly educated. She had known Dan since she was 3 years old. He was a frequent guest at her father's home. She was strongly attracted to his maturity, accomplishment and worldliness, which set him apart from other young men closer to her age.

With a new wife to support, Sickles looked for a job that would enrich him financially more than his position in the New York State Assembly. Using his extensive network of friends, he secured appointment as the Corporation Attorney for the City of New York. In that capacity he began several battles that would eventually improve New Yorkers' quality of life and give him a lasting legacy with its citizens. He chaired a commission that carved out a large tract of undeveloped scrub land near the city's center for use as a public park. After Dan had moved on, the commission's work was adopted by the city and New York began construction of Central Park. Dan also fought for an improved method by which people could move about the ever growing metropolis. As a result of his pioneering efforts, the Omnibus system was adopted as the first urban mass transit system in New York, and eventually copied in many other cities.

Busy as he was as Corporate Attorney for New York, Dan soon resigned to take up an even better opportunity. His friend in the White House, Franklin Pierce, had just named James Buchanan, Pierce's political rival, to be head of the US legation to London (precursor to Ambassador rank), and Buchanan had requested as his Secretary, a bright young fellow he had met at the 1852 convention, Dan Sickles. Pierce, eager to get his rival out of the country, was only too happy to approve Buchanan's request and see him off to England.

Sickles served as secretary to James Buchanan and the US legation in London for two years and then came back home. He began working in earnest for the nomination and election of James Buchanan as President. He also simultaneously ran for a seat in Congress from New York. Buchanan went on to beat John C. Fremont in the national election, and Dan Sickles won a seat in Congress from New York.

At James Buchanan's Inaugural Ball, Dan and his wife Teresa met the recently widowed US Attorney for Washington DC, Phillip Barton Key. Considered one of the handsomest and most eligible men in the city, Key was the son of the composer of the Star Spangled Banner, Francis Scott Key. Over the next few years, Key and Dan Sickles grew to be close friends, and in the case of Dan's young wife, something more.

Sickles' work in Congress kept him at the Capitol quite late, and he travelled frequently. During these absences Key began, with Dan's blessing, to escort Teresa Sickles to social functions around Washington. Soon Washington began to speculate about them. Dan remained unaware of their growing relationship until 1859, when he received an anonymous letter describing the details of Teresa and Key's affair.

Sickles confronted his wife that day and extracted from her a full written confession, even going so far to have the written document witnessed and signed by Teresa's friend Octavia Ridgely, who was visiting them at the time. By chance Phillip Barton Key had come to Lafayette Park just as Teresa's dramatic confession was playing out at the Sickles home. Located just across the street from the White House and directly opposite the Sickles' home, Lafayette Park was a perfect place for Phillip Barton Key to give Teresa a signal telling her they should meet. Unfortunately for Key, Dan Sickles now knew of their affair, and of their secret signal, the waving of a white handkerchief. When Sickles saw Key in the park, he rushed from his house, confronted Key and shot him twice, fatally wounding him.

Dan Sickles was arrested and taken to the county jail to await trial. His team of eight defense lawyers were amongst the best then practicing law in the US, including his former mentor Edwin Stanton. The defense that they created centered on the concept of temporary insanity, a plea never before used in this country. After a lengthy trial whose daily dramatics were faithfully recorded in the headlines of nearly every newspaper in the country, the jury conferred for only 7 hours before announcing their verdict. In 1800's America, a wife committing adultery was considered one of the worst of crimes. Dan was found not guilty.

Dan refused to divorce his wife, but they never reconciled. Teresa lived like a prisoner in their home while Dan lived elsewhere, rarely visiting her.

The coming of the Civil War changed Dan Sickles' life. On this great stage Dan would play a part that would guarantee him lasting fame, or infamy, depending on whose opinion you share.

***

After Confederate forces fired on Fort Sumter in 1861, Dan became anxious to somehow contribute to the effort to preserve the Union. At a dinner at Delmonico's in New York, a Tammany Hall friend, William Willey, suggested that he would raise, arm and equip a regiment of troops if Sickles would agree to lead it. Dan agreed and within a few weeks the regiment was formed. When Sickles presented his regiment to the Governor of New York, the Governor requested that Sickles and Willey should do more, and recruit a full brigade. Rather than react with shock, the two agreed and by mid- May 1861, they had completed the recruiting of a full brigade, with Dan serving as their acting Brigadier General. In July the brigade completed its initial training and was sworn in as the Excelsior Brigade, named after the Latin motto for the state of New York. The brigade became part of Joe Hooker's division, attached to the 3rd Corps, Army of the Potomac.

The Excelsior brigade was not formed in time to participate in the Union Army's disastrous defeat at Bull Run. Just days after, they moved into camp near Washington DC with the shaken remnants of the defeated army. While stationed there, Sickles was invited to a reception at the White House, There he met and befriended the nation's new First Lady, Mary Lincoln. He managed the introduction through yet another friend, a fellow of questionable character who went by the grandiose name of Chevalier Wyckoff. Wyckoff had ingratiated himself with Mrs. Lincoln through lavish flattery and shady financial advice. Through Mrs. Lincoln Dan was introduced to President Lincoln.

***

In May, 1862, Dan and his brigade fought well in several battles on the Yorktown peninsula where the Union army led by George McClellan had landed in a surprise amphibious movement. The Union forces managed to get within sight of the church spires of Richmond before they were struck by Robert E. Lee's troops in a vicious series of attacks that drove them back away from the rebel capital. The boldness of these attacks convinced McClellan that he was facing a greatly superior rebel army (he was mistaken in this), and he ordered the evacuation of the army from the Yorktown peninsula back to Washington DC.

Back in Washington DC, President Lincoln, upset with McClellan's timidity in the face of Lee's army, removed him from command. Other staff changes were made as the army recruited soldiers to replace its casualties. Joe Hooker, Sickles' division commander, was promoted to command of the 3rd Corps. Sickles, whose steadiness under fire had been appreciated by Hooker, was given command of the division. Dan was now a Major General.

Chaos at the top of the command chain continued for the Army of The Potomac. Ambrose Burnside, who had replaced McClellan, fought and lost badly at Fredericksburg, Virginia. Lincoln replaced him with McClellan yet again, as Robert E. Lee led his army north to invade Maryland. McClellan managed a victory of sorts by halting the invasion at Sharpsburg, Maryland, but failed to crush the badly damaged rebel Army, allowing it to escape south. In frustration, Lincoln removed McClellan and promoted Joseph Hooker, Dan's corps commander to lead the army. Dan now had a friend as his commanding general. That friend promptly named Dan to lead the 3rd Corps.

***

Hooker proved to be very skilled at reorganizing the army, reinvigorating its pride and fighting spirit by allowing each corps to design its own distinct shoulder patch to wear. He was confident that he could do what none of his predecessors could - defeat Robert E. Lee's army. He came up with an audacious plan and convinced President Lincoln to let him set it in motion.

Lee's army was entrenched at Fredericksburg, where it had defeated Ambrose Burnside's attempt to dislodge it. Hooker's men were just opposite them, across the Rappahannock River. Hooker's plan was to leave a strong force at the river, skirmishing daily with Lee's men, convincing them that the whole army was soon to cross the river and attack. This would pin Lee's troops in place. Hooker would then march most of his troops west several miles, cross the river, move back east toward Fredericksburg and trap Lee between a hammer and an anvil.

The flank march by Hooker worked. What Hooker's plan didn't allow for was how much of a gambler Robert E.. Lee was. When Hooker got behind him, Lee did what the textbooks said was unthinkable. He divided his smaller army. Leaving a token force to hold Fredericksburg and convince the Federals that Lee's whole army was still there, Lee marched toward Hooker's main force. Then Lee doubled down, dividing his force yet again. While Hooker had his army resting in the woods near a crossroads called Chancellorsville, preparing for what he believed would be a glorious advance to victory in the morning, Lee sent Stonewall Jackson's full army corps (more than half the strength of his already divided force) on a long march through thick woods to surprise the far right flank of the Union forces. Lee nervously waited in front of Hooker's much larger force, for Jackson to get in position to attack. Had this maneuver been found out, Hooker could have crushed Lee's divided units piecemeal, and the war might well have been over.

Fate played with Union fortunes that day. Dan Sickles saw Jackson's men marching west through the woods near his men's position and mistook the flanking movement for the retreat of Lee's army. This is what he reported to Hooker's headquarters. Hooker was considering what to do about this unexpected turn of events when he heard the sound of rolling volleys of rifle fire to the west. It soon became evident that the whole Union right flank was collapsing under heavy attack. So too was Hooker's plan for an assault the next morning on Robert E. Lee's position. Hooker's only concern now became saving his army from compete destruction. Lee had won again. Sickles' men had fought well in this battle, but Dan, not trained in strategy and tactics, had misread a flanking march as a retreat, and this certainly contributed to the embarrassing Union defeat at Chancellorsville.

***

As Hooker's army restored and rebuilt its weakened ranks, Robert E. Lee planned yet another invasion of the North. President Jefferson Davis approved the strategy, and Lee began secretly disengaging his troops from their camps directly across the Rappahanock River from Hooker's army and headed them north, one corps at a time. Hooker eventually realized that Lee was on the move, but the Southern army had a head start and Hooker was not sure where he was headed. Might it be Baltimore, Philadelphia, or even Washington DC? His orders were clear; stay between Lee's army and Washington. But where exactly was Lee's army?

Dan Sickles'. Third Corps began moving north along with the rest of the Union army. Lee had kept his final destination unknown to everyone on his staff until his lead divisions were just across the Susquehanna River from Harrisburg, Pennsylvania. Knowing that Hooker was somewhere to his south and closing the distance between their armies, Lee informed his generals that he expected to give battle somewhere near Gettysburg, Pa. Orders went out to begin concentrating forces there, but to bring on no battle until the army was concentrated. Then he would catch Hooker's army strung out in pursuit and destroy it piece by piece as it rushed north to find him.

In Washington President Lincoln, frustrated with Hooker's inability to locate and bring Lee's army to battle, dismissed him from command and appointed George Meade, the only corps commander willing to take the job, to replace him.

***

On July 1st, 1863, elements of Lee's 2nd and 3rd corps reached Gettysburg and a small force of infantry was sent to the town to gather a large supply of shoes that were supposed to be warehoused there. Lee's troops discovered the road to Gettysburg blocked by two small brigades of Union cavalry, guarding the key roads into the town. The cavalry put up a stiff fight, slowing the Confederate advance. John Buford, the cavalry commander, sent an urgent request for support to the closest troops he knew of, the Union First Corps. That corps, commanded by John Reynolds, was the vanguard of the scattered Union army rushing north. Both sides were unsure if they were facing anything but a small force. Meade was hoping to entice Lee to attack him at Pipe Creek, south of Gettysburg, where his engineers had constructed a strong defensive position. Lee's forces were not yet concentrated, so he did not want a major battle. Despite the plans of both commanders, a battle was starting at Gettysburg.

Fighting became heavier as both sides were reinforced by more troops streaming into Gettysburg. Lee's troops enjoyed the early advantage as they concentrated faster, and were able to mass more men for the attack. Lee finally reached Gettysburg late on July 1st and saw that his army had the numerical advantage. He quickly surmised that he could do just what he had originally planned, defeat each new Union element piecemeal as it reached the battlefield. Throughout the day Union troops were driven back off the hills west of town, then through the town of Gettysburg and finally up onto the hills east of town. As night fell, confused and shattered remnants of two union corps found their way up Cemetery Hill, where they dug in, awaiting a final assault and probable destruction.

Lee chose not to launch a final major assault that night. It was dark and his troops were exhausted from marching and fighting all day. Even though he had not wanted to give battle here, his troops had swept the field, and the whole Union army had not yet concentrated to oppose them. Lee decided he could finish the job the next day, with a grand attack that would flank the Union position and drive them off the hill. Then he could pursue the disorganized survivors and crush the remains of the Union Army as it reached Gettysburg too late to help.

***

During the night, most of the remaining elements of Lee's army reached Gettysburg. The major exception was the bulk of Lee's cavalry, which was still finding its way back to Lee after an ill-considered raid farther north. A mile outside of the town, on Cemetery Hill, the Union Army was slowly regrouping. Their new commander, George Meade, was still not at Gettysburg. He was at Pipe Creek supervising the completion of the powerful defensive works he hoped Lee would shatter his army trying to overcome. He had begun to receive reports about an action north of him at Gettysburg between his cavalry screen and some Confederate troops. He had been disturbed to receive news that John Reynolds 1st Corps had ignored his orders to concentrate at Pipe Creek and had instead responded to an urgent call for help from the Union cavalry at Gettysburg. Late reports confirmed that a heavy engagement was taking place, and that Confederate forces seemed to be there in large numbers. Should he march all troops to Gettysburg, or call them back to the Pipe Creek defensive line?

Dan Sickles' 3rd Corps arrived in Gettysburg in the evening of the first day of battle. He had marched there in response to a frantic call for assistance from General Oliver O. Howard, commander of the Union 11th Corps and the senior general on the field at Gettysburg. By doing so he had chosen to ignore army commander George Meade's order to head for Pipe Creek. Once Sickles arrived at Gettysburg, he surveyed the defense that Howard had established with the remnants of the 1st and 11th Corps. The troops were deployed in a fishhook shaped line, pointed north to south, with the hook and barb at the north end, anchored on a forested knob called Culp's Hill. The center of the line, at the bend of the hook, rested on Cemetery Hill, named for a small cemetery located there. Its prominent feature was a large stone arch marking the entrance to the cemetery. From there the Union line ran south along a gradually flattening Cemetery Ridge. At its southern end the ridge was little more than a slight rise. There the Union line ended. Next to it sat two hills, the smaller called Little Round Top and the larger called Big Round Top.

Lee's army was posted in a broad arc around the Union position, enveloping it from Culp's Hill to the end of Cemetery Ridge. The Union army had interior lines of support while Lee had to shift troops across the wide expanse of the arc his army held.

Dan Sickles and Oliver O. Howard thought the Union position was a strong one. Sickles sent a message to his commanding officer, George Meade, saying "it is a good battlefield for us, though weak on the left flank." George Meade arrived on the field of Gettysburg late in the night of July 1ˢᵗ and immediately surveyed his army's disposition. He was not as confident of the strength of the position as Sickles and Howard. As he considered what to do next, more and more of his army arrived on the field and filed into position alongside the survivors of the first day's battles.

***

The morning of July 2ⁿᵈ found most of the Union Army, save for the 6ᵗʰ Corps, up on the ridges east of Gettysburg. Meade was still not convinced that this was where he should fight Lee's army, but circumstances were rapidly forcing him to make a final decision. Should he stand and fight on defense here, or retreat to his Pipe Creek defensive line several miles south, or even consider launching an attack from his right flank against what seemed to be Lee's weakest position, the Confederate left flank?

Dan Sickles was not a happy man. George Meade had assigned the 3ʳᵈ Corps to the weakest part of the Union line, the far southern end of Cemetery Ridge, where there was barely any advantage of elevation. Sickles saw higher ground some 1500 yards ahead of him near a peach orchard along the Emmitsburg Road. It was closer to the enemy, but a better place to set up artillery. Dan worried that if his troops did not occupy it the Rebels would, and then they could set up artillery there that would dominate his lower position on Cemetery Ridge and cause heavy casualties to his corps. Sickles dispatched an aide to go to Meade's headquarters and ask the general for permission to advance the 3ʳᵈ corps off Cemetery Ridge to occupy the Peach Orchard area. The aide soon returned with the answer. Sickles and his troops were to stay put on Cemetery Ridge, preserving the continuity of the Union line. If the 3ʳᵈ Corps moved forward it would break the Union line and leave a large gap between Sickles' right flank and the left flank of Winfield Hancock's 2ⁿᵈ corps up on Cemetery Ridge. For the next two hours Sickles sent message after message urging Meade to reconsider. He got no reply. Finally Dan mounted his horse and rode off to the commanding general's headquarters to argue his case in person. Dan found a perturbed Meade busy with details of army logistics and pressed him to take the time to visit Dan's position and see for himself what Dan saw. Meade bluntly refused, saying he was far too busy. Meade and Sickles were temperamental and political opposites and did not like each other at all. Dan realized he could not budge Meade, so he asked if Meade would agree to send the army's chief engineer and head of artillery, Henry Hunt, to look over the situation to determine whether Sickles might dispose of his troops according to Sickles' judgment. Meade agreed, adding "certainly, within the limits of the instructions I have given you."

When Henry Hunt surveyed the proposed new position Sickles wanted his 3rd Corps to occupy he liked it, but said Dan would have to wait for Meade's approval before moving to it. With that Hunt rode off to inform Meade of his findings. Sickles' agitation increased over the next hour as word of Meade's approval still had not come. Skirmishing along the 3rd Corps front was increasing and Dan worried that this was a sign that the Rebels were preparing to occupy the high ground near the Peach Orchard. Rationalizing that Meade had approved his realigning his troops as he saw fit (and ignoring the part about staying within the limits of instructions given), Dan ordered his infantry corps forward along with its artillery support.

 Union generals on Cemetery Ridge watched in confusion and surprise as the 3rd corps marched from its position on the ridge and out nearly a mile forward to its new defensive line.

The 3rd Corps took up a position that included the Peach Orchard and several patches of thick woods. It was a strong position if manned by twice the number of troops Sickles commanded. In reality the 3rd corps was stretched far too thin, with both of its flanks unsupported and some 1500 yards and a shallow creek separating them from the rest of the Federal army.

While Meade and Sickles remained at odds about the proper positioning of the Union 3rd Corps, Robert E. Lee was preparing to attack. His plan was to strike the Union left at the low point of Cemetery Ridge with elements of General James Longstreet's Confederate 2nd Corps. They would push Federal troops off that part of the ridge, then pivot the attack north up the spine of Cemetery Ridge and roll up the entire Union position. Sickles had providentially or disastrously moved his corps right into the path this attack would take.

George Meade, as yet unaware of Sickles' repositioning of the 3rd Corps, called for a conference of all his corps commanders. New to army command, he wanted his subordinate general's opinions as to whether the army should fight at Gettysburg or retreat to Pipe Creek.

Sickles replied to the summons saying he could not come because he expected action on his front to be imminent. Meade insisted that he attend the meeting. By the time Sickles arrived at army headquarters Confederate artillery were booming out the opening salvo of Longstreet's assault. Meade heard the sounds also and told Sickles to return to his troops, and that he, Meade, would join him after the conference. By the time Sickles got back to his troops they were already giving ground to Longstreet's attack. Longstreet had been surprised when his men ran into Sickles 3rd corps. A reconnaissance of the area that morning had shown the area to be unoccupied, yet here was a full Union infantry corps waiting for them. It took some time to adjust to this circumstance, but quickly Longstreet's superior numbers took their toll on Sickles badly strung out troops. By the time Meade arrived he took stock of the unexpected position of Sickles Corps and said "You are too far out from the main line, General." But as they were fully engaged, no repositioning of the 3rd corps was possible. Meade promised to send what support he could and rode off to rearrange the main line of the army to compensate for the large gap Sickles had created by moving his corps forward. Reinforcements came, but they were not sufficient to slow up Longstreet's attack. Sickles was on his horse near the center of his collapsing defensive line when he felt a spherical case artillery round hit the ground near him. It slowed down enough so that Dan could see it as it bounced toward him at too fast a pace to dodge. It struck Sickles right leg, shredding it below the knee and leaving the lower limb dangling by thin threads of flesh. As he was borne off the field on a stretcher he asked an aide to give him a lit cigar to puff on. His troops cheered him as he was carried away. He returned their show of affection with a sharp salute. Dan Sickles' role as a field general in the Civil War had ended.

***

A surgeon at the field hospital removed the lower portion of Dan's leg, and was about to dispose of it when the patient, awake and lucid, said that he had recently read that the Army Medical Museum in Washington was in need of samples of amputations for instruction purposes. Per Dan's instructions, the leg was wrapped in cloth, placed in a box and shipped to that institution. It was used for instruction, and then put on display where it remains to this day. The wound was thought to be fatal, but to everyone's surprise Dan survived the amputation. A shockingly rapid recovery followed.

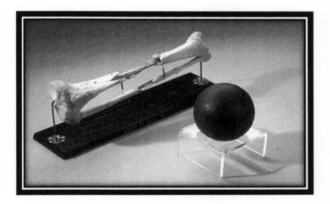

Two days after the repulse of Pickett's Charge at Gettysburg and the subsequent retreat of Lee's army from the north, Dan Sickles arrived by train in Washington DC. His post-operative pain was being controlled by doses of opium that left him semi-conscious. In that daze he could not appreciate the cheers of the crowd gathered at the train station to welcome his arrival. His life was still in danger, as death by gangrene infection was common amongst Civil War amputees.

He began his recovery at a home on 8th Street that had been secured for him by his friends. President Lincoln and his son Tad visited Dan soon after he settled in, and thanked him for his heroic service to the country. While other generals were already debating the folly or genius of Sickles actions at Gettysburg, President Lincoln supported him. Lincoln was livid that General Meade had failed to destroy Lee's army as it retreated following the battle. Sickles' aggressiveness and propensity for taking the initiative were just the traits that Lincoln looked for in his generals.

***

Dan's next great fight had already begun. His defense of his actions at Gettysburg would continue for the rest of his life and find him gathering powerful enemies and surprising allies. When Lincoln first met with Dan he was anxious for details of the great battle, and Dan used this opportunity to frame his arguments in defense of his actions. General Meade, in his official report of the battle, which the President had already read, stated that Sickles had misinterpreted his orders, wrongly moving his 3rd Corps nearly a mile in front of the main Union defensive position. This error, Meade maintained, led to the destruction of a large part of the 3rd Corps and a near breaching of the Union position on Cemetery Ridge. Sickles explained to the President that Meade never had a clear plan of battle that afternoon, and that he was contemplating a retreat. It was Sickles advance to secure the high ground in his front before the rebels could that had prevented a complete disaster for the Union forces. As Sickles spun his argument for the President he frequently interrupted his narrative to have an orderly mop his brow and moisten the bandaged stump of his right leg. By the time the President departed he had received the whole story - as Dan Sickles saw it. It was a grand opening salvo in the battle to save and build his reputation for posterity.

Dan's recovery from the amputation of his lower right leg, considering the limitations of medicine at the time, was remarkable. He spent the first week at the 8th Street house in Washington DC., where a continuous stream of visitors stopped in to hear his tales of the great battle. Chevalier Wykoff, a close friend of the first lady, met with Dan several times to relay news of current politics, public opinion on the war and, of course, Washington DC gossip. Army comrades gave him updates on the state of affairs in the field. Members of his old legal team visited too, bringing him some of his favorite foods. Dan never invited his wife Teresa to visit.

When Edwin Stanton, Secretary of War, stopped in, Dan questioned him about his 3rd Corps, fearing they had suffered heavy casualties in action fighting Lee's army as it retreated from Gettysburg. President Lincoln himself sent Dan a telegram reassuring him that no such action involving the 3rd Corps had taken place. In a subsequent visit to Sickles, the President was overheard to say to Dan that General Meade had allowed Lee's army to retreat across the Potomac unmolested, thus assuring the continuation of the war. Lincoln considered that failure by Meade to crush Lee's forces as the greatest disaster of the war to date.

Three weeks after being wounded, Sickles departed Washington D.C., travelling by train, then boat, back to New York City.

***

Despite his stump still healing and hurting, especially in wet weather, Dan was full of nervous energy and anxious to return to command his 3rd Corps. He wrote to the Secretary of War asking whether Stanton could secure that position for him. While waiting for a chance to rejoin the army in the field, Dan enjoyed great popularity as a guest of honor and speaker at various events. He spoke in favor of generous rather than vengeful treatment of the South once the war was over. This put him at odds with the radical Republicans in Congress, but in accord with most Democrats and President Lincoln, who was intent on bringing the southern states back into the Union as soon as possible.

In October, 1863, Dan Sickles headed south to meet with the commander of the Army of the Potomac, his former superior, George Meade. The two had been waging a written war about each other's conduct at Gettysburg – and there was little cordiality between them. Sickles asked Meade to re-appoint him head of the 3rd Corps. Meade deflected the request, suggesting it was too soon for Sickles to return to active field duty, as Dan could not yet ride a horse or march. A very disappointed Sickles visited with his 3rd Corps troops, was cheered heartily and presented with a gift of a small coach and two horses. He made a few remarks of appreciation, saluted the men, climbed into his new coach and headed back to Washington. He would not see the 3rd Corps again.

Once back in Washington, Sickles met with President Lincoln and Secretary of the Navy Gideon Welles to discuss Sickles' all-consuming, favorite topic, Gettysburg. Sickles argued that he and Oliver O. Howard, commander of the 11th Corps had chosen the ground to fight on at Gettysburg on the evening of July 1st, not George Meade. Meade had not yet reached the field. Secretary Welles agreed that Meade was wanting as a commanding general.

In February of 1864, the Joint Committee on the Conduct of the War convened at the Capitol to probe the actions of Sickles' friend Joseph Hooker, former commander of the Army of the Potomac, as he pursued Lee's army north. They also investigated the actions of George Meade, the Union army's commander during and after the battle of Gettysburg. Dan testified before the committee, and his comments painted a positive portrait of Hooker and a decidedly negative one of Meade. He stated that Meade, upon arriving at Gettysburg and surveying the army's position there, asked his chief of staff to draft orders for a retreat to Meade's preferred defensive position at Pipe Creek several miles away. Sickles claimed that only his actions in moving his corps forward, and the subsequent attack by James Longstreet's Confederate corps on July 2nd stopped Meade from abandoning the field.

Sickles went further in his criticism of Meade when the committee asked him whether the Union army – after Lee retreated from Gettysburg – should have pursued and attacked them. Sickles answered in the affirmative.

George Meade was called to testify before the committee and he defended his actions, stating that he had no fixed plan to retreat from Gettysburg on July 1st or 2nd. The retreat order he drafted was to be used only if absolutely necessary. He replied to the committee's query about why he did not attack Lee's army as it retreated across the Potomac by stating that Lee had superior numbers (he did not) and a strong rearguard – and that such an attack could have led to a disaster for the Union army.

In the end the committee recommended that President Lincoln relieve Meade from command, with possible replacement by Joseph Hooker, Dan Sickles' old friend.

Dan anxiously waited for President Lincoln's decision. With Hooker back in command of the Army of the Potomac, Dan could be reinstated as 3rd corps commander.

Lincoln, realizing the volatility of the situation and disliking the thought of appearing to be coerced into an action recommended by a Congressional committee that had been a thorn in his side for years, chose a clever alternate path. First, he left Meade in operational command of the Army of the Potomac. Then he created a new position, General in Chief of all Union Armies – and appointed Ulysses Grant to fill it. Grant was a stubborn Illinoisan known for being offensive minded. He had just completed a hard fought and brilliantly executed campaign to capture the vitally important city of Vicksburg, Mississippi. This victory guaranteed Union control of the entire length of the Mississippi River, effectively cutting the western confederacy off from its eastern sister states. Grant thanked Lincoln for his trust and announced that he would make his headquarters wherever the Army of the Potomac travelled, thus superseding Meade in any decisions regarding army strategy. This left Meade as a purely administrative, not tactical or strategic leader.

Sickles had won a partial victory over Meade, who felt publicly embarrassed by the new command arrangement. But Sickles failed in his attempt to regain command of the 3rd corps. When Grant took overall command of Union forces he gave Meade permission to disband what was left of the 3rd Corps, merging those troops into Winfield Scott's 2nd Corps. Sickles beloved 3rd Corps ceased to exist.

***

Lincoln knew that his friend was sorely hurt by the disbanding of the 3rd Corps, so he found him something else to occupy his ever- restless mind. He asked Dan if he felt able to travel south to check on the condition of the Union armies in the field. He also wanted Sickles to meet with the newly appointed Governor of Tennessee, Andrew Johnson. Johnson was making speeches arguing for harsh treatment of former rebels and Lincoln wanted to know whether Johnson could be moved to a more conciliatory tone, in keeping with what Lincoln had in mind for post- war reconstruction.

Dan's reports shed light on the problems Lincoln would face after the war. As the Union regained control of areas in the South profiteers descended upon the starving local populous, raking in huge profits on artificially high prices charged for necessities like food, clothing and medicines. Sometimes this was done with the collusion of corrupt Union officers in command of these areas. Not surprisingly, Dan also reported on the deep hatred of the North pervading areas of the South just retaken by Union forces.

By the time Dan returned from his inspection duties down south the Presidential election of 1864 was on the near horizon. Lincoln was re-nominated by the Republicans with Andrew Johnson as his Vice Presidential running mate. Johnson had apparently taken to heart Dan Sickles' suggestion that he accept President Lincoln's softer stance on the handling of the South. The Democrats nominated George McLellan, former commander of the Army of the Potomac, a pro-peace candidate and one-time patron of young Dan Sickles. Despite their past friendship Sickles supported President Lincoln for re-election, joining Democrats for Lincoln. To the surprise of a great many, including Lincoln himself, the President was re-elected that fall.

***

By winter of 1864, President Lincoln sought to find a new task to challenge Dan Sickles, and keep him from causing further mischief about a field commission with the Army. He asked Dan to travel to Columbia, South America. He would have two tasks to accomplish while there. First, he was to seek Columbia's approval for Union troops to cross the Isthmus of Panama. Second, he was to seek Columbian approval for his plan to move many freed blacks now streaming into northern cities to Columbia, where they could form their own colony. Before the war, when Dan was in Congress, he had gotten on well with the Columbian counsel to the US. That counsel was now President of Columbia. While in Columbia Dan could also work on behalf of the commissioners who ran Central Park in New York City. They wanted him to gather flora, fauna and animals native to South America and ship them back to New York for use in the park.

In the 1860's a trip to Panama (then part of New Grenada, a large area including the Isthmus of Panama and parts of South America, all under the control of Columbia) was a life threatening excursion that included rail, steamer, mule and oxcart travel. By March, 1865, Dan was on his way. The trip was arduous and exhausting for a healthy citizen, let alone one recovering from an amputation, but Dan managed it without further injury.

Once in Panama he met with civil authorities and received assurances that the issue of US troops marching across the Isthmus would be seriously discussed if a $14 million payment was made. This was compensation for past damages done to Panamanian property by American drunks and ruffians. Dan asked for and received agreement from the U.S. State Department for that payment to be made. With one objective achieved in Panama, Dan moved on to the capital, Bogota, Columbia. This trip was as dangerous as the first leg, and the last 70 miles of it was done with carts pulled by mules up increasingly steep paths that wound their way up the plateau on which Bogota was situated. For large parts of the trip Dan strapped on a prosthetic leg and rode a donkey.

Once settled in the Columbian capitol Dan went to the Presidential Palace located next to the city cathedral and met with his old acquaintance, the former counsel to the US and current President of the country, Manuel Murillo. After welcoming ceremonies they discussed the main objectives of Dan's trip. Murillo agreed to do all in his power to make sure that regional governments approved passage of US troops across Panamanian soil. He also agreed in principle with the relocation of recently freed US slaves to Columbia. Once the US had created legislation to accomplish this, Murillo promised to present it to his cabinet for approval.

Sending messages from Columbia to Washington DC and receiving replies took well over a month. Dan sent news of his diplomatic successes to Secretary of War Stanton, and made a point of how well he had handled the rough journey, hoping it would convince Stanton and the President that he was now physically ready to serve with the army in the field, but much had changed in the US since Dan's departure. Union forces had finally trapped the shrunken and starving army of Robert E. Lee and forced it to surrender. Richmond, the capitol of the Confederacy was now in Union hands, and the war was rapidly coming to a close.

Not yet knowing any of these things, Dan departed Columbia with his mission accomplished, looking forward to a possible new command in the army. He led a caravan out of Columbia that carried with it travertine stone, sloths, jaguars, monkeys, tapirs, agoutis, trees, plants and exotic flowers-all bound for Central Park in New York. Not long after departing Bogota, and while still in Columbia, Dan learned of the assassination of President Lincoln, the attempted assassination of Secretary of State Seward, the accession of Vice President Johnson to the Presidency and the surrender of the Confederacy's main army at Appomattox. Dan would be returning to a very different US than he had left months before.

***

Back in the United States, Dan made one of his rare visits to his wife Teresa at their home, Bloomingdale, where she had been living in isolation since Dan's trial for murder in the 1850's. He had visited her occasionally over the years and corresponded, but they were a couple only in the legal sense. He now found her in the middle stages of consumption, breathing with some difficulty. Her widely praised beauty was darkened by a grey pallor and her youthful vitality was clearly gone. She shuffled about the big house with slow and careful steps. The reunion was brief. By summer's end Dan was offered a position as Military Governor of South Carolina. Now that the South had been defeated, Congress had divided it into military districts to be governed by military men as the states sought to regain full status within the Union. Dan was assigned to manage a district that included the most rabidly anti Northern area of the South, the very wellspring of the late rebellion. He left for Charleston and once again chose not to take his wife Teresa with him.

South Carolinians had created a series of laws and regulations called the Black Codes, which effectively served to keep freed slaves under the thumb of their former masters. Once Dan took over his new post he declared the Black Codes null and void. He also insisted on the same judicial recourse for black as well as white citizens. Wherever he could he intervened in subversions of justice. When he heard that a district court had sentenced a white man to be whipped for associating with blacks, he sent troops to stop the sentence from being carried out. Dan and all his fellow Military Governors were caught in a terrible political mess that existed after the war. Radical Republicans, in control of Congress, wanted the South dealt with harshly, while the white South saw its judicial system survive the war intact and wanted no Northern interference with its view of justice. Military governors saw the number of their troops continually decrease as the nation slowly disbanded its armies. While this weakening of Northern military presence occurred, bands of white southerners called "regulators" (a forerunner to the Ku Klux Klan) rode through the countryside terrorizing blacks. His calm and fair administration of the South Carolina District gained Dan a promotion to the Military Governorship of the newly formed 2nd Military Department, which included North and South Carolina. This in some ways lessened Dan's burden, as North Carolina contained many more citizens willing to peacefully acknowledge the primacy of the Union and end of the Confederacy.

Dan got word from New York that Teresa's health was continuing to decline. He did not visit her. This ongoing failure to acknowledge their marriage in any public way drove a serious wedge between Dan and his now 13 year old daughter Laura, who lived with Teresa. Laura's seemingly constant need for activity, her stubbornness and her quickness to judge reminded Teresa very much of Dan. Despite their similar temperament, Laura held her father partly responsible for her mother's deteriorating health.

Ever the charmer and attractive to ladies even with one leg gone, Dan kept company in South Carolina with a young woman named Allie Grant. She received considerably more than her share of ration certificates issued from Dan's offices to those in need.

By November, 1866, President Andrew Johnson declared that the rebellion of the South had officially ended, and by 1867 many functions performed by the Military Governors were taken over by local authorities.

By the winter of 1867, Teresa's illness grew steadily worse. With a swiftness that caught everyone by surprise, Teresa died at 31 years of age. Once again her name was in all the papers as it had been so embarrassingly a decade before. Shunned for decades by the nation as a fallen woman, she was now mourned. Dan Sickles finally came to her side now, as she had so long hoped he would, only to participate in her funeral. As in life, newspapers paid more attention to him than to her. His public grief was reported as "Christian submission to the decree of Divine Wisdom."

Dan returned to South Carolina from Teresa's funeral to attend to his duties. He had, by virtue of several decrees he issued there, placed himself at odds with President Johnson. Johnson did not object to the content of the decrees, but to the fact that Sickles had not consulted him first before issuing them. After unsatisfactory discussions about the limits of a Military Governor's power, the President demanded the resignations of Dan Sickles, Phillip Sheridan, and John Pope. When Sickles did not promptly reply the President dismissed him.

Never one to turn the other cheek, Sickles headed for Washington DC to help the Radical Republicans in Congress to impeach the President. Their history making attempt failed by only one vote, but Andrew Johnson's Presidency never recovered from the political damage.

***

With the sitting President politically emasculated, Sickles busied himself working for the election of Ulysses Grant to the Presidency in 1868. Grant, the general who had secured victory and an end to the Civil War won election easily. In return for his strong support, Grant named Sickles Minister to Spain. This was an important diplomatic posting, for Spain's queen Isabella II had just been forced from the throne and replaced by a general, Juan Prim. The President hoped that this new leader of Spain might be open to discussing the possibility of the United States buying Cuba. As soon as Dan assumed his new position he began discussions with General Prim, who was amenable to the idea. But he would have to consult with his cabinet and obtain their approval. Despite Prim's recommendation the Spanish cabinet refused to consider the offer. Cuba was off the table.

While in Spain, recently widowed Dan Sickles' love life did not suffer. At an Ambassador's Ball he met and began to court Caroline DeCreagh, a dark haired Spanish-Irish beauty. While courting one woman might be enough for some men, for Dan it was not excitement enough. While travelling to Paris on business Dan made the acquaintance of the former Spanish Queen, Isabella II. Each found the other attractive and soon an affair blazed hot.

In 1871, despite his affair with Isabella, Dan married Caroline DeCreagh. In less than a year a letter was written to the US Secretary of State by an American just back from Spain. The letter accused

Sickles of consorting with child prostitutes and carrying on yet another affair, this one with a Senora Domeriquy, supposedly a spy for Cuba. The writer called Sickles an embarrassment to the United States and demanded his removal.

Despite those kinds of criticism Dan survived in his post until 1874, when he finally left Madrid and his position as Ambassador to Spain. He moved to Paris and lived there for 4 years with his wife Caroline, his mother Susan and his daughter (from his first wife) Laura. Caroline bore him a son and daughter. The lean and wiry Dan Sickles of the Civil War had now grown heavier and lost some of his dark curly hair.

By 1879 Dan was ready to leave Europe. His marriage to Caroline DeCreagh was falling apart over the issue of Dan's infidelity. She refused to go back to the US with him. He left for America without her and their children. His daughter Laura was already back in the states, having moved in with her grandmother after a short, unsuccessful marriage. She spent the support money Dan sent her on drink. When Dan found this out he cut her off financially.

***

Once back in the states Dan needed a steady income, and he determined to land a government job by campaigning for U.S. Grant in the 1880 Presidential elections. For one of the few times in his life, Dan backed the wrong man. Grant failed to get the Republican nomination, and a compromise candidate, James A. Garfield, was nominated and went on to beat the Democrat, Winfield Scott Hancock, in the general election. With no ally in the White House, Dan received no government position.

After the election, the Battle of Gettysburg erupted again in print. Several books and articles were published by battle survivors, each retelling the events of those days in July, 1863, from the author's perspective. Dan plunged into the battle with pen blazing. He argued that his high ground position at the Peach Orchard surprised and weakened the attack of James Longstreet's Confederates on July 2nd, and prevented them from gaining a foothold on Cemetery Ridge that would have led to the collapse of the entire Union position.

In a bizarre turn of events Dan's strongest ally in arguing this point was his adversary on that second day of the battle, James Longstreet. Longstreet had been under much criticism from Southerners for his hesitation in properly executing Robert E. Lee's orders during that campaign. Longstreet had been vocal in his disagreement with Lee over Lee's insistence on taking the offensive at Gettysburg. Longstreet repeatedly, and in front of many witnesses, had tried to talk Lee into maneuvering around Meade's flank at Gettysburg, getting between him and Washington DC and forcing Meade to attack Lee at a place of Lee's choosing. Longstreet was badly hurt by his own people blaming him for what he considered Lee's failings at Gettysburg. He saw the Sickles controversy as a way of deflecting criticism toward Meade, who was now 10 years dead and unable to defend himself. In defense of Sickles, Longstreet wrote "I believe it is now conceded that the advanced position at the Peach Orchard taken by your Corps and under your orders saved the battlefield for the Union cause."

In the midst of this war of words, Dan was appointed chairman of the New York State Monuments Committee, charged with designing and building monuments to New York State regiments that participated in the battle of Gettysburg. The battlefield had been neglected since the end of the war and was in a deplorable state. Dan would spend much of his remaining life improving it so that future generations could learn of the sacrifices made there. The scene of his life's greatest moments would be made into a place where heroes were remembered and honored—and Sickles hoped his reputation would shine in their reflected glory.

By 1891, Sickles' daughter Laura (by his first wife Teresa) had died of either tuberculosis or alcoholism. Dan's father had died a few years before. While he still lived, George Sickles had tried to get his son to help Laura, but Dan refused. "I have done my whole duty toward the person in whose behalf you write" Dan replied to his father. "As far as I am concerned she is dead and buried." And now she was. Dan did not attend her funeral.

While giving a speech dedicating yet another monument at Gettysburg, Dan was awarded the Congressional Medal of Honor for "conspicuous gallantry on the battlefield, vigorously contesting the advance of the enemy and continuing to encourage his troops after being himself severely wounded." While accepting the medal and unveiling the monument, Dan announced his candidacy for Congress. One of his main campaign issues would be the need for federal control of the Gettysburg battlefield. Private groups and state committees had proven themselves ineffective. This hallowed ground needed to be better preserved.

In 1892, at the age of 75, the still vigorous Dan Sickles was elected to Congress and took his seat during the Presidency of Benjamin Harrison. His stay was short and disappointing. He lost re-election in 1894. Afterward, he continued to practice law and chair the New York State Monuments Commission.

1898 saw him campaigning again, this time for Republican William McKinley. He travelled on the official campaign train that carried McKinley surrogates across the US, often waving to the crowds from the back platform along with other aged Civil War heroes. McKinley won and once again Dan had a friend in the White House.

Sickles appeared at several veterans' reunions with former Confederate General James Longstreet. They had become good friends. All the anger they may have felt toward each other as generals on opposing sides had been worn away with the passing of the years. During one of their visits to Gettysburg they found themselves helping each other climb up the steep slopes of little Round Top, the feisty one legged Irishman and the Southern hero without honor in his own land, locked arm in arm. "Sickles", Longstreet said, "you can well afford to help me up here now. If you had not kept me away so long on July 2, 1863, the war would have lasted longer than it did."

In 1896 they again appeared together at William McKinley's second inauguration. In 1902 at West Point, they met again for the last time to join a review of Spanish-American War veterans. By 1904 James Longstreet, first an enemy, then a friend, was dead.

In his last years Dan was looked after by two servants and a middle-aged widow named Eleanor Wilmerding. It was clear that she shared more than an employee-employer relationship with Dan. Even at his advanced age, Dan had appetites. One drawer of his bedroom dresser was found to be filled with stockings and ladies gloves, trophies carefully gathered from admiring female visitors.

In his eighties Dan met and became friends with Mark Twain, the famed humorist. Noting Dan's penchant for telling stories of his exploits at Gettysburg, Twain said "the general valued his lost leg by a way above the one that is left. I am perfectly sure that if he had to part with either one of them he would part with the one he has got."

Dan was never one to count money carefully. In his last years he foolishly loaned money to several women and incurred debts he never repaid. His most embarrassing financial difficulty came in 1912. It was discovered that over $28,000 was missing from the funds allotted to the New York State Monuments Commission-of which Dan was the longtime chairman. Plans were made to arrest the old man. James Longstreet's widow Helen, stating that Sickles was her late husband's close friend, promised to raise the money necessary to repay the missing funds, and to raise it from "the ragged, destitute, maimed veterans who followed Lee. The Republic whose battles you fought will not permit your degradation." Despite Helen's noble effort, Dan was placed under house arrest. Bond was set at $30,000 and bail was arranged. The issue was not settled, but Dan was free again.

In 1913 Dan attended the 50th anniversary encampment at Gettysburg Pennsylvania. Thousands of old men who formerly faced each other in blue and grey attended. Dan was one of the main attractions. Many attendees sought to meet him and shake his hand. The climax of the gathering was a recreation of Pickett's Grand Charge, with the Confederate survivors of it, now white haired and feeble, slowly making their way across the open field from Seminary Ridge to the crest of Cemetery Hill, where a small copse of trees still stood as it did the day of the battle, marking their furthest advance into Union lines. As the old men tottered to the top of the hill they were greeted not by rifle fire and grapeshot, but by the cheers of the Union veterans gathered there. The former enemies joined together into one mass, handshaking, backslapping, swapping stories and reminiscing.

Less than a year later Daniel Edgar Sickles' tumultuous life came to an end. On May 3, 1914, just after 9pm, he suffered a cerebral hemorrhage and passed into history.

***

Dan Sickles lived a truly event filled life. His marital strife, illicit affairs, political intrigue, embezzlement, military successes and failures all blended together to produce a man whose legacy is still debated by historians. But Gettysburg National Park would not exist as it is without him. Had he not championed its development, Central Park might have remained for years an ugly, rock filled scar of land in central New York City. And the insanity plea as a defense in murder cases might never have been tried.

Whatever else his life was, it was not ordinary.

6

LEADER OF THE LOST CAUSE

Jefferson Davis

A tall, gaunt figure entered St Paul's Episcopal Church in Richmond Virginia on the morning of April 2, 1865 and took an aisle seat. Throughout the past four years of war the President of the Confederate States of America and his family had occupied the same pew while listening to services conducted by Reverend Dr. Charles A. Minnegerode. What drew some attention from the congregation today was the absence of Jefferson Davis' wife and children from his side. Without public notice, Davis had sent his wife, Varina Howell Davis, and their four children south to Charlotte, North Carolina, three days earlier in anticipation of the eventual fall of the Confederate capitol to surrounding Northern forces.

The scent of spring flowers and fresh cut grass passed through open windows to fill the church, lifting the spirits of its members who had for weeks been struggling with the ongoing horrors of the war that was rapidly closing in on them. Soon after President Davis entered St. Paul's, a messenger walked into the church and strode quickly up the center aisle to the side of the President, delivering a message directly into his hands. Jefferson Davis calmly opened it and, careful to control his features and body language, began to read. It was from Robert E. Lee, commander of all Confederate forces, sent through the Secretary of War, John C. Breckenridge. Lee explained that the Army of Northern Virginia, the most powerful and successful Confederate army still in the field, could no longer hold back the much larger Union army surrounding Richmond. Lee's army would soon have to abandon the trenches around the capital and retreat. The city would need to be evacuated immediately.

Davis finished reading the dispatch, stood up, and slowly walked out of the church. By the time Davis entered his carriage to return to the Confederate White House, rumors were already spreading in the streets that the Yankees were coming.

***

Four years earlier, Jefferson Davis had arrived in Richmond, the capital of the newly formed Confederate States of America, and had taken up the reins of power as its first President. He was much better known nationally than his counterpart in Washington DC, Abraham Lincoln. Davis was a graduate of West Point, a Colonel of infantry in the Mexican War, and was wounded in battle while leading a charge of his Mississippi Rifles regiment. He was a plantation owner who was elected to Congress, then the US Senate. While in the Senate, he was instrumental in helping in the creation of the Smithsonian Institution, and supervised a major expansion of the US Capitol building. He served as Secretary of War in the cabinet of President Franklin Pierce and was frequently spoken of as a future Democratic candidate for President of the United States. When southern statesmen began to seriously talk about seceding, Davis argued that southern rights could be better defended by fighting for them in Congress rather than on a battlefield. After the states of the South chose to ignore his counsel and leave the Union, they recognized in Davis the military and political skills the new country would need in its leader and chose him as their President.

Davis looked the part of a wartime leader. His training at West Point made him an excellent equestrian, sitting ramrod straight in the saddle. His erect soldierly posture made him appear taller than his 5- foot-eleven-inch height. Many people commented that with his prominent nose and clear, penetrating gaze he resembled an eagle. Though he looked robustly healthy he suffered from neuralgia and frequent bouts of malaria which he had contracted while on duty with his regiment in Mexico.

***

Once back at his small office in the Confederate White House, Davis issued orders to the heads of his various government departments to gather all papers necessary to continue governance of the Confederacy and prepare them for rail transport to Danville, Virginia, where a government in exile would be set up. All confederate assets, paper currency, gold, and silver were to be transported by a second train immediately following Davis' departure. By 11 pm that evening all was ready and Davis boarded a train ready to head 145 miles west to Danville, Virginia. With him were his aides: Francis A. Lubbock, former Governor of Texas, William Preston Johnston, son of Davis's old friend the late General Albert S. Johnston, John Taylor Wood, grandson of President Zachary Taylor and Micaiah Clark, Davis' chief clerk. To help run his government from Danville many of his cabinet boarded as well, including Secretary of State Judah P. Benjamin, Attorney General George Davis, Secretary of the Treasury George Trenholm, Postmaster John Reagan and Secretary of the Navy Stephen Mallory. As the two trains pulled out of Richmond, the city was dark and quiet. Soon it would be lit in flames and ravaged by roaming groups of looters. The last days of the Confederacy and Jefferson Davis' freedom had begun.

When Union troops took over the city the next day, General Godfrey Wetzel asked President Lincoln what orders he had for dealing with the conquered rebels. "If I were in your place" Lincoln replied, "I'd let 'em up easy."

By 3pm April 3rd, Davis's train arrived in Danville Virginia. Here Davis hoped to restart the business of governing his country. Rail lines out of the city were still intact, as were telegraph lines to facilitate communication with the remaining forces in the field. He hoped to concentrate these forces against the armies of the North to deny them victory. Three hours after pulling into the Danville station, a log cabin had been erected along with numerous tents to provide office space for the cabinet. The Confederacy once again had a functioning government.

Varina Davis and her children reached Charlotte, North Carolina the next day. Burton Harrison, an aide Davis had dispatched to ensure that his family reached Charlotte safely, left Varina and her children to return to Jefferson Davis in Danville. That same day, Jefferson Davis issued a proclamation to the people of the Confederacy from Danville.

We have now entered upon a new phase of the struggle...It is my purpose to maintain your cause with my whole heart and soul; ... I will never consent to abandon to the enemy one foot of any one of the states of the Confederacy...Let us meet the foe with fresh defiance, with unconquered and unconquerable hearts.

On April 9th, Davis sent a message from Danville to General Robert E. Lee. "I hope to hear from you soon at this point, where offices have been opened to keep up the current business, until more definite knowledge would enable us to form more permanent plans. May God preserve, sustain and guide you." Davis had no way of knowing that Lee had met that very day with Ulysses S. Grant to discuss terms under which Lee might surrender his Army of Northern Virginia to avoid further bloodshed before what he saw as his inevitable defeat. Grant offered generous terms and Lee surrendered his army, the most powerful remaining force still in the field defending the Confederacy.

The next morning, Washington D.C. shook from repeated cannon fire, but there was no panic over an enemy attack. The city was beginning to learn the news of Lee's surrender. They knew this meant the end was near. Two weeks earlier, in anticipation of this day, President Lincoln had met with Generals Grant and Sherman. They asked what was to be done with the rebel leaders, such as Jefferson Davis, when the war ended. Sherman quoted Lincoln as saying "he was hardly at liberty to speak his mind fully, but intimated that he(Davis) ought to clear out, 'escape the country,' only it would not do for him to say so openly. As usual he illustrated his meaning by a story. 'A man once had taken the total abstinence pledge. When visiting a friend, he was invited to take a drink, but declined, on the score of his pledge; when his friend suggested lemonade, which was accepted. In preparing the lemonade, the friend pointed to the brandy bottle, and said the lemonade would be more palatable if he were to pour in a little brandy; when his guest said, if he could do so unbeknown to him, he would not object.' From which I inferred that Mr. Lincoln wanted Davis to escape unbeknown to him."

All day on April 10th, Jefferson Davis and his cabinet heard rumors circulating in Danville that General Lee had surrendered his army. Absent any official confirmation they doubted the news, but out of prudence decided to act on the possibility. The portable Confederate government was once again packed onto trains, and by 11pm was heading further south, hoping to stay between Grant's army to the north and Sherman's army to the southeast.

The Davis' train headed for Greensboro, North Carolina, travelling all night and the next morning. Along the route they missed a unit of Union cavalry by just 5 minutes, pulling into Greensboro around 2pm. The people of the town stayed behind closed doors as their President passed through their streets because they knew that Union forces were in the immediate area and feared reprisals if they offered any help to President Davis and his cabinet.

A wealthy citizen of the town finally agreed to provide accommodations for Davis and his government in exile while they were in Greensboro. On April 13th Davis finally received a message from Robert E. Lee detailing the surrender of his army to U.S. Grant. Lee's son, Robert E. Lee Jr. was in Greensboro with Davis, and observed the effect his father's dispatch had on the President. "After reading it, he handed it without comment to us: then, turning away, he silently wept bitter tears. He seemed quite broken at the moment by this tangible evidence of the loss of his army and the misfortune of its general." The next day Davis penned a letter to his wife, who was in South Carolina, also heading further south. "Dear Winnie, I will come to you if I can. Everything is dark. – you should prepare for the worst…." His cabinet was urging him to flee the country, but he refused to do so as long as any organized body of troops, regardless of their size, remained to resist the federal advance. Relocation of the Confederate government (not retreat) would continue, but not by train. There were no trains available, so the cabinet, his staff and others rode horses or climbed aboard carriages to depart Greensboro on April 15th. The travel would be slow, as heavy rains had turned the roads into a quagmire. Davis had no knowledge of the fact that Abraham Lincoln had died that morning, a victim of an assassin's bullet delivered into the back of his head as he sat watching a play at Ford's Theatre. There was a firestorm of anger growing in the North directed at the man they felt was responsible for the assassin's attack, Jefferson Davis. Even worse, the man who would now assume the office of President of the United States, Andrew Johnson, harbored a deep hatred of the Southern planter class that Jefferson Davis epitomized.

Two days later the Davis party arrived in Salisbury, North Carolina, still unaware of Lincoln's death. They were also unaware of the fact that Confederate General Joseph E. Johnston had met with Union General William T. Sherman to discuss terms for the surrender of Johnston's army. While in Salisbury Davis received a letter signed by several high ranking officers asking his permission to disband their troops and send their men home. Davis replied that the situation was not yet so grave that such a move could be approved. He denied their request, asking them to continue to do their duty to their country as he was. Davis and his entourage rested and regrouped on April 18th, then headed south again, riding into Charlotte, North Carolina on April 19th.

Charlotte gave the Presidential party a cool reception. Heavy casualties suffered by its soldiers during four years of war had eroded their morale. With some difficulty, the Davis party found one citizen willing to give them shelter during their stay. When a large group of citizens and soldiers gathered outside their quarters, Davis emerged to give a brief speech. In it he thanked them for their loyalty, but showed no remorse for the decisions he had made. "I am conscious of having committed errors, and very grave ones; but in all that I have done, in that I have tried to do, I can lay my hand upon my heart and appeal to God that I have had but one purpose to serve, but one mission to fulfill, the preservation of the true principles of constitutional freedom, which are as dear to me today as they were four years ago. I have nothing to abate or take back; if they were right then they are right now, and no misfortune to our arms can change right into wrong. Again I thank you."

Soon after the speech Davis received a telegram from his Secretary of War John C. Breckenridge, telling him of Lincoln's assassination. He immediately shared the news with his cabinet, and all agreed that the death of the moderate Lincoln and the ascension to the Presidency of

Andrew Johnson was very bad news for the Confederacy. To his Secretary of the Navy Stephen Mallory he said, "I certainly have no special regard for Mr. Lincoln; but there are a great many men of whose end I would much rather have heard than his. I fear it will be disastrous to our people, and I regret it deeply."

Several units of Confederate cavalry arrived in Charlotte, giving Davis new hope. General Wade Hampton, one of his cavalry commanders, urged Davis to head west across the Mississippi, where together with scattered units now slowly coalescing in various areas of the south, they might form a western Confederacy and continue the fight. Davis was tempted, but decided that he could not yield one inch of Confederate territory while there was breath left in his body. He would continue a strategic retreat south, hopefully gathering more troops as they progressed, and then, at an opportune moment, turn and lead an attack against the pursuing enemy.

He penned a letter to Varina, from whom he had been separated for three stress- filled weeks.

Dear wife,

This is not the fate to which I invited you when the future was rose colored to us both; but I know you will bear it even better than myself and that of us two I alone will ever look back reproachfully on my past career…Farwell my dear; there may be better things in store for us than are now in view, but my love is all I have to offer and that has the value of a thing long possessed and sure not to be lost. Once more, and with God's favor for a short time only, farewell—

Your Husband

On April 26[th,] Davis was made aware that General Joseph Johnston had surrendered his army to Union General William Sherman. This was the last Confederate infantry force of any size left east of the Mississippi River. Also, unknown to Davis, John Wilkes Booth had, this morning, been trapped, shot, and killed in a tobacco barn on Garrett's farm near Port Royal, Virginia. While Lincoln was alive he did not direct any troops to pursue Jefferson Davis. Once Lincoln was killed the focus of Union Secretary of War Edwin Stanton and the troops he directed was on bringing in John Wilkes Booth, Lincoln's assassin. With that task completed Union forces were now being ordered to capture Jefferson Davis. Davis again wrote to his wife Varina and told her to continue her travel without him. There would be too much danger surrounding him now as he also headed further south toward Abbeville, South Carolina.

In Washington D.C., Edwin Stanton was directing an extensive search not only for Jefferson Davis, but for the wagons containing what remained of the Confederate treasury, thought to be as much as $5,000,000 in gold and silver. Orders went out to Union General George Stoneman's cavalry units to head toward Charlotte, North Carolina, and further south "to intercept Jeff…and follow him to the ends of the earth, if possible, and never give him up."

As Federal troops began to stream south in search of him Davis moved on horseback with cavalry troops and staff toward Abbeville, which his wife had left some days before. On April 28[th,] Davis' Treasury Secretary, John Reagan, saw him pause at a wayside cabin "…where a lady was standing in the door. He turned aside and requested a drink of water, which she brought. While he was drinking, a little baby hardly old enough to walk crawled down the steps. The lady asked whether this was not the President Davis; and on his answering in the affirmative, she pointed to the little boy and said, 'he is named for you.' Mr. Davis took a gold coin from his pocket and asked her to keep it for his namesake." This was the last coin he had. Jefferson Davis was now officially penniless, despite the money laden wagons that were following him south. They contained government funds, property of the Confederate States of America, which he refused to use for his personal needs. If his escape was to succeed, he would have to rely on the hospitality of his fellow southern citizens.

General James Wilson was leading the Union cavalry pursuit of

Jefferson Davis in the Carolinas. He deduced that Davis' wagon train could not head east to the Atlantic coast or west toward a crossing of the Mississippi River from anywhere in North Carolina. His Union troops were spread out in a broad arc north, east and west of the suspected location of Davis. The Confederate President would have to head further south into South Carolina before trying for the Atlantic Coast or Mississippi River. Davis might even head to some area of coastline in Florida in the hopes of locating a vessel to take him to Cuba. Wilson directed troops to Atlanta and Florida in hopes of trapping the Davis wagon train.

Jefferson Davis' reliance on the hospitality and continuing support of southern citizens was proving well-founded. Slave owners along Davis' path of travel were giving their slaves false information about where the Davis group was headed, believing that as soon as they could the slaves would contact pursuing Union troops and relay to them the information they had received. This strategy succeeded for some time in misdirecting and delaying Union cavalry pursuit.

The Davis party reached Abbeville, South Carolina on May 2nd, a few days after Varina Davis and her children, per her husband's insistence, had headed further south into Georgia. The caravan carrying Confederate gold and silver, guarded by a contingent of naval cadets led by Captain William Parker, had arrived ahead of the Davis party. Parker met with Davis that day and observed

I never saw the President appear to better advantage than during these last hours of the Confederacy. He showed no signs of despondency. His air was resolute; and he looked, as he is, a born leader of men.

Davis' confidence received a powerful blow when Parker told him that Secretary of the Navy Mallory had instructed him to disband his men. He was further disheartened when he learned that a great number of the cavalry travelling with him as escort could no longer be relied upon in a fight. They believed the struggle was over. Secretary Mallory and Captain Parker urged Davis to focus his flight on reaching the Trans-

Mississippi region. They told him Union cavalry was closing fast on them, and that he should leave immediately. Davis refused to consider it, saying he would never abandon his people.

After hearing yet another plea on May 2nd from Captain Parker for him to leave immediately, Davis convened his cabinet and told them to prepare to move by nightfall. He would not agree to head for the east coast of Florida, but would move further south. At 11pm that night Davis, his cabinet and staff, the treasury wagons and an escort of cavalry left for Washington Georgia.

At a crossing of the Savannah River, Davis learned that Federal cavalry had ridden into Washington, Georgia looking for him. He and his entourage decided to rest for some time, until they received word that the Union troops had left the area they were headed toward. While the horses were being fed and breakfast was being prepared, the troops escorting Davis and the treasury train made it known to their officers that they wanted to be paid. They knew that the wagons they were guarding were loaded with gold and silver, and they simply wanted their back pay. They would not go on without it. Secretary of War John C. Breckinridge, who had been travelling with the Davis group for some time, gave in to their demands. It was at the Savannah River crossing that Secretary of State Judah Benjamin decided to leave the group and head out on his own. He believed that Davis was travelling far too slowly to avoid capture. Treasury Secretary Reagan asked him where he was going. "To the farthest place from the United States," he replied, "if it takes me to China."

Despite the reports of Federal troops in the area, Davis and his party continued on to Washington, Georgia, arriving on May 3rd. They found that the stories of Union cavalry there had been false. They remained for a few days, resting and seeking information on the whereabouts of pursuing Union cavalry. General Breckenridge and Secretary Reagan tried to convince Davis to head to Florida, board a vessel there for Cuba, then head from Cuba to the mouth of the Rio Grande in Texas where they promised they would meet him with whatever troops they could rally. He refused, saying "I shall not leave Confederate soil while a Confederate regiment is on it."

Jefferson Davis was fast becoming the focal point of searches by both the military organizations and civilians, fueled by the proclamation Andrew Johnson had just signed offering a $100,000 reward for Davis's capture. This was the highest reward ever offered in American history. His pursuers were now not only driven by duty, but a huge sum of money. Davis would not learn of this reward for days.

Davis was still in Washington, Georgia, on May 4th, when a townswoman, Eliza Andrews recorded the town's response to the presence of their President.

Father and Cora went to call on the President, and…father says his manner was so calm and dignified that he could not help admiring the man. Crowds of people flocked to see him, and nearly all were melted to tears.…The village sent so many good things for the President to eat that an ogre couldn't have devoured them all, and he left many delicacies, besides giving away a number of his personal effects to people who had been kind to him."

As Davis left Washington, Georgia, on the night of May 4th, Eliza Andrews grew sad with the thought, "This, I suppose, is the end of the Confederacy." She was right. The very next day Union cavalry entered and occupied her town, hot on President Davis' trail. To move more quickly Davis had decided to proceed with his cabinet, and separate from the treasury train. He had with him his personal secretary, his staff officers and a ten man cavalry escort.

Near Dublin, Georgia, on May 6th, Jefferson Davis and his small party happened on a campsite in the woods. It contained his wife Varina, their children and servants. After nearly a month of exhausting and anxious flight apart from each other, the Davis family was reunited. They would spend the night sleeping fitfully, exchanging stories of their ordeals apart. Morning would bring continuation of their journey.

Travelling sometimes together, sometimes in two separate groups, Jefferson and Varina Davis crossed some 30 miles until they came to a halt for the night in a stand of pine trees just off the road near Irwinville, Georgia. They had about 30 soldiers with them, all that was left of a once several-thousand-strong escort. They posted no guard for the night. Davis did direct a group of soldiers to scout ahead while the group ate a simple meal and rested as best they could. The plan was for Davis to again separate from Varina and the children, taking only 3 or 4 of his staff, and make for the Trans- Mississippi region. For reasons not known, Davis spent the night with his wife at the campsite rather than leave the campsite immediately. By 4am they were surrounded by elements of the 4th Michigan cavalry, and were forced to surrender. The only casualties that occurred were when two converging Union forces mistakenly fired at each other, each thinking they were firing at resisting Confederates.

***

Jefferson Davis and his family were loaded into a single wagon and sent to the headquarters of General James Wilson, commander of the Union troops pursuing Davis, in Macon, Georgia. There Davis and his family were treated with respect. General Wilson agreed to let Davis' family travel with him. They assumed they were headed for Washington DC, and a trial for treason. Enroute north, the group stopped in Augusta, Georgia, where Confederate Vice President Alexander Stephens joined them. They boarded the steamer William P. Clyde for the next part of their journey, which, by May 20th, brought them to Hampton Roads, Virginia. Confederate Treasury Secretary John Reagan, who had for some time been travelling with Davis, rejoined him here after being captured by Union forces in his home town. Stephens and Reagan were immediately taken away, to what would become their places of incarceration. Two days later Jefferson Davis was also moved. Varina Davis said that she and her children were only given 5 minutes notice that he was to be separated from them. Davis was placed in a small boat and rowed across the harbor to nearby Fortress Monroe, where the new prison commandant, General Nelson A. Miles, awaited his famous prisoner. Federal officials feared that Davis might try to kill himself or escape, so they gave Miles the authority to place Davis in irons if he deemed it necessary. Davis entered the Fortress prison on May 22, 1865. Davis was placed in an interior room with two guards posted outside and one posted inside, with him at all times. Furnishings included an iron hospital bed, chair and table, a moveable stool, Bible and prayer book. The room remained lit at all times with a single lamp, and meals were prepared in the Fortress hospital. No knife or fork was allowed. The only eating utensil provided was a spoon. One day after his arrival there, Davis was placed in heavy iron manacles. Four soldiers held him down as a blacksmith hammered the irons closed around both of Davis' ankles. His guards took to calling him "Jeffy" or "the rebel chieftain."

When word leaked out to the public that Davis had been placed in irons, Secretary of War Edwin Stanton began receiving protest messages from citizens of note in both Northern and Southern states. After suffering only 5 days of such protest letters, Stanton ordered Miles to remove the irons, which he promptly did. After 2 months of good behavior from him, Miles removed the guard from Davis' cell and discontinued the practice of burning a candle there all night. The prisoner was allowed to exercise outdoors, but was allowed communication with no one but prison personnel.

By October, 1865, Davis was moved to a larger cell with more amenities. He now enjoyed a folding screen for privacy when using his chamber pot, a water basin and pitcher, a shelf for books and a wall peg on which to hang his clothes. Most appreciated was the small fireplace which would lessen the cold and damp of oncoming winter. He was also allowed to receive gifts. Varina sent him night shirts and an overcoat. Friends sent him cigars and brandy.

The government, not willing to open itself up to charges of ignoring the health of its prisoner, instructed a physician, Dr. George Cooper, to visit Davis regularly to monitor his health and provide any needed treatment and medications.

President Andrew Johnson sent Secretary of the Treasury Hugh McCulloch to check on the health of the former Confederate President. McCulloch reported back to Johnson that Davis' "gait was erect and elastic," and that "He had the bearing of a brave and high bred gentleman…." McCulloch further reported that while Davis recalled being treated very harshly at first, he now had no real complaint.

By late 1865 Davis was allowed to meet regularly with his former pastor from St. Paul's Church in Richmond, Virginia, Reverend Charles Minnigerode. The two men prayed together, and the pastor brought Davis much appreciated news of how his friends and family were faring in the chaos of the post-war south.

A powerful group of supporters began to organize efforts to defend Davis from whatever charges the federal government might bring against him. Former U.S. President Franklin Pierce and members of his cabinet, one of whom Davis had been, joined together in efforts to aid Charles O' Conor, a state's rights Democrat who had appointed himself Davis's unofficial legal counsel. O'Conor feared that Republicans, if unchecked, would run roughshod over the constitution in their attempt to punish the rebel leader any way they could.

O'Conor's fears were provoked by the military trial of Henry Wirz, the former commandant of Andersonville Prison in Georgia. Thousands of Union soldiers had died there while in captivity, starved and diseased, without decent water, food or shelter. Wirz was convicted as a war criminal and hung. Rumors were circulating that Wirz had been offered life in prison in exchange for his testimony implicating Davis as accessory to what happened at Andersonville. Wirz supposedly had denied any dealings with Davis.

O' Conor and Davis' supporters waited anxiously for the U.S. government to prosecute Jefferson Davis. Andrew Johnson's cabinet and the Chief Justice of the Supreme Court, Salmon P. Chase, could not agree on a course of legal action against Davis. The prosecutors of the conspirators in President Lincoln's assassination had, after much investigation, failed to discover any direct evidence of action taken by Jefferson Davis to aid in that crime. It was also unclear whether a trial of Davis should be held in a civil or military court.

While President Andrew Johnson tried to find a path through the swamp of conflicting legal advice he was receiving to successfully prosecute Jefferson Davis, the prisoner sat in his cell at Fortress Monroe, patiently awaiting his fate. Varina Davis was not so patient. She and her children were living under house arrest in a hotel in Savannah, Georgia. She feared for their safety. The summer heat was coming soon, and with it outbreaks of malaria and other diseases. Her 3 ½ year- old had had a black soldier level a gun at his head after the child had referred to him as "Uncle," a term wealthy southerners used to refer to older slaves. She decided to seek approval to send her children away. The government granted the request, and she sent her 3 oldest children, along with her sister Margret, to Montreal, Canada to live with Varina's mother, Margret Howell. She kept the baby, Varina Anne, called Piecake, with her in Savannah. She was able to live comfortably there with funds sent to her by former Confederates living in England.

Once her children were safe and funds for her living expenses had been secured, Varina petitioned the government to allow her to move to a friend's home in Augusta, Georgia with her baby. Her request was granted and she left Savannah for a healthier and friendlier climate. There she immediately set about to fight for her husband's freedom. She wanted to prove that he had no connection to Lincoln's assassination, get him better treatment at Fortress Monroe, and gain permission to visit him there. She sent letters to President Andrew Johnson, General Ulysses S. Grant and newspaper editor Horace Greeley. She failed in these efforts, but the government did finally give her permission to leave the country and rejoin her children in Canada, which she did in January, 1866.

Varina continued her efforts to help her husband. In April, 1866, she again sent a letter to President Andrew Johnson. "I hear that my husband is failing rapidly. Can I come to him? Can you refuse me? Answer." This alarmed the President and he immediately sought out Secretary of War Edwin Stanton for advice on how to answer Varina Davis' request. Stanton, who had, up to now, firmly refused to let Varina visit her husband, relented. Despite warnings from the prison commandant, Nelson Miles, as to how dangerous Varina Davis could be to the government, Stanton advised the President to grant Varina's request. On May 3, 1866, Varina and her baby daughter Piecake arrived at Fortress Monroe. There she had to sign a document swearing to in no way assist in helping her husband escape from his imprisonment. She signed the document and began regular visits with her husband as frequently as authorities would allow. Soon she decided to move into the Fortress to remain with him.

When he first came to Fortress Monroe Jefferson Davis was assigned a doctor, Lt. Col. John J. Craven, to care for him. Davis and Craven soon formed a close relationship, which eventually cost Craven his position. Nelson Miles, the prison commandant, disliked the closeness between the two men and requested that Craven be replaced. Craven, once removed, retired from the Army and began to write a book about his friend Jefferson Davis and his stay at Fortress Monroe. The book, published in June of 1866, was entitled "Prison Life of Jefferson Davis, Embracing Details and Incidents In His Captivity." The book whipped up a great surge of interest in and sympathy for Jefferson Davis. Upon reading of Davis' captivity, the Pope sent Davis an inscribed photograph and a crown of thorns. Three months after the publication of Craven's book, Nelson Miles was re-assigned to a different post in the Army. Miles would suffer no long standing harm to his reputation as a result of his tour of duty as Jefferson Davis' chief jailer. He eventually became the commander of all U.S. armies in the late 1800's.

By the spring of 1867, the federal government was still undecided about what to do with their famous prisoner. He was a sympathetic figure to many, a living reminder of treason and assassination to others. The government did not want to try him. They feared a legal debate of the principle of state's rights that might ensue, for while the force of arms had ended southern secession, no legal finding had ever been established to prevent it in the future. Some of the best defense attorneys in the nation were ready to represent Davis. If the government prosecuted and failed to convict Davis, the central reason for the war which took hundreds of thousands of lives might be disproved and the foundation principle of the Confederate States of America upheld. If Davis was found guilty, the South would have a powerful martyr, whose death could rekindle all the hatred and violence that the nation was only now seeing dissipate .

President Johnson concluded that the wisest strategy was to release Jefferson Davis and let the nation's healing continue. On May 13, 1867, Davis posted $100,000 bail and was released from federal custody. He travelled to Hollywood Cemetery in Richmond, Virginia, and placed flowers on the grave of his son Joseph E. Davis, who had been killed in a fall from the second story of their home during the war. He also placed flowers on the graves of Confederate soldiers. As he moved through the streets of his former capital, men removed their hats and women waved their handkerchiefs in silent salute to their former President.

Robert E. Lee sent Davis a letter in June saying "…that the rest of your days may be triumphantly happy is the sincere and earnest wish of your most obedient, faithful friend and servant."

***

Now Jefferson Davis was faced with the hardest questions he had to answer since the end of the war. How would he earn a living? Where would he and his family live? How would he be received by the people of the North, against whom he led a rebellion, and the people of the South, whom, he believed, he had failed?

For the next two years Davis pursued several business opportunities, but none brought long term stability and financial security. He gave his brother Joseph permission to sell his Mississippi plantation, Brierfield, for $300,000. The buyer was to pay over a nine-year period, thus insuring an income to Davis and his family. The new owners proved highly unreliable in their payments. Davis also got involved in some mining ventures that failed to produce expected returns. He continued to search for a more secure means of earning income, but he was limited in what he might do by what he had decided he would not do. He would not accept charity. Too many of his southern brethren were in much worse straits than the Davis family. He would do nothing that might bring shame or embarrassment on the South. He would never again seek elected office, and would never again set foot in Washington D.C.

Prospects for him seemed brighter in Europe, where many high-ranking former Confederates had fled and were now well-established in business and society. In August of 1867 Jefferson Davis and his family embarked for England and stepped off the boat in Liverpool. Judah Benjamin, his former Secretary of the Treasury, who had been with him during his flight from Union forces after the fall of Richmond, greeted him at the dock. Benjamin was already well known in England, and well-liked by Queen Victoria. Benjamin promised to help Davis with introductions to the wealthy and powerful friends he had made in the business community. Davis' hope at this time was to gather investors and form a business brokering US cotton sales to England.

His very first concern was to set his family up in comfortable quarters, which he accomplished within several months. Then he decided to travel, as a way of rebuilding his mental and physical strength, which were so severely taxed while in captivity. He visited many historical sites in England and held many business meetings as well. No investors were yet forthcoming, so Davis decided to extend his travel into Scotland, with a travelling companion, Dr. Charles McKay, whom he had met along the way. McKay had told him that the bracing climate and beautiful scenery there would help him regain his former vitality. The cool breezes of the Scottish Highlands and the great pleasure he derived from visiting Edinburg Castle, Holyrood and Saint Andrews did help him regain a more positive frame of mind than he had held in years. Steeled with this new optimism for the future, Davis returned to his family in England and announced that he was returning to the United States. He was sure now that he would find there the employment opportunity and regular income that had eluded him before, and when he did he would send for them.

On October 10, 1868, Jefferson Davis' ship docked in Baltimore, Maryland, where he was met by his brother, Joseph. After some days rest Davis left for New Orleans, where he visited relatives, then Vicksburg Mississippi, then Memphis, Tennessee. The Carolina Insurance Company had sent him word that they wanted to discuss with him a possible position in their growing organization.

Davis met with the company's owners and was offered a position as President of the Carolina Life Insurance Company, at a salary of $12,000 a year. The President of the United States made $25,000 yearly, so Davis was very pleased and accepted quickly. Back behind a desk, Davis showed his skill: as an administrator, straightening out the company books; as a leader, recruiting many former Confederate offices to serve as new sales agents; and as a strategist, in planning for the future growth of his company. An epidemic of plague broke out in the South, killing many policyholders and causing a catastrophic drain on the company's financial resources. Despite his urgent efforts to avoid failure, the company soon went out of business. Davis once again found himself out of work, devoid of income, and embarrassed.

Robert E. Lee, the great Confederate commander, died in 1870. Jefferson Davis was called upon to speak at his memorial service. It was on this occasion that Davis found his future calling. He would be the keeper of the flame, the symbol around which veterans and relatives of the fallen could rally and with whom they could remember. Davis began to write articles, maintain correspondence with former associates in his cabinet and armies, and serve as a living archive of facts, explaining the military, political and diplomatic efforts of the Confederate States of America.

***

During the 1870's, Davis watched America change from a rural Jeffersonian society to a major industrial power, from a nation fighting itself to one waging a war of expansion against Indian tribes on the western plains, from a nation that barely existed beyond the Mississippi River to one that stretched from the Atlantic to the Pacific. He watched as his South suffered through Reconstruction, and observed the struggles of newly freed slaves trying to find their place in society. As the North and South carefully, fitfully rewove the bonds of union, he remained a constant reminder of what America had been before the horrors of war reshaped it.

Jefferson Davis continued through this period to search for a secure financial future for his family, and a permanent home in which they could find peace. In 1877 he finally made progress. After he paid a visit to an old friend, Sarah Dorsey, at her plantation Beauvoir, near Biloxi, Mississippi, she informed him that he could stay there as long as he wished, and bring his family. The aging widow explained that she planned to deed him her properties when she passed.

At Beauvoir Davis finally had security and peace. There, on the shores of the Gulf of Mexico, calmed by gentle breezes, Davis began work on the story he had been anxious to tell. Robert E. Lee had died before he could pen his memoirs. History was cheated of the insights he might have provided about his decision to quit the Union out of loyalty to Virginia, the state he loved more. He might have shared his thoughts about when he won the great victories at Fredericksburg and Chancellorsville, or when he realized the appalling loss of life sustained by his army at Gettysburg. Davis would make sure that history was not denied the reasons behind his decisions during the Civil War.

For four years Jefferson Davis pored over his government's documents, reread old correspondence with his generals and cabinet and reviewed his own personal notes jotted down during the war. He organized his thoughts and committed them to paper. In 1881 he published a two-volume memoir entitled Rise and Fall of the Confederate Government. Unfortunately Davis chose to make his work a legalistic defense of state's rights and secession. There was little warmth or personal detail in it. It revealed his brilliant legal mind, but not his human genuine emotion. The book sold 20,000 copies, mostly in the South and became a regional rather than national best seller.

Davis now settled into a quiet life. Newspaper reporters visited to interview him for articles they were writing about the war. Guests and friends came to share a cool drink with him on the veranda overlooking the Gulf. Many left surprised at his lively conversation and general good humor, having expected to meet an old man bitter over his fate.

Davis began to consider that in two years he would reach eighty years of age. He had not expected to live as long as he had. His health had always been up and down, once near death when plague struck him and killed his first wife, constantly suffering from neuralgia, recurring bouts of malaria, constant eye pain and headaches. His plans now were to stay at Beauvoir with his wife and children. There were no plans to travel, speak, or even appear at public events. This serene existence lasted less than a year.

The citizens of Montgomery, Alabama, had gathered donations to build a monument to Alabama's fallen soldiers. They were ready to dedicate it, and sent a query to Jefferson Davis: would he consent to appear and speak at the ceremony? Davis was worried about his health, but felt he could not refuse the request. Montgomery, Alabama, was the first capital of the Confederate States of America. At the courthouse there, 25 years before, Davis had been sworn in as provisional President of the Confederacy. Davis boarded a train with his daughter Winnie and began a journey to Montgomery that would, by its end, bring a drastic change to what he expected would be his last years.

***

On April 28, 1886, Jefferson Davis and his daughter arrived in Montgomery, Alabama. There to greet him was a crowd of thousands. They had just heard from John B. Gordon, one of the Confederacy's most successful generals. He had given a passionate speech of introduction to the crowd about their former leader.

Let us, my countrymen, in the few remaining years which are left to our great captain, seek to smooth and soften with flowers of affection the thorny path he has been made to tread for our sake.

As his train pulled in, the crowd roared and cannon fired. Unfortunately heavy rains caused the planned public reception at the station to be cancelled. Instead Davis traveled by carriage to the Exchange Hotel. As he passed through the streets on his short ride he saw the city lit with electric illuminations and bonfires in his honor. As he entered the hotel he stopped and briefly addressed the large crowd gathered there, thanking them for their kindness. Then he entered the very same hotel he had stayed in the night before he was sworn in as the first President of the Confederacy twenty-five years before.

That night, at the state capitol, the mayor of Montgomery introduced Davis by calling him "...that most illustrious type of southern manhood and statesmanship, our honored ex-President...." The roars of the crowd drowned out Davis' first few words, but he continued on, trying to calm the crowd. "Brethren," he would start, and the roars would begin again and roll over him. People stomped their feet, cried, laughed, waved their handkerchiefs. "Brethren," he would start again. Finally the crowd seemed to quiet down.

He spoke of their tribute as one surely not meant for him, but for a greater idea for which their sons had died. Then he did what he had failed to do in his memoirs, he spoke from his heart.

Well do I remember seeing your gentle boys, so small, to use a farmers phrase, they might have been called seed corn, moving on with eager step and fearless brow to the carnival of death; and I have also looked upon them when their knapsacks and muskets seemed heavier than the boys, and my eyes, partaking of a mother's weakness, filled with tears. Those days have passed. Many of them have found nameless graves....But they are not dead-they live in memory and their spirits stand out a grand reserve of that column which is marching on with unfaltering steps towards the goal of constitutional liberty.

When Davis took his seat, all was quiet for a few heartbeats. Then, as a reporter from the Atlanta Constitution, who was on the scene recorded

...such a cheer followed the speaker that cannot be described. It was an outburst of nature. It was long continued. Then a lone Confederate veteran shouted 'Hurrah for Jeff Davis!' as loud as the old rebel could yell and within moments, thousands of voices repeated the salute.

Back at the hotel many well-wishers came to see and, if possible, touch him. That evening Davis decided to accept an invitation he had recently received to speak at the dedication of a statue of a civic leader in Atlanta, Georgia. His experience in Montgomery had scattered his earlier thoughts of approaching death and left him with an eagerness to hold high the banner of what was now being called "The Lost Cause."

At every refueling stop between Montgomery and Atlanta, crowds turned out to greet him, cheering from the first moment they saw his train until he was too far away to hear. When he arrived in Atlanta, more than 50,000 people were on hand to see him. Along his mile-long ride from the station to his room for the night, 8,000 children lined the road and 2,000 Confederate veterans marched behind him. At the statue dedication he was introduced with these words:

This outcast...is the uncrowned king of our people...the resurrection of these

memories that for twenty years have been buried in our hearts have given us the best Easter we have seen since Christ was risen from the dead.

From Atlanta he travelled to Savannah, Georgia, in response to yet another invitation to speak. The audience response to his speech here was just as it had been at previous ones, an explosive release of pride for the Southern way of life that had been suppressed for two decades. Davis was shocked by the reception he had received at every stop on this trip, but also pleased and thoroughly exhausted. Before he had begun the trip he feared how the people he believed he had failed would respond to him. Now he knew that he was remembered, revered and even loved.

In 1887 Davis was invited to attend and speak at the Georgia State Fair in Macon, where there was to be a reunion of Confederate soldiers. Varina Davis, worried that the strain of the trip could kill her 79-year-old husband, came with him. Local papers ran stories calling for all citizens that could to attend the Fair at Macon, as it could be Davis' last appearance in public. Thousands of people did come to Macon, and marched to the home where he was staying, calling on him to appear. He obliged them by stepping out onto the porch. There he observed someone holding a Confederate battle flag up to him. He took hold of it and spoke to the crowd

I am like that old flag, riven and torn by storms and trials. I love it as a memento; I love it for what you and your fathers did. God bless you! I am glad to be able to see you again.

Then he began to wave the flag back and forth, causing the crowd, many of them veterans, to cheer wildly.

In 1888, defying his age and infirmity, he agreed to appear in public yet again. He was to address a group of young people in a town very near Beauvoir. Since it was a very short trip, and he particularly loved meeting with young people, he felt it was worth the risk. His speech there was short, but revealing

The faces I see before me are those of young men; had I not known this I would not have appeared before you. Men in whose hands the destinies of our Southland lie, for love of her I break my silence, to speak to you a few words of respectful admonition. The past is dead; let it burn its dead, its hopes and its aspirations; before you lies the future - a future full of golden promise; a future of expanding national glory, before which all the world shall stand amazed. Let me beseech you to lay aside all rancor, all bitter sectional feelings, and to make your places in the ranks of those who will bring about a consummation devoutly to be wished — a reunited country.

The man who not so long before was waving a Confederate battle flag and driving a crowd into a frenzy of southern pride, now spoke of leaving the past behind and re-uniting the country. Perhaps feeling the approaching end of his life, Jefferson Davis was ready again to embrace America as one nation.

On June 3, 1888, Jefferson Davis reached the goal he had set for himself years before, his 80th birthday. He could reflect on a very active and event-filled life, and one that had travelled a full circle. He had served Mississippi as a leader of its militia in the Mexican-American War and as its Senator in the U.S. Congress, he had served his country as Secretary of War in the administration of President Franklin Pierce and then led a failed rebellion against his country as the President of a Southern nation. Now he was ending his life urging young southerners to pledge their future to the United States of America, just as he had in his youth.

In November of 1889 Davis left the comforts of his gulf side home at Beauvoir to inspect the plantation he still owned at Brierfield in Mississippi. Soon after he began the journey he fell ill with Malaria, which had periodically recurred since his time served in the Mexican-American War. His wife Varina rushed to his side to care for him. His health fluctuated for weeks, finally settling into a decline. As Varina sat at his bedside spooning medicine into his mouth, he waved it away saying "I pray I cannot take it." He fell asleep then, holding Varina's hand. Around midnight she felt his hand slip from hers. Jefferson Davis was dead.

Varina decided that his resting place would be in Richmond, Virginia, at Hollywood Cemetery. Committees began to form almost immediately to solicit funds for a fitting memorial to Davis. In 1907 work on the components of the monument was completed. On June 3rd, Davis's 93rd birthday, it was dedicated.

Some 200,000 people lined the parade route in Richmond that day, more than had lined Pennsylvania Avenue for Lincoln's funeral procession. Davis' last living daughter, Margaret Davis Hayes, unveiled the eight-foot-tall bronze statue of her father. Behind it stood a 65-foot-tall column whose base held three plaques: one inscribed with the Latin words "Deo Vindici," (the states' war time motto, Under God, our Vindication), one inscribed "Jure Civitatum" (for the rights of states) and one inscribed "Pro Atris Et Focis" (for hearth and home). A bronze tablet was affixed to the base of an eight-foot-tall bronze figure of Davis. It bore the following words

Jefferson Davis

President of the Confederate States of America

1861-1865

***

Jefferson Davis began his public life as a man sworn to uphold the Union. He fought the idea of disunion, then accepted leadership of a Confederacy of seceded states, feeling it was his duty to his native South. For four years he presided over a rebellion that caused the greatest bloodletting in the nation's history, and became its living symbol after defeat. Then, with his own death approaching, he sought to heal the wounds caused by that rebellion.

Was he a defender of slavery or a man of principle, convinced of correctness of state's rights? He was both. And as a result, judgement of the man has as much to do with the person making the judgement as it has with to do with the man himself.

THE POWER COUPLE

Salmon P. Chase and Kate Chase Sprague

There are some historical figures whose lives are so inextricably entwined that they must be examined together or the real nature of their separate characters can never be understood.

***

They were one of the most famous couples in a city full of famous people. As the two strolled down the avenue, many passersby stopped and stared, most men removing their hats to him as a sign of respect, most women admiringly, if not jealously, nodding their acknowledgement of her. Salmon P. Chase, 66 year old Chief Justice of the U.S. Supreme Court and his daughter, Kate Chase Sprague, widely considered one of the most fashionable and beautiful women in Washington D.C., had decided to walk the 20 minutes from the home they shared on Sixth and E Street to the Capitol grounds. This spring day in March, 1868, would be of historic importance to them and the country. They wanted this time to discuss all the political ramifications of what was to come.

Salmon Chase and his daughter Kate were always close. He had lost three wives and two other children to diseases over the course of his life, and Kate was all the more precious to him as a result of those tragedies. His experiences had taught him the fleeting nature of life, and he frequently reminded his headstrong daughter that she must always strive for moral and intellectual perfection in the short time she had on this earth. Kate appreciated his concern for her and constantly strove to please him. That proved to be a frustrating task, for Salmon Chase pointed out her faults and imperfections as a means of lecturing her on improvement. Rarely did he acknowledge her many achievements. His criticism was gentle, but direct and frequent. She loved him despite his lectures and always hoped for signs of his approval.

Once they reached the Capitol, Salmon Chase disappeared into the cloak room of the U.S. House of Representatives to don his judicial robes. Kate made her way to the viewing gallery above the floor of the House to take her seat. Filling the chairs around her were the ladies of Washington society, foreign diplomats, and newspaper reporters, all come to see the extraordinary event about to unfold. Members of the U.S. House of Representatives had passed 18 articles of impeachment against President Andrew Johnson. Now the Senate as a body would listen to the charges, hear witnesses, view evidence and render a verdict to sustain the President in office or remove him. This had never been attempted in the 80 year history of the republic. Presiding over this political spectacle, as spelled out by the Constitution, would be the Chief Justice of the United States, Salmon Chase.

Kate looked down onto the floor of the House from her seat in the crowded gallery as the members of the Senate entered the chamber. Last onto the floor was her father. Standing six feet two inches tall, posture stiff, with a high Roman forehead, thinning hair, piercing eyes and an ever serious visage, Chase looked the very personification of dignity. His contemporaries knew him to be aloof, displaying little humor or empathy. He had once been described as "all light and no heat." He took his chair and signaled to the House prosecutors for the proceedings to begin.

***

Salmon Chase was born on January 13, 1808 in Cornish, New Hampshire, the third youngest of the 10 children of Ithamar and Janet Chase. The family worked a farm, but Salmon never seemed to embrace the manual labor required to sustain it. When his father died he was taken in by his uncle, Philander Chase, an Episcopalian Bishop from Worthington, a town near Cincinnati, Ohio. The uncle was a stern taskmaster, who tended to view the world in black and white. He demanded perfection of young Salmon and if not satisfied by the boy's efforts, beat him or locked him up, quoting scriptures as justification for his actions. Despite this harsh treatment, Salmon looked up to his uncle as a good man worthy of emulation.

In 1829 Salmon Chase completed his legal studies and was admitted to the bar. He left the east coast, to return to Ohio, explaining to Charles Cleveland, a Dartmouth College friend, that he would rather be a big fish in Cincinnati than a small one in the bigger pool of Baltimore. To another he confided, "I have always thought that Providence intended me as the instrument of effecting something more than falls to the lot of all men to achieve."

After graduating from the boys school his uncle ran, Salmon enrolled at Cincinnati College, where he received a classical education in Latin, Greek and Euclidean geometry. In 1823 Philander Chase left America and headed to England to raise funds for the establishment of an Episcopal seminary in Ohio, which eventually became Kenyon College. Salmon Chase, aged 15 years, then left Ohio to teach school in Keene, New Hampshire. He was fired from that job after parents of the students complained that he administered excessive corporal punishment. At age 16 years, Chase entered Dartmouth College, graduating Phi Beta Kappa. He moved to Washington D. C. in 1829 at age 21. In order to pay for his legal studies, he again began to teach. His first students included the son of Senator Henry Clay and the sons of several of President John Quincy Adams' cabinet members. His interest in politics began to grow during these years. His opposition to the institution of slavery grew as he observed the squalid misery of the slaves held in pens scattered all around the Capitol, awaiting their time on the selling block. He considered at this time that the best solution to the problem was to colonize African Americans somewhere on the Pacific coast or back in their native Africa. He told his friend, Henry Sparhawk, that one day he expected to "see this Union dissolved and I do not know that New England has much reason to deprecate such an event."

Ten years after his move back to Ohio, Salmon Chase's life had changed dramatically. He had gained a reputation as a lawyer willing to represent runaway slaves and was involved in so many such cases that he was known as the "Attorney General for Runaway Negroes." He garnered national fame for arguing against the U.S. fugitive slave law that required a citizen to assist in the return of any Negro shown to be a runaway slave to his master when asked to do so. Chase thought it unconstitutional, as it was "contrary to natural law."

Chase's domestic life in the 1840's could be compared to the biblical trials of Job. He married twice, losing his first wife in 1835 to complications following childbirth, then losing his first daughter to scarlet fever five years later. In 1839 he married again, and his second wife bore him another daughter in 1840, whom they named Catherine Jane, but called Kate. By 1842 the family grew again with the birth of their third daughter, Lizzie, named after her mother. Lizzie died within three months of her birth.

***

While his domestic life was being torn by constant losses, Salmon Chase's career in public service was blossoming. In1840 he was elected to the Cincinnati City Council as a member of the Whig Party. He served there until he was defeated due to his support for temperance. Chase then helped form the anti-slavery Liberty Party.

***

Until she was five years old, Kate Chase enjoyed a stable home life. Her father was busy with local politics, but home mostl evenings. Her mother, Lizzie, tended to her needs as she grew into a precocious child. In 1845 Kate's pleasant, secure life was shattered when her 23 year old mother Lizzie died. Her father continued to care for her alone, reading to her each evening from the Bible. He knew that she could not at her tender age understand the words, but the rhythmic sounds of his reading seemed to soothe her. In 1846 the widower married his third wife, Sara "Belle" Ludlow, from one of the founding families of Cincinnati. Within a year Kate had a new little sister, Janet Ralston Chase, known to the family as Nettie.

***

In 1849 Salmon Chase's political career was pulling him away from his family more and more. He was elected to the U.S. Senate under unusual circumstances, the damage from which he would suffer for decades. The Whigs and Democrats in the Ohio state legislature were warring for control. Each had insufficient strength to muster a majority on any vote. Chase's small Liberty Party held sufficient votes to tip the balance. Chase struck a deal with the Democrats. He guaranteed them enough Liberty Party votes in the legislature to control it in return for them voting him into the U.S. Senate. He convinced himself that this was a principled move because he had extracted from the Democrats a pledge to repeal Ohio's "black laws," which denied free African Americans the right to vote, hold office or testify against whites in court. Many members of the Whig and Liberty Party saw the move as a selfish one, moving Chase up onto the national stage at their expense. As Chase prepared for his move to Washington D.C. to take his seat in the Senate, Belle and Nettie were saying goodbye to Kate, who had been enrolled at Miss Haines School For Girls at 10 Gramercy Park, New York. The school was considered one of the nation's finest institutions for the education of young ladies.

***

Nine-year-old Kate Chase took up residence at the Haines School as one of the few actual boarders there. Most of the girls came from local New York families, and returned home each night. Kate was also one of the youngest students, and while her father was now a U.S. Senator, she was clearly not of the same social rank as many of her classmates, whose parents were descended from the oldest Dutch founding families of New York. For her to make her mark here she would have to excel.

The girls awoke at 5:30am each morning , studied for an hour, went to prayers, enjoyed a simple breakfast, took a brisk walk, then headed to class for lessons. Bedtime was at 8pm sharp. Instruction included training in the table manners of proper society along with a curriculum of subjects such as French, Latin, geography, history, math, grammar, spelling, penmanship and composition. There were also piano instruction, cotillion dancing and lessons in elocution.
While in cosmopolitan New York, surrounded by children of affluent parents, young Kate grew to appreciate and desire the finer things of fashion and entertainment. She once ran up bills for clothes that totaled almost $8,000 in 2015 money. Unable to conceive of how a young girl Kate's age could run up such an expense her exasperated father asked her to confirm this huge amount. She coolly replied, "I have examined the bill and find everything correct."

During these years Kate received constant lectures by letter from her father. "You have said a good deal in your letters in excuse of your delays and bad writing. I do not like excuses," he wrote. Later she received this remonstrance. "You do not always speak the exact truth. This is a very-very bad habit. If you do not overcome it, it will grow upon you and will ruin you forever." Even though he continually corrected her and withheld praise, he recognized much of himself in her. "You, I think, are like me. I wish you could put a little more life into your letters, but I cannot blame you much seeing there is so little in mine."

***

Salmon Chase's term in the U.S. Senate coincided with growing national debate over the issue of slavery. In 1850, Senator Henry Clay fashioned a bill (known later as the Compromise of 1850) designed to cool the national fever and bridge the divide between northern and southern interests. It called for admission of one new territory as a free state, one as a slave state, and for the strengthening of the existing fugitive slave laws. Chase spoke against the Compromise, as he was opposed to any enforcement of fugitive slave laws. The bill passed into law, calming both sides enough to avert open conflict. In 1854 Democratic Senator Stephen A. Douglas, seeking to fashion his own solution to the continuing national crisis over slavery, proposed the Kansas-Nebraska Act, in which the two territories would be admitted as states with their citizens free to choose between slave and free status for Negroes. By applying the principle of popular sovereignty Douglas hoped to curry favor with the south while not alienating northern and western factions. This, he hoped, would gain him support in the upcoming Presidential contest of 1856. Chase argued against the bill in a pamphlet that was widely read across the nation. He gained a considerable following with it
among anti-slavery factions, who later adopted it as part of the platform of the newly formed Republican Party.

In June, 1852, yet another family tragedy occurred, with Chase's wife Belle passing away from tuberculosis. He would never again marry.

***

Two years after her mother Belle passed, Kate left Miss Haines School and its rigidly dictated lifestyle for what she hoped would be a freer atmosphere at Aston Ridge School outside Philadelphia, Pennsylvania. Soon after arriving there, Kate began to complain to her father about the headmistress, Maria Eastman, who had criticized Kate for some unacceptable conduct. Her father supported Miss Eastman, telling Kate that "sometimes you may deserve it." Now age fourteen, Kate was beginning to catch the eye of young men. One asked her in a note if she might consider sitting next to him at a gathering that Sunday evening. Her response is not known. Another wrote her a poem comparing her to the goddess Venus. Her father was aware that her intelligence and manners were improving, but with his well understood fatalism, he lectured her on guarding her physical health. "Be as much in the air as possible," he wrote, "avoid stooping. Take such exercise as will expand the chest and give freest motion to the lungs."

***

Salmon Chase chose not to run for re-election to the Senate. Instead he left the Liberty Party and ran for Governor of Ohio as a member of that state's newly-founded Republican Party. He told a friend that he feared the new party might not last long, but despite his misgivings he was elected the first Republican Governor of Ohio by a narrow margin.

***

Kate returned to Ohio after her father's election and took up residence with him for the first time in seven years. A widower, Chase looked to Kate to be his official hostess, maintain his home and assist with his official correspondence. She thrived in these roles, eagerly displaying the fruits of her excellent education by entering into conversations with him and his guests as they discussed politics, state and national affairs. She also played the piano for his guests, and directed spirited games of charades. Other evenings when they were alone together she played backgammon with her father to distract him from his daily burdens.

Kate was now beginning to show a tendency to stand up for herself and ignore public opinion. Some saw her attitude as haughtiness. To any who crossed her she replied with words sharp enough to wound like an arrow. "She was not as diplomatic in her youth as she later became," a friend later recalled. She began to be seen in public with a 28-year-old married man, riding around Columbus with him in his carriage. After hearing from her father how she had disappointed him with her "false conduct," Kate ended the relationship. She could easily tolerate negative public opinion, but not from her father.

***

Salmon Chase's time as Governor of Ohio could have been frustrating if he were a lesser driven man. The state constitution gave the governor little actual power, so he diligently used his office to champion a progressive agenda that mirrored the Republican national platform. He spoke out in favor of education reform, prison improvements, and rights for the mentally disabled and for women. Above all, he spoke out against slavery. This made him the foremost anti-slavery man in the west. As such he felt he should be seriously considered for his party's nomination as the first Republican candidate for President. The party saw him as too stridently anti-slavery and therefore unelectable. They chose instead a political neophyte, the handsome former explorer of the western plains, John C. Fremont, whose views on slavery were more opaque than Governor Chase. While contemplating his loss, Chase and Kate must have observed that Fremont's wife, Jesse Benton Fremont was a major player in his campaign for the nomination. An intelligent, attractive woman could be an invaluable asset to a man's quest for the ultimate seat of political power. Salmon Chase spent little time brooding over his loss. In 1857 he was re-elected Governor of Ohio.

***

In January, 1857, Kate appeared with her father and her little sister Nettie at the dedication of Ohio's new Governor's mansion in Columbus, Ohio. Chase gave Kate the job of furnishing and decorating their new home. "I fear that I am trusting a good deal to the judgement of a girl of 17, " he told her, "but I am confident I may safely trust yours." He then proceeded, despite the trust he claimed he had in her judgement, to micromanage her efforts, detailing how much to spend, what to buy, and urging her to keep detailed accounts of her actions so that he could review them. Along with these tasks, Kate was also acting as mother to her 10-year-old sister,, Nettie. Their relationship was made difficult by the fact that from age 2 to age 9 Nettie had lived separate from Kate, who was away at boarding schools.

It pleased Kate very much at this time that she was more and more involved in discussions with her father about his political plans. Carl Schurz, the Republican activist and former German revolutionary, met Kate at this time while visiting her father. In later years, he recorded his impressions.

Soon she came, saluted me very kindly, and then let herself down upon her chair with the graceful lightness of a bird… She was then about eighteen years old, tall and slender and exceedingly well formed. Her features were not at all regularly beautiful according to the classical rule. Her little nose, somewhat audaciously tipped up, would perhaps not have passed muster with a severe critic, but it fitted pleasingly into her face with its large, languid but at the same time vivacious hazel eyes, shaded by long dark lashes, and arched over by proud eyebrows…She had something imperial the pose of her head, and all her movements possessed an exquisite natural charm…After the usual polite commonplaces, the conversation at the breakfast table, in which Miss Kate took a lively and remarkably intelligent part, soon turned upon politics, and that conversation was continued during a large part of the forenoon in the Governor's library.

Schurz was charmed by her, and for the rest of their lives they would remain friends. She was becoming a powerful ally in her father's climb up the political ladder.

***

Salmon Chase was already looking ahead to the next Presidential contest, in 1860. In 1857 he sent a request to a friend, Charles Cleveland, asking him to sound out public opinion in the east about his support for the Republican nomination. He said it was not because he sought it, but because so many others had been urging him to be available. He also asked Cleveland to make sure that he (Chase) was not identified as the one asking for the information.

In 1859 the nation was shocked by the actions of an anti-slavery zealot, John Brown. He and a small handful of followers had attempted to seize the weapons stored in a federal arsenal at Harpers Ferry, Virginia. Brown's plan was to take the weapons south and distribute them amongst thousands of slaves who would escape their plantations and rally to him. He would then lead this growing army deep into the South, freeing all slaves who had the courage and opportunity to join him, forcing the nation to confront head on the issue of slavery. Slaves never learned of his presence at Harpers Ferry, and the US government quickly dispatched troops to surround and capture Brown and his cohorts. After the incident and John Brown's trial, it was reported that Salmon P. Chase, along with several wealthy east coast anti-slavery men, had contributed money to Brown's failed campaign. Chase deftly handled the potential crisis by publicly condemning Brown's violent tactics, but not his end game of changing the nation's posture toward slavery.

With the Republican convention opening soon in Chicago, Illinois, Kate convinced her father to meet with members of east coast congressional delegations, many of whom would be delegates to the upcoming convention. The Chases adopted a realistic strategy. Both knew he was not the delegates' first choice for the nomination, as that position was held by Senator William Seward of New York. They planned to ask the delegates to make Chase their second choice if and when Seward faltered. Kate and her father attended several gatherings in Washington DC, at which Chase, as usual, appeared to most aloof and distant. Kate, on the other hand, charmed most, and probably did more good for their cause than her father.

Salmon Chase knew himself to be a polished writer of cogent and compelling legal arguments, and a master at shaping statements of party principle. He also knew that as a public speaker he was mediocre at best. That realization led him to refuse an invitation by influential Republicans to speak at New York's prestigious Cooper Union Institute in the winter of 1859. Abraham Lincoln, a man Chase had campaigned for when Lincoln ran against Democrat Stephen A. Douglas for the US Senate in 1858, accepted the invitation that Chase had refused. The speech Lincoln gave there boosted his following in the east, invigorated his national campaign, and moved him from a longshot to a contender for the Republican nomination.

When the Republican convention was gaveled to order in the newly built Wigwam building in Chicago, Illinois, in May, 1860, it was apparent to Chase and his daughter that they would not gain the nomination on any early ballot. Senator William Seward of New York was the odds on favorite going into the conclave. He led on the first three ballots, with Chase starting in fourth place and slowly slipping lower with each ballot. Unknown to Chase, Lincoln's managers had devised the same strategy that Chase had. They asked delegates to make Lincoln their second choice, after their favorite failed to build enough support to win. After the third ballot, delegates began switching from their favorite to Lincoln, not Chase. Lincoln finally took the lead after the fourth ballot, with a delegate count just short of what he needed to win. The votes that finally put Lincoln over the top, much to Chase's chagrin, came from his own Ohio delegation. It was a bitter, if not shocking, defeat. Chase would always blame his Ohio delegation and its leader Ben Wade, for his loss. He felt they should have held firm voting for him until both Lincoln's and Seward's support faded.

***

Kate saw the truth behind her father's failure to gain the nomination. She planned to use the lessons learned in Chicago to manage her father to the Presidency in 1864. Lincoln's campaign was much better organized and staffed. He took moderate, not extreme positions, even on slavery. Lincoln and his team worked ceaselessly and relentlessly to win. They were fully committed to the task. Kate would not let her father down. She would counsel him to make better political moves so that he would be ready when the time was right.

***

Salmon Chase put aside his bitterness and started on two campaigns after the loss at the convention. He stood again for election to the Senate from Ohio and won, and he simultaneously campaigned around the north on Lincoln's behalf in the Presidential election. The Democratic Party at its convention split apart over how to address the slavery issue, and now two Democrats were running against Lincoln. John C. Breckenridge, the incumbent Vice President under James Buchanan, was running as the candidate of Southern Democrats, advocating state's rights and continued tolerance of slavery. Senator Stephen Douglas of Illinois was also running, as the candidate of the Northern Democrats, advocating popular sovereignty as the solution to the slavery issue. A fourth party sprung up as well, the Constitutional Union Party, fielding as its candidate John Bell of Tennessee. His party tried to take a moderate approach to the issues of the day by calling simply for adherence to the Constitution and maintenance of the Union.

The breakup of the usually dominant Democratic Party allowed Lincoln to amass enough electoral votes from the Northeastern and Midwestern states to achieve election, even though his name did not appear on the ballot in several southern states. The Republican won with only 39% of the vote, but a majority in the Electoral College. Between the end of the election and his inauguration in March, 1861, Lincoln began the task of building a cabinet.

The President-elect was not by nature or experience, an administrator. He had never run anything other than a simple village grocery and a two-man law firm. He also was aware that he was not yet the dominant political force within his own party. With this in mind, he began to build a cabinet that historian Doris Kearns Goodwin would later call "The Team of Rivals." Lincoln would offer cabinet positions to the strongest men within his party. These bright, ambitious men could deal with the day to day complexity of running the government, leaving Lincoln to focus on how to avoid disunion and civil war. If they did their jobs well, the country would be better off and he would garner credit for having chosen them. If they failed, their reputations would suffer more than his, they would cease to be threats, and he could replace them. He was confident that he could manage their ambitions better with them inside his administration than outside it.

With the probability of war increasing with each passing day, the resiliency of the nation's economy would be of vital importance. Soon the country's military spending would exceed $1.5 million a day. President Lincoln knew his attention would be needed on a host of other problems, so he offered Salmon Chase the office of Secretary of the Treasury. Though Chase had little experience with high finance, Lincoln had none at all. Chase did not accept immediately. Lincoln pressed him saying "You understand these things; I do not." Chase had hoped to be offered the senior position in the cabinet, that of Secretary of State, but Lincoln had given that position to his chief rival for the nomination at Chicago, William Seward of New York. Chase, reasoning that he could have more influence over Lincoln's policies from within the cabinet than out, accepted the Treasury position.

***

Kate Chase was in full agreement with her father's decision. He would be a member of the President's cabinet at a crucial time in the nation's history. She would have four years to help him burnish his already shining reputation, and then he would replace the man who she believed to be inferior to her father in every way, Abraham Lincoln. And while she helped her father attain the White House, she would begin her own campaign to become the acknowledged mistress of fashion and culture in Washington society. For her to achieve her goal she would have to steal the spotlight from the woman traditionally ceded that honor, the wife of the President.

Mary Todd Lincoln came to Washington D.C. feeling she had achieved all that she had ever hoped for as a young girl coming of age in Springfield, Illinois. There she was courted by all the most eligible bachelors in the state capital, including Stephen Douglas, then a rising star in the Democratic Party. She had told her family as a little girl that the man she married would one day become President, so they all were shocked when she chose as her mate an uncultured, self- educated local lawyer, Abraham Lincoln. They were a very odd couple: he with a penchant for telling off color jokes accented with his distinctly Kentucky drawl; she conversing fluently in French, garbed in the latest fashions. He stood 6 feet four; she stood barely 5 feet three inches. He called them "the long and short of it." He frequently answered knocks at their door himself in his stocking feet, while she yelled at him that they had a servant to do that. Now her husband was indeed President and she planned on reigning over society in Washington D.C., just as she had dreamed as a little girl.

Before the Lincolns even reached Washington, gossipers there complained that a country bumpkin and his washer woman wife were coming from the uncouth west to camp out in the White House. Lincoln's campaign had portrayed him as the rail splitter, and too many people took that description literally. Many of the most prominent women in Washington were aghast that such a pair would actually attempt to act as their peers, or even more intolerable, their betters.

In March, 1861 the Lincolns hosted their first state dinner at the White House. All of official Washington was there to see the new first couple, and pass judgement. Mary Lincoln was wearing a Paris- designed gown reflecting the height of current fashion, though some observers commented that it was far too low-cut for a woman of her years. The event went smoothly, with the Lincolns leaving a much better impression than any of the attendees had expected. Kate Chase was there, on the arm of her father, working the room with confidence, gathering in a circle of admirers that drew the envious attention of Mrs. Lincoln. A widely circulated story about that evening relates that Mrs. Lincoln spoke to the Chases as they were leaving, saying to Kate, "I shall be glad to see you at any time, Miss Chase," to which Kate replied "Mrs. Lincoln, I shall be glad for you to call on me at any time." From that night to the end of President Lincoln's life, the two women competed, each attempting to attract the better guests, host the more lavish party or gain the better reviews of their gowns and entertainments. They would never be friends.

***

As Southern states began one by one to secede from the Union, both sides began to build up their armies. For this action, much greater revenues were needed than had ever been raised before. The actions of the Treasury Secretary became much more crucial to the government's survival than they would have been in times of peace. To answer this growing need for money Salmon Chase conceived the idea of a national banking system, and then successfully lobbied Congress to pass the proposal into law. This gave structure and stability to the nation's financial operations, and created enough confidence in the minds of investors for them to buy up the nation's debt in the form of bonds. He also instituted the first paper currency, called "greenbacks." These greenbacks were made legally binding tender for payment of debts, backed only by government credit instead of gold coin. When the artwork for the first of these bills was created, Chase seized an opportunity to further his political career by instructing the artist to place his image on the denomination of currency that would be most widely distributed, the $1 bill. As war costs continued to rise and the prompt collection of taxes became imperative, Chase created the Bureau of Internal Revenue to facilitate the effort.

Despite the heavy Treasury Department workload Chase dealt with during the war, he always found time to advance his political fortunes. He sometimes used his treasury agents around the country to perform political tasks for him, contrary to accepted government practice. James A. Garfield, a frequent guest at the Chase home, heard many criticisms of President Lincoln coming from the Treasury Secretary. He heard that Lincoln was well meaning but too
weak, that he was too slow in granting emancipation to slaves, too hesitant in waging war, and was a failure at picking successful generals. And all the while, Chase would complain, the President failed to fully recognize the miraculous feat Chase had achieved in financing the war

effort. In many of his letters to friends another refrain was repeated, that there was no real cabinet advising the President. Instead, there was a group of managers who met occasionally and were expected to run their respective departments "as if they were heads of factories supplying shoes or cloth."

By December, 1863, powerful friends of the Treasury Secretary formed a Chase for President Committee. The war was dragging on far longer than anyone had expected, and there was no end in sight. Casualty lists posted in public squares around the nation caused heartache in nearly every household. People were tired of death and deprivation, and were losing faith in the President's ability to deal with the situation. Chase saw the upcoming election of 1864 as his chance to replace the overmatched Illinois lawyer in the White House. The Chase for President Committee produced a pamphlet highly critical of the President, intended to be sent secretly to supporters favorable to the Treasury Secretary. Somehow the pamphlet, known thereafter as "the Pomeroy Circular," was leaked to the press. The public perceived it as a traitorous backstab of the President by a member of his own team, and Chase quickly attempted to minimize any damage it might do by disclaiming any responsibility for it. This was difficult for anyone to accept, as his daughter Kate was a close friend of many members of the committee. After issuing numerous public denials of involvement, Chase offered the President his resignation. Lincoln refused the offer, content that Chase had done himself enough damage to minimize his credibility as an opponent in 1864.

Though Lincoln recognized Chase's talents and gave him relatively free reign over the nation's financial health, his relationship with his Treasury Secretary was anything but cordial. Several times in Lincoln's first term of office Chase, angered by perceived slights, threatened to resign. Once he used this strategy when he could not convince Lincoln to appoint a political protégé to a lucrative government position in New York. He offered his resignation again during the Pomeroy Circular fiasco. He offered it for the last time in in June of 1864, when he could not convince Lincoln to make a patronage appointment he had promised to a supporter. In the past Lincoln had always refused to accept his resignation, citing Chase's invaluable service to the cause of the Union. This time Lincoln held on to Chase's resignation note, making no attempt to read it. Later Chase was shocked when he received a note sent from the President in which he stated that their official relations had reached a point of mutual embarrassment and that Chase's resignation was accepted.

***

When her father took up his position in the Lincoln cabinet in 1861, Kate Chase set about creating a home in Washington worthy of her father, his high government position and even greater aspirations. Her father had rented a three story brick mansion ten blocks from the White House. She spent a small fortune decorating it.

Every Tuesday evening and Saturday afternoon Mrs. Lincoln held gatherings at the White House which were, by tradition, open to the public, and therefore were not deemed as desirable by the high society of the Capitol. Parties held by cabinet officials were private affairs and invitations to them were more sought after by the crème of Washington society. The most sought after invitation in Washington quickly became one for any event hosted by Kate Chase and her father. She established a regular routine of daily breakfasts and Wednesday afternoon dances at their home, which she called "matinee dansantes." They concluded with a dinner and reception for her father. The guest lists that she created focused on the men who could best serve her father's political interests. Despite her intent for these parties to further her father's political goals, she was more often the center of attention than he was. In later years Mrs. Daniel Chester French, an occasional attendee at these gatherings, described how the crowd would react when Kate made her appearance.

Kate Chase "was more of a professional beauty than had at that time ever been seen in America, with a beauty and regal carriage which we called 'queenly,' but which no real queen ever has…She was tall and slim-the universal art of being slim had not been discovered in those days-with an unusually long white neck, and a slow and deliberate way of turning it when she glanced about her. When she appeared, people dropped back in order to watch her."

Lord Lyons, English ambassador to the United States, worked hard to gain her attentions and affection. John Hay, President Lincoln's private secretary, was a frequent guest. Kate liked Hay, admired his intellect, and used him to gain as much information for her father about the President as she could. Hay, who found her both charming and intelligent, used her in equal measure to gain information he might pass on to the President about Secretary Chase's political maneuverings. Despite their using each other as targets of political espionage Kate and John Hay remained friends for the rest of their lives.

Kate was known to radiate both friendly interest in her guests and an aloofness that kept them at a discreet distance. The powerful men with whom she loved to debate issues of the day reported that she "never came out second" in the exchanges.

Unlike Mary Lincoln, Kate Chase avoided the blood and gore of military hospitals, preferring instead to raise morale by visiting army camps. It was during one of these visits early in the war that she renewed her acquaintance with William Sprague, the 31 year old "boy governor" of Rhode Island. They had first met at a dance in Cleveland Ohio the year before.

Sprague was ten years older than Kate, and at only five feet, was two inches shorter than Kate. When she met him for the second time in 1861 he was Brigadier General of a regiment he himself had raised, equipped and trained. He was wearing a splendid new uniform set off by a bright yellow sash, sporting a yellow plumed hat with his longish black hair tucked under it, mounted on a white horse. Quite a sight for a girl of barely twenty to take in. "It was a case of instant and mutual infatuation," a close friend of her father said.

***

William Sprague was the second son of Amasa and Fanny Sprague of Cranston, Rhode Island. When Kate met him he was worth an estimated $10 million dollars. His family had built up vast holdings in textile mills and print works. As William grew, his father had him work menial jobs at the family businesses to learn about their companies from the bottom up. He made fires, swept floors, clerked at the company store, and eventually moved up to keeping accounts worth hundreds of thousands of dollars. By age 22 he was an acting partner in the business. By age 26, following the deaths of his father and uncle, William built the business from a worth of $3 million dollars to $19 million dollars. He also diversified family business investments to include large shares of stock in a railroad, a steamship company, a sheet iron company and farm equipment.

In 1860 Sprague was elected Governor of Rhode Island. A year later, when President Lincoln issued a call to the governors of the states to raise 75,000 volunteers to serve in the army to put down secession, "the Boy Governor," as Sprague was called, answered by recruiting a regiment and quickly marching it down to Washington. His Rhode Island troops were the first fully trained and equipped troops to enter Washington DC in response to the President's call. With this swift action, he became a personal favorite of the president and First Lady.

Kate and William Sprague began to appear all around Washington together. Salmon Chase began to think that Sprague might just be the kind of man his daughter should choose as a suitable mate.

The young Brigadier General's wartime exploits in the field were limited to only one engagement, the battle of Bull Run, in July 1861. There, while trying to rally his retreating troops, he had his horse shot out from under him. He struggled to his feet and shouted "I am not dead; forward, boys of Rhode Island!" Brave as he was, he could not rally his regiment. The entire Union army collapsed, surprised by a sudden attack of fresh new rebel reinforcements.

Sprague would remain in the army, but inactive, while he fulfilled his role as Governor of Rhode Island. He and Kate resumed their courtship, but it was slowed by Sprague's need to remain in Rhode Island to attend to his official duties and family business. Kate, without informing her father, travelled to Providence to see him. Perhaps she was spurred to this action by newspaper reports linking Sprague romantically to the daughters of several other prominent men. Salmon Chase admonished her for the trip, saying that unless they were more than friends she should not have gone, and that if she and Sprague were more than friends, he should have been informed. Chase was not yet fully convinced that Sprague was the right man for his daughter to marry. Kate's sister Nettie, on the other hand, urged her to marry Sprague sooner rather than later.

Kate was attracted to Sprague for all the ways he differed from her father. Salmon Chase was spare with praise and affection. Sprague simply and openly adored Kate. Her father did not smoke or drink. Sprague did both, the latter to great excess occasionally. Kate was refined, but not wealthy. Sprague was rich and uncultured. He was, in modern terms, a "bad boy," and Kate found him fascinating, but she found reasons to hesitate in yielding to Sprague's desire to marry. She was a person who reasoned out her actions carefully, while he often acted erratically, on impulse. He always chose action over words. And then there was the drinking, though he seemed to have it under control.

Sometime in early May, 1863, Kate and William Sprague, recently elected a U.S. Senator, became engaged. Their wedding would take place later that fall. In the intervening months Kate showed signs of uncertainty, delaying the sending of invitations. Sprague pleaded with her by letter from Rhode Island to trust that his love was true and steady, and wrote to Salmon Chase to recruit her father in convincing her that all should proceed as planned. Salmon Chase, now reconciled to the idea of losing his daughter to William Sprague in marriage, joined him in reassuring Kate that her decision to marry was correct. Chase's pain over losing his daughter was perhaps eased by William Sprague's declaration to him that he was, through the marriage, gaining access to the Sprague family fortune.

On November 12, 1863 Kate Chase and William Sprague were married at the Chase mansion in Washington D.C. She had already received nearly $100,000 in wedding gifts, not including the $6,500 Tiffany jewelry set Sprague had bought for her. President Lincoln attended the wedding alone despite his wife's insistence that he stay home with her. Fifty other guests were invited, including most of the President's cabinet, many Senators and several foreign ambassadors. Kate had no maid of honor. She was attended by her sister Nettie, a cousin and a niece. Sprague's groomsmen were three officer friends from his regiment. The brief Episcopal ceremony was over within 30 minutes, after which all the guests moved into the main parlor for a lavish dinner and a serenade by the Marine Band. Washington newspapers reported the affair a dazzling success.

That night the new bride found time alone to write in her diary about the momentous day, and how she had felt when William Sprague finally embraced her as her husband.

I felt a sense of ineffable rest, joy and completeness. It was like a glimpse of Heaven for purity and peace. All strife ended, all regret silenced…Every thought, every desire, every feeling merged with the one longing to make him happy. Not a reserve in my heart, not a hidden corner he might not scan, the first, the only man that had found a lodgment there.

Soon after the wedding, William Sprague left Kate in Washington with her father and sister and headed up to Rhode Island to tend to family business. Seven weeks after their wedding she wrote to him:

The sunshine has gone from our beautiful home. Paradise is no paradise without a God and my Eden is indeed deserted...Oh darling, I hope these separations will not come often. They are so hard to bear.

Managing the family businesses would preoccupy Sprague and take him from her side frequently in the years to come.

***

June, 1864, found Salmon Chase out of a job. Lincoln had been re-nominated for President by the Republican Party, with Andrew Johnson of Tennessee as his running mate. Yet another chance at grabbing the golden ring had eluded Chase. As the summer wore on, the war was still going badly, with U.S. Grant and his Union Army of the Potomac frustratingly stalemated in its drive to capture Richmond by Robert E. Lee and his outnumbered, underfed and ill-equipped Army of Northern Virginia. Grant's heavy casualties were the talk of the North, with long lists of killed and wounded appearing daily in local papers all around the country. He was being called "Grant the Butcher" in some newspapers. The people were losing faith in President Lincoln's attempts to bring the war to a conclusion, and there was talk amongst some powerful Republicans of holding another special convention to replace Lincoln as their candidate for President. Chase began to hope that there was still a chance, narrow at best, to claim the nomination he so relentlessly coveted. Kate increased the number of parties she held at the Chase mansion, inviting any politician who might control delegate votes at a convention, while her father wrote to William Sprague, eschewing any desire for the office himself, but declaring that "a man of different qualities from those the President has will be needed for the next four years." William Sprague, knowing his wife's devotion to her father's political success, quickly wrote to her arguing they would have to plan something soon to derail Lincoln's re-election bid. He knew that this pledge of loyalty, with its implication of financial help for the campaign, would win him greater affection from her than any else could.

Chase's hopes fell almost as quickly as they were raised. Where there had previously been only bloody stalemate, Union armies began to achieve victories. William Sherman's Army of Tennessee captured the key southern city of Atlanta in early September. Then Admiral David Farragut's fleet won a naval victory that closed off Southern use of Mobile Bay on the Gulf of Mexico. Soon after that, Phillip Sheridan's forces destroyed an opposing rebel army that had been protecting the south's chief agricultural center, the Shenandoah Valley. These victories bolstered Lincoln's leadership image and insured that in two months he would be re-elected. There would be no special convention, no radical Republican coup to replace him on the ticket, no chance in 1864 for Chase to grab the Republican Presidential nomination.

In the fall, with the election only one month away, fate finally intervened in favor of Salmon Chase. Roger Taney, the aged Chief Justice of the Supreme Court chosen by President Andrew Jackson, died. President Lincoln needed to name a replacement. He offered the position to his former Treasury Secretary. He felt that by elevating Chase to this high but non-political office he could eliminate a constant thorn in his side and give the country a man who could honorably and ably serve the nation. Chase accepted the appointment in December, following Lincoln's re-election. He confided to a friend that he viewed accepting the position of Chief Justice as "an experiment," and that after some time he might resign. That would make Chase eminently available for the Presidency in 1868. He would never stop reaching for the highest office in the land.

***

It is not clear how Kate, now pregnant with her first child, felt about her father accepting the position of Chief Justice. There were rumors that she was angry about him being shelved, but Kate Chase took pride in always keeping her composure, publically at least. President Lincoln was reported to have asked Supreme Court Justice Stephen J. Field, a friend of the Chase family, "…how Mrs. Sprague would like the appointment of her father;" and that he had heard the remark attributed to her that her father "...was not to be set aside by a place on the bench.." Kate probably agreed with her father's decision to accept the appointment, for she knew very well that she and her father would not let the judicial appointment halt their political maneuvers to achieve the Presidency.

***

Four months after Salmon Chase became Chief Justice of the United States, Abraham Lincoln was assassinated, and Andrew Johnson was elevated to the Presidency. Kate and her father began to recalibrate their plans based on this unexpected turn of events. Andrew Johnson had been chosen by Lincoln himself to join him on a National Union ticket in 1864. As a Democratic Governor of Tennessee who chose to remain loyal to the Union rather than side with the South, Johnson was a symbol of the country Lincoln hoped it could become after the war ended. Their ticket represented a whole republic, North and South, re-united. The choice made sense at the time. The war was winding down, and Lincoln was only 54 years old and in relatively good health. Now, with Lincoln dead, a Democrat was President. Yes, he had agreed to run with Republican Lincoln, but how sound was he on Republican principles? Chase saw an opportunity for 1868. Who was better to lead the Republican Party into the post war reconstruction? A former lifelong Democrat or a founder of the Republican Party, the wartime leader of the country's finances and the Lincoln-appointed head of the judicial branch of government?

Within weeks of Lincoln's assassination, Kate and her father headed south on a trip through the former Confederacy to report back to the President on conditions as they found them there. This was the official explanation for the junket. Its other purpose was to influence the President, by the reports they sent him, to support reconstruction policies that reflected Chase's plans. The Chases were greeted joyously by ex-slaves everywhere they went. Chase saw them as a huge potential voting block for him in 1868 if he could get the President to support legislation in favor of black suffrage. This strategy became a non-starter as Chase watched Johnson veto all major civil rights legislation passed by the Radical Republican controlled Congress.

***

Kate had to leave her father before the completion of their southern trip, to prepare for the birth of her child. She joined her husband in Narraganset, Rhode Island where, in June, she gave birth to a son, William Sprague V. The "bright, black-haired and handsome boy" would be known to the family as "Willie." His birth was widely reported in newspapers around the nation, with regular installments to follow that reported Willie's first words, steps and growth.

Salmon Chase constantly preached to his daughter Kate that she should be loyal, supportive and deferential to her husband. The latter admonition was particularly difficult for Kate to accept. They fought regularly about the great amount of time Sprague was away tending to family business. When she complained of this in letters to her father, Chase always counseled her to accept her husband's actions as necessary to insure the family's future. Chase grew even closer to his son-in-law when Sprague, in his capacity as a U.S. Senator, voted in support of black suffrage. Chase told his daughter that her husband was "independent, and manly as well as intelligent; and real manliness and intelligence are rare qualities in these days."

When the war ended in 1865, social events in Washington began to take on their pre-war extravagance. Kate and her father hosted numerous receptions at their house on Sixth and E Street. As always, her guest list included the best of Washington society and invitations to her affairs once again were the most sought after in the capital. The leading society columnist of the day, Emily Edson Briggs, stated that no ball or reception held in the capital that year was more impressive than the affairs hosted by "our accomplished country woman, Mrs. Senator Sprague."

Senator Sprague did not attend many of the parties his wife organized. He was spending a lot of time in Providence, Rhode Island, attending to family business. Whether these trips were really necessary is debatable. He and Kate had been fighting again. An unsubstantiated story circulating at the time relates that at a State dinner given by President Johnson, Sprague had been drinking too much. A person at his table said "a pair of bright eyes" were staring at him. He replied,

"Damn them, they can't see me." Kate immediately said "Yes they can see you, and they are heartily ashamed of you."

Kate felt that her best strategy was to put some distance between them for a time, for Sprague always seemed to come to his senses following such separations. She embarked on a trip to Europe for the summer, taking little Willie, his nurse and her sister Nettie with her.

***

By 1866, Salmon Chase had been a widower for fourteen years. With both his daughters and his grandson away in Europe he decided to visit New Hampshire and his old college at Dartmouth. There he spent time with Charlotte Eastman at the home of a friend. Chase had met Charlotte Eastman, the widow of a former congressman, in Washington D.C. in 1862. They saw each other at many parties there, and rumors circulated at the time about them possibly becoming engaged. Kate was very protective of her relationship with her father, and did not look kindly on the amount of time Mrs. Eastman was spending with him. He wrote to Charlotte Eastman in 1863 to say "so sorry that you and Katie - one so dear to me as a friend and the other as a daughter, don't exactly get along." Unknown to Chase, Kate was intercepting and destroying letters to her father from Eastman and other interested Washington ladies before he could read them. Once he became aware of what Kate was doing he asked his female acquaintances to send their letters to him at the Treasury department rather than to his home.

Chase was shocked when his friend Senator Charles Sumner, a life-long bachelor, suddenly married a young woman half his age. It gave him pause to consider his own life. Sumner's marriage lasted for less than a year, when his young wife was found to be seeing another man. Kate surely breathed a sigh of relief when she learned from her sister Nettie that Chase had confided to her, "I am still and still likely to remain a widower."

***

Kate's strategy of putting distance between her and her husband did not work quite as she hoped it would. She began to receive a stream of disconcerting letters from him.

I am depressed past weakness.

Expect to hear of my doing all sorts of things during your absence. You know I am fond of the ladies and you must not blame me for indulging my fondness. I know you will not if you reflect but will rather commend me for it.

I must I think get some young woman to live with me. Do you consent?

Are you not sorry you have deserted me?

He confessed to her that he had begun to drink heavily again. The newspapers were reporting it to the nation. One article called on him to pass a constitutional amendment to stop him from using his shirt collar as a funnel. He began to write to Kate that he was thinking of resigning his seat in the Senate.

Kate had heard all of his self-pitying litanies before, and knew that he had been unfaithful before, but he had never suggested resigning his seat. This told her he was in a serious depressive spiral. She wrote to him immediately and offered to return home to help him regain his composure. Her possible return startled him into some semblance of normality. He wrote back thanking her for her offer, pledging his love and affection. Kate judged that he was finally out of the depression that had gripped him, and felt safe continuing her travels around Europe.

She and Nettie met with royalty, toured castles and cathedrals, and corresponded frequently with their father, who admitted to them both that they were every bit as qualified to take part in public affairs as he was at their age. This was high praise indeed from their usually critical father.

Sprague was beginning to worry about his attractive wife, alone amongst the many single male members of the European royal courts. He wrote her asking if she had forgotten her "lord here at home?"

Do you need his presence to keep you in the faith? I think you are undergoing serious temptations and if you survive and surmount them, how glorious will be the conquest?

In early October, Sprague left for Europe to bring Kate and Willie back home. While he was gone, newspapers began to speculate about a possible divorce, due to "gross immoralities on his part." Salmon Chase, incensed by the accusations, called on old friends at other newspapers to write articles demanding a retraction of the scurrilous stories.

Sprague reunited with his wife and son in Germany and returned with them to the states. Nettie remained in Europe to study art. On December 10, 1866, Kate, her husband and son were together again with Salmon Chase at their shared home on Sixth and E Street in Washington.

After the 1866 European trip, everything began to change for the Spragues. The Senator completed the purchase of a 300 acre farm in Narragansett, Rhode Island, and Kate began to direct all aspects of the construction of what she hoped would become the grandest villa in America. The summer home was completed (though some parts of the huge mansion would never quite be finished) after two years. They named the four-story high Victorian Gothic mansion Canonchet, after a native chief who had camped on the property two hundred years before. It featured a sauna, a bowling alley, an octagonal glass domed main salon, a hand carved staircase imported from Italy, a telegraph office, a blue room reminiscent of the one in the White House, and a separate apartment for Chief Justice Chase.

Kate, by this time, knew of an affair her husband had conducted with the nurse of their little boy Willie, and she suspected he was having an on-going affair with a woman named Mary Viall. Whether they fought over these indiscretions is not known, but Kate years later recorded in her diary that 1866 was the year her marriage became a constant burden.

Perhaps as compensation, Kate began hosting regular Saturday afternoon receptions at their Washington D.C. home. She attended any dancing parties to which she received invitations, frequently staying out until three or four in the morning without her absent husband.

In 1867 Kate left her husband in the states and travelled to Europe once again to bring her sister Nettie back from her studies. The sisters extended their stay to visit Paris, returning home to America in the fall.

***

With his daughter back in Washington, Salmon Chase's mind turned, as it so predictably did in the past, to presidential politics. He told Nettie in 1867, "…it does look now that, if there were no military names before the public the choice of the people might fall on me." Unfortunately for Chase there was a military name – a big one- before the public. Ulysses S. Grant, hero of the Civil War, was looming as a possible candidate for the Republican nomination for President. How could Chase surmount such a formidable obstacle to the Republican nomination? The answer was revealed in February at the most unusual of places, a party hosted by Kate Chase Sprague. She had been busy since her return from Europe gauging what support her father might have for the Republican nomination. Reporters took note of her activities describing her in news accounts of the day as "the most splendid woman at the present time amid Republican politicians and courtiers of Washington." Unfortunately for Salmon Chase, what Kate heard as she made the rounds in Washington was a constant refrain of Grant, Grant, and Grant. It was time once again for them to reset their strategy for how to gain the Presidency. Consequently, at a reception she held on February 22 she was heard by many party attendees to say "unreservedly that she thought President Johnson was right in his controversy with Congress" and that she would do all she could to help the Democratic Party in the struggle for control of reconstruction.

Two days later President Johnson was impeached by the Radical Republican controlled Congress.

***

For six weeks the nation's attention was focused on the prosecution and defense teams as they presented evidence and witnesses to bolster their cases. The lines were clearly drawn, with very few people holding no opinion. On one side was President Andrew Johnson, who in the past three years had alienated most of the Republican Party that had chosen him, at Abraham Lincoln's request, as their Vice Presidential nominee in 1864. Supporting President Johnson were most Democrats, whose party he belonged to when Lincoln chose him as a running mate on a Union Party coalition ticket. On the other side were the Republicans, controlled in Congress by their radical faction. These radicals were bent on placing the executive branch in a position subservient to the legislative branch, thus thwarting the President's attempts to control the ongoing Reconstruction of the South, which they saw as too lenient. President Johnson favored allowing former high ranking army officers and government officials of the Confederacy to run for office in the very government that they had tried for years to destroy. Even worse in their opinion, Johnson was not willing to support laws passed by Congress to protect recently freed slaves from legal and physical assault by their former masters. The Radical Republicans' chosen weapon to defeat the President was the Tenure of Office Act, a law they had recently passed, giving Congress the authority to override Presidential cabinet dismissals. Johnson had fired Secretary of War Edwin Stanton and replaced him with a person more amenable to the President's views on Reconstruction. Congress then invoked the new Act, and Stanton, a Radical Republican, barricaded himself in his office at the War Department and refused to leave. When Johnson tried to have him removed he was found in contempt of Congress and was brought up on impeachment charges.

Chase presided over the trial, but not as a judge. The Constitution outlined his role as more of an arbiter, ruling on admissibility of evidence and procedural motions. Even with this limited role he was under intense scrutiny, each side looking for any signs of partiality he might display.

The Impeachment trial brought considerable stress to the Chief Justice's family. Salmon Chase intensely disliked the President Pro-Tempore of the Senate, Benjamin Wade of Ohio. Chase felt that back in 1860 at the Republican convention Wade, as chairman of their state's delegation should have delivered favorite son Chase the entire Ohio delegate vote. Instead Wade allowed his delegates to split their vote between Chase and Abraham Lincoln. That, Chase felt, gave Lincoln's effort to gain the nomination an important boost and eventually led to Chase's defeat. If Johnson's impeachment succeeded and he was removed from office, Wade would become President because there was no sitting Vice President and the Constitution specified that the President Pro-Tempore was next line of succession. That was a nightmare scenario for both Chase and his daughter Kate.

If Wade became President prior to the Republican convention, it would be almost impossible for Chase's supporters to deny Wade the nomination to run for a full term of his own.

Kate's marriage also complicated matters. Her husband, now a Senator from Rhode Island, was sitting on the House floor listening to prosecution and defense arguments. He would have to vote for or against President Johnson. The public assumed that due to his close relations with his father-in-law the Chief Justice, Sprague would vote against impeachment, denying Ben Wade a chance at the White House. Sprague was also part of the Radical Republican block in Congress, and so was under intense pressure to vote for impeachment by his colleagues. Kate knew that her husband had not yet decided how to vote.

***

After three weeks the prosecution and defense teams had completed their arguments. All that was left was the vote. To remove the President an affirmative vote by 35 members, or 2/3 of the Senate was necessary. As the roll was called it was clear that the vote would be closer than was expected. Most people believed that President Johnson would be impeached. The first surprise occurred when William Sprague voted for impeachment. His fellow radicals had been sure of his vote, and probably by that day Kate and her father knew which way he would cast it. What discussions took place in the Chase household that night are not known, but it is doubtful that his vote did anything to strengthen his already shaken marriage. The deciding vote was cast by Edmund Ross, a first term Republican Senator from Kansas. He was expected by his radical colleagues to vote for impeachment, but he did not. By supporting President Johnson he assured that the Radicals would fall one vote short of removing President Johnson from office, with the final tally being 34-19.

Edmund Ross paid a high price for his vote in support of President Johnson. Radical Republican leaders discovered that the President had brought Ross into the White House on several occasions during the impeachment proceedings and offered to give Ross's friends and relatives positions in government as a means of buying his support. Whether this explains Ross's vote, or, as Ross later justified it, it was simply a matter of his honest judgment that President Johnson deserved to remain in office, cannot be determined beyond reasonable doubt. It is clear what happened to Ross. The Republican Party in Kansas refused to re-nominate him for a second term and he never held elective office again.

Chief Justice Chase ruled on issues of evidence and procedure carefully, and to the general public, without bias. Some influential national Republicans felt that he was too partial to the defense. Radial Republicans in Congress saw his actions differently. Future President James A Garfield, then a Congressman from Ohio, and Chase's old friend Senator Charles Sumner publically declared that the Chief Justice was a traitor to the Radical Republican cause.

The 1868 Republican Presidential convention to choose their nominee was only weeks away. Salmon P. Chase's chances of becoming that nominee were slim before the impeachment trial. After it, they were non-existent. Ulysses S. Grant was easily nominated.

***

After the Republicans nominated Grant, Kate began to work in earnest on convincing anyone she could, including the Chief Justice, of his availability for the Democratic nomination for President. One Georgia newspaper reported that Kate was "pulling the wires with great effect." Another newspaper in that state praised her powers of persuasion, saying "Can it be that by winning her talented father over to the sound doctrines of the Democratic Party, Mrs. Senator Sprague has pointed out the road to prosperity and political reconciliation for this now distracted Republic? I am told that she actually controls the entire affair." Friends of the Chief Justice around the country began to urge him to run for the Democratic nomination.

Many Republicans viewed Chase's apparent change of party allegiance with bitterness. Joseph Foraker, a former Governor of Chase's home state, Ohio, commented in later years, "It is probably safe to say that Chase had membership in more political parties...with less mutual obligation arising therefrom than any other public man America has produced."

Kate and her father used the weeks leading up to the July 4th opening date of the 1868 Democratic Convention to allay any suspicions that the party might have about his loyalty and commitment to its principles. He supported free trade and lower tariffs, just as they did. He advocated small government, just as Thomas Jefferson, founder of the party, did. Only on the issue of slavery did he differ from the Democratic Party's principles. Unfortunately, that was not an insignificant difference. Chase addressed that troublesome problem quickly, arguing that Democrats in their party platform should endorse universal suffrage (full voting rights for white and black men) in principle, but leave its application up to the states, consistent with Democratic belief in state's rights.

With Chief Justice Chase's new position on universal suffrage softening opposition to his candidacy, Kate left for New York City to manage her father's campaign for the nomination. Her sex dictated that she could not appear on the convention floor at Tammany Hall, where the gathering was taking place. It would be unseemly for a woman to be seen rustling about ankle deep in the muck of male dominated politics. She would remain seated in the public gallery of Tammany Hall while the delegates were in session, where she would receive constant updates from her father's floor managers and dispatch orders to them through notes. After the convention recessed each day she would go back to her suite at the hotel and manage from there.

Kate and her father had developed what they hoped would be a winning strategy. They believed that the front runners would not be able to gather sufficient votes to gain the nomination on any early ballots. As some contenders began to fade and the nerves of delegates began to fray, Chase's name would be placed in nomination and the real scramble would begin. Kate had worked out an agreement with the chairman of the convention, former New York Governor Horatio Seymour. He would, at the right time, announce that New York's 33 votes would switch from their original choice, Indiana's Thomas Hendricks to Chief Justice Chase. Then Samuel Tilden, Seymour's right hand man on the floor, would call in the promises of key state delegations to switch their votes to Chase also. Kate believed that Seymour and Tilden were the right men for this important job. Both were popular and influential with fellow New Yorkers. The only reason the New York delegation was not voting for Seymour himself for President was because he had strongly and repeatedly disavowed any desire to be the nominee of his party. He said he was plagued by illness and believed he was too weak to campaign effectively.

After the first day of the convention was gaveled to a close, Kate was asked by a reporter what she thought about her father's chances to gain the nomination. "It is all a question whether the Democratic Party has the sense to seize its opportunities, she said. "I fear that when the South seceded the brains of the Party went with it. Since then it has rarely missed an opportunity to blunder."

A few days later Kate wrote to her father with an update. "The excitement here is intense-the outside pressure is very great and 'Chase' is the pass word in the throng gathered about Tammany Hall." She saw "...snares and pitfalls everywhere," but, "...the feeling improves every hour and there is a growing confidence everywhere that you will be the Ultimate choice."

By the fourth day of the convention, July 8, twelve ballots had been cast and the contest was still undecided. Winfield Scott Hancock, a Pennsylvania Democrat and Civil War hero on many battlefields, was slowly gathering strength. Thomas Hendricks' support was fading with each new ballot, and the former leader of the balloting, George Pendleton of Ohio, was losing his support to other contenders.

Now was the time. As the California delegation announced its vote, it concluded with the words "and one-half vote for Salmon P. Chase." Cheers began to erupt around the hall, and a demonstration continued for a full ten minutes, surprising many delegates. Kate stood and applauded, her eyes misting with pride. The goal that she and her father had so long sought was just ahead on the horizon.

The plan called for New York to switch its votes to Chase at this point, but for reasons unknown it did not. Kate could only watch from the gallery, scribbling urgent notes to Seymour and Tilden. Winfield Scott continued to gain delegates across six more ballots. Horatio Seymour, the convention chairman, called for an adjournment so that the growing Hancock momentum could be halted. Hancock's total stood at 144.5, with Hendricks at 87, Pendleton at 56.5 and Chase at ½ vote.

A group of New York delegates, along with some from Ohio, gathered late that night at Delmonico's restaurant to plot their next moves. It was an evening of brandy, and cigars, and politics. Women were not invited. Kate remained in her hotel room, directing her convention managers, including Horatio Seymour and Samuel Tilden, to seek out potential new Chase supporters. They did not receive an invitation to the Delmonico's meeting.

The next day, July 9th, balloting began again. Chase picked up support from the Massachusetts delegation. New York still continued to vote for Thomas Hendricks, even though it was clear he could not win. They seemed to be waiting for some dramatic break that would point to a potential winner.

Seymour had led Kate to believe that on the 22nd ballot New York would finally switch its vote to her father. She listened to them report their delegate count. It remained with Hendricks. Then Ohio, her father's home state was called. The spokesman for the delegation, George McCook, not a fan of Chief Justice Chase, announced that, "I rise at the unanimous request and demand of the delegation from Ohio, and with the consent and approval of every public man in the state... to place in nomination, against his inclination, but no longer against his honor, the name of Horatio Seymour of New York."

Kate sat in the gallery, shocked, as loud cheers and applause greeted the Ohio vote. A blow to the Chase cause had been dealt, but perhaps not a fatal one. Seymour, who had assured her of his unwillingness to be the nominee, had yet to be heard from.

Horatio Seymour, seemingly stunned by this turn of events, stepped up to the podium and addressed the frenzied convention. "Gentlemen, I thank you and may God bless you for your kindness to me, but your candidate I cannot be." He then excused himself and left the stage. In that moment Kate must have breathed a sigh of relief, but it was premature.

Another Ohioan was recognized by the chair to speak. Clement Vallandigham, a former enemy of Chase during the war years who had only recently come around to support him in early ballots, addressed the convention. "Ohio cannot – Ohio will not accept his declination, and her twenty-one votes shall stand recorded for his (Seymour's) name."

Now many voices shouted for recognition from the chair as delegation after delegation switched its votes to Horatio Seymour. Soon he had the required number of delegate votes and Horatio Seymour was the nominee of the Democratic Party for President.

That evening back at her hotel, Kate wrote a letter to her father, showing her bitterness over the loss. "You have been most cruelly deceived and shamefully used ... You can form no conception of the depression here." She was convinced that Samuel Tilden and Horatio Seymour had played a duplicitous game at the expense of her father.

Chase received word of his defeat while playing a game of croquet on the lawn outside his home in Washington. His first words were "Does Mrs. Sprague know? And how does she bear it?"

One of Chase's clerks at the Supreme Court later said of Kate, "I think she was more disappointed by the failure of the Presidential dream than her father was, for he was still a leading figure in the world - the head of a department of government, but she was only the wife of William Sprague."

One newspaper editor best explained what actually happened to Chase's bid at the convention when he wrote that Chase "was on every man's tongue, but in no man's heart."

Former Republican friends of the Chief Justice expressed complete disgust when speaking of his run for the Democratic Party nomination. Frederick Douglas, the handsome former slave and powerful spokesman for Negro rights, said that Chase had fallen further than "any of his predecessors in treachery." Henry Ward Beecher, the eloquent abolitionist minister whose sister wrote Uncle Tom's Cabin, was quoted as saying that Chase's switch to the Democratic party showed that his "ambition was consuming the better elements of his nature."

***

In the months following the Democratic convention, without her father's political future to occupy her, Kate allowed herself to drift into self-examination and self-pity. She had kept a diary in her youth, stopping entries sometime around 1862. Now she began writing again. Estranged from her husband, separated from her father by his work at the Supreme Court and without any close female friends, she could only reveal her emotional distress in her diary.

It is long since when I have appealed to you for relief as I used to in the old days when I was alone, and trouble overtook me. So I come back to you for that silent sympathy that even a listener may give.

When her husband suffered a broken leg in a riding accident, she was quick to act as his nurse, offering soothing words and medicines. But the peace between them did not last. When he accused her of manipulating him to obtain money, she called him "small and mean," with a "littleness of soul." In most of these disputes and differences, her father's counsel was always the same. "There can be but one head to a family."

Sprague began to accuse Kate of infidelity, saying he knew things about her "which, if true, would make you (Kate) unworthy to be a wife – any man's wife." He even went as far as flinging in her face her own weakness before their marriage in giving in to his sexual demands, calling her actions "weakness and sin." The double standards of the day regarding men, women and chastity were stunningly unfair to women.

At Christmas that year another incident occurred that brought Kate to despair. She had gone to great lengths to pick out personal gifts for her father and husband. In return her husband had given her money and her father, for the first time in their lives, had given her nothing. He had either forgot to or thought it unnecessary. In her diary she recorded that she would not allow herself to display "the old bitterness of spirit" that she disliked in others. She would show no one how much they had hurt her. She would no longer even confide it to her diary. She stopped writing in it that day, December 27th, 1868.

Kate and her husband were both caught in an emotionally draining cycle of loving, fighting, reconciling, and repeating. Neither was yet ready to or able to end it.

***

William Sprague, who had always taken his responsibilities as a Senator lightly, placing them second to the demands of his family business interests, shocked his colleagues and his wife by making a major speech in March of 1869. The shock came not only from his actually speaking out after months of sitting quietly in the Senate chamber, but from what he chose to say. He attacked the members of the Senate, his father-in-law's Supreme Court, the Founding Fathers, Wall Street bankers, monopolists, journalists, and his former commanding officer in the Civil War, Ambrose Burnside. It appeared as if all his emotions, so long pent up, finally exploded in superheated verbal pyrotechnics. He even aimed arrows at his own wife, if veiled in generalization. He reviled "…Americans who travel abroad (as his wife so often did) and mix and mingle in that filth and come home here to inculcate the immoralities that they have seen upon their own society." It was reported by some present that day that at this point Sprague appeared to look up into the Senate gallery, where his wife Kate was seated. She quickly gathered up her shawl and exited the building.

Kate left the city and joined her sister at a resort in North Carolina, humiliated by Sprague's public rebuke. Chief Justice Chase finally gave his daughter the emotional support she hoped he would, writing to her that he knew she had been "sorely tried" by Sprague's "unkind words and unkind acts." He called on both of them to work on their marriage. "You have both erred greatly and ought to do all that is possible towards reconciliation."

Throughout this unfortunate time, Kate kept secret the fact that she was pregnant with her second child. In October, she delivered a daughter, Esbelle, known thereafter to the family as Ethel. Sprague would in later years claim that Ethel was not his, but studies of his and Kate's travels put them in the same place together during the probable time of the child's conception. Ethel also bore a strong resemblance to her father.

***

When William Sprague fired a servant at the Washington D.C. home he shared with Salmon Chase and Kate, and replaced her with "a very fine looking Englishwoman," the Chief Justice finally had all he could take of the eccentricities of his son-in-law. Using the excuse of needing to give his youngest daughter Nettie an opportunity to run a household, the Chief Justice announced that he was moving out of the Sixth and E Street home to a rented apartment while a new home was being built for him. "Edgewood" would be a Federal style manor built on 50 acres of farmland that had a fine view of the Capitol dome some three miles away.

Salmon Chase would never again give marital advice to Kate, or tell her to submit to her husband. He knew by 1869 that she would never find happiness in that union.

After Sprague's diatribe on the Senate floor, he saw his popularity with the general public grow as his influence amongst his fellow Senators completely disappeared. That realization caused him to lose all further interest in his Senate career, though he still had four years left to serve in office.

***

Kate's personal problems weighed on the Chief Justice, but he was distracted by the heavy work load facing the Supreme Court. In Hepburn vs. Griswold the Court found that Chase's own "greenback" policy to help fund the Civil War was unconstitutional. He wrote the majority opinion. While this seemed like a complete turnaround of position for Chase, it was actually more reflective of his true conservative fiscal nature. He had never liked resorting to the printing of paper money, but did it only out of wartime necessity. Months later, the Court, now filled with new appointees of President Grant, reversed the decision. In Ex parte Milligan, the Court decreed that a military trial of a civilian was unconstitutional. In Texas vs White, the court dealt with the issue of secession, declaring that Texas would always remain a state, even though the government and its citizens might have formed "an alien group."

Kate was summering at Canonchet, following her new life style of being wherever her husband was not. While staying with her there, the Chief Justice, exhausted from his Court work and probably distressed by the state of his daughter's marriage, suffered a mild stroke. He was unable to speak or write for some time, depending on Kate to be his private secretary. She later referred to this summer as a "laborious and trying" time.

Upon his recovery Chase headed back to Washington, but he was a changed man. He spoke little at the dinner table, letting his daughter Nettie lead discussions. He hosted only two parties that season, both, as his private secretary Eugene Didier recalled, "...solemn affairs, too dignified for laughter, not pathetic enough for tears." Chase seemed, Didier said, "...oppressed by the burdens of life, or crushed by disappointed ambition."

***

Throughout the winter of 1870 and early spring of 1871, Kate Chase Sprague was pleasantly distracted from her marital troubles by her 23 year old sister Nettie's engagement to William Sprague Hoyt, a young cousin of Kate's husband. Nettie was considered the plainer, sweeter and more playful sister, while Kate was acknowledged, even by Nettie, as the more beautiful, educated and charming one. When she was sixteen years old Nettie saw her future as one of "old maidism and forty cats." John Hay, Lincoln's private secretary, future Secretary of State under Theodore Roosevelt and longtime friend of Kate, described Will Hoyt as "a very nice fellow – and no end of cash." Hoyt's family owned dry goods businesses that sold the textiles manufactured by William Sprague's mills.

Once their mother died, Kate began acting as Nettie's surrogate mother. She gave Nettie guidance and advice, and much like her father, criticism. While Kate spent thousands each year on the latest fashions, she was telling Nettie that $300 should suffice for her yearly school spending on clothes. The two sisters were close, but never overly affectionate in their relationship. Seven years age separated them, and very different temperaments.

Nettie's wedding took place on March 23, 1871, at St. John's Episcopal Church, known as "the Church of the Presidents," directly across from the White House. William Sprague paid for the entire affair even though he played no part in it, staying in the background. The Chief Justice, looking thin and haggard from his recent stroke, was there to give his daughter away. The reception that followed took place at Sprague's house on Sixth and E Street. As with any affair hosted by Kate, much of Washington's elite were in attendance, including President Grant, members of the Supreme Court, Senators, and foreign ambassadors. Nettie wore a white gown that her sister picked out for her, adorned with natural orange blossoms. The bride is generally the center of attention at these wedding receptions, but Kate, as always, drew the gaze of most attendees. Leading society gossip columnist of the day, Miss Grundy, remarked that Kate looked "if possible, more regal and more graceful than ever," in a green silk dress with a pink silk train.

Perhaps it was the happiness of her newlywed sister that caused Kate and her husband to get back together again, if briefly. Less than a year after Nettie's marriage, in early February, 1872, Kate gave birth to her third child, named Katherine. Kate and William Sprague called her Kitty, after the nickname of Salmon Chase's first wife. Kitty was an attractive child, said to favor her mother. Unfortunately, as she grew older it became apparent that Kitty was not maturing intellectually. Kitty's mind remained that of a seven year old. As was the custom of the time, Kate kept Kitty out of the public eye for the rest of her life. She is seen only in a few family group photos.

***

In April of 1872, Kate hosted another reception for her father at the Sprague's Washington home. A Presidential election was approaching, and the Chief Justice and Kate had not yet given up on their dream of occupying the White House. Their objective at this gathering was to convince politicians and newsmen that the Chief Justice was still physically up to the job. Kate told party goers that her father had walked to the Sixth and E Street home that evening from Edgewood, two miles away. It is doubtful that anyone believed her. As Chase stood in the receiving line with Kate greeting guests, it was hard for him to hide the fact that his hands were trembling, as they had been since his stroke. Carl Schurz, a Republican Senator in attendance that night later commented on Chase's "...futile efforts to appear youthfully vigorous and agile," calling them "...pathetically evident."

Kate and Chase were looking to secure his nomination by either the newly formed Liberal Republican Party or the Democratic Party. Ulysses S. Grant had been elected President in 1868, easily defeating Horatio Seymour, the man who thwarted Chase's hopes at the last Democratic convention. Now Grant was running for re-election, but his first term had been marred by accusations of wide spread corruption amongst his cabinet members and other appointees. There was hope that the nation might be looking for someone to clean up government. Forces opposing Grant within the Republican Party split away to form the rival Liberal Republican Party. The Democrats nationally were in disarray, with no one in the party able to command majority support to oppose Grant. There appeared to be an opening for a man like Salmon P. Chase, who still enjoyed national recognition and a reputation as morally sound. William Sprague, in a not so subtle bid to regain his wife's and father-in-law's favor, dumped large sums of money into their effort to build support for Chase. He dispatched friends and workers to the Liberal Republican convention in Cincinnati, Ohio to aid in the effort to gain the nomination for Chase. Despite all their efforts, that nomination went to the famed newspaper editor Horace Greeley. After failing to agree upon a candidate from their own ranks, Democrats also turned their backs on Chase, and chose to nominate Greeley as a fusion candidate, hoping the combined strength of Democrats and disillusioned Liberal Republicans could defeat Grant in November.

Salmon Chase's long quest for the Presidency was over. Carl Schurz said of Chase's lifelong fixation on the White House, that he "...continued to nurse that one ambition so that it became the curse of his life to his last day."

Chase and Kate campaigned for Greeley, an old family friend, after the Chief Justice failed to gain the Liberal Republican or Democratic nomination. Their support did little to help Greeley, who Grant went on to defeat in a landslide that November. Three weeks later, Greeley fell ill and died.

***

In the spring of 1873, Chase's health began to fail. Once the term of the Supreme Court ended in May, he travelled to New York City to visit his daughter Nettie. There, on May 6, he was found unconscious in bed after suffering a massive stroke. Kate and William Sprague rushed to New York to be at his bedside. The next day, May 7, 1873, Chief Justice of the Supreme Court Salmon P. Chase died, surrounded by his family.

In the weeks that followed, the nation's newspapers were filled with eulogies for Chase. He was hailed as "one of the two great financiers in our history." He had declared himself an abolitionist at a time when such beliefs were reviled, believing that in time many would "join the advancing host of Liberty," and lived to see his position adopted as law.

Throughout the triumphs and tribulations of Kate's life, Salmon Chase had been her anchor. When her actions grew too reckless his letters admonished her and brought her back to reality. When she suffered hurts, his home was always there as a refuge where she could heal. Now, married to a husband for whom she had little respect and from whom she received little emotional support, she would have to face life on her own.

***

At this time in their lives, William Sprague was no longer a husband to Kate. They lived apart most of the time, and appeared together publicly only when it benefitted them both socially. William did, however, continue to support Kate's lavish lifestyle. Soon after Nettie's wedding, Kate purchased a French silk gown from Paris for $18,000. She sent a $1,000 bouquet to President Grant to decorate his second inaugural ball. Sprague's mother, who very much wanted their marriage to remain intact, gave $250,000 to each of Kate and her son's children when they were born, adding $50,000 for Kate herself.

Kate was one of the wealthiest women in America, until September 18, 1873. It became known as Black Thursday, the day when the Panic of 1873 began. Railroad stock prices had been rising constantly for decades, and now, overinflated in value, they began to drop. Sell offs ran out of control, runoffs occurred at banks across the country, businesses that sold goods to railroads collapsed, and huge numbers of workers lost their jobs and fell into poverty.

The banks that had been supplying credit to William Sprague lost confidence in his leadership, influenced by their observation of his extravagant lifestyle at Canonchet, his huge new mansion. He was forced to step down as president of his company in favor of his brother, who would run A&W Sprague Manufacturing under a trusteeship of the banks. William would receive a salary as an employee of his brother.

During this crisis, and despite their estrangement, Kate became pregnant with their fourth child. In November 1873, Portia was born. She was given her name as tribute to Kate's father, whose middle name was Portland.

A court case brought by the Hoyt family in 1874 drove a permanent wedge between Kate and her sister Nettie. Will Hoyt, Nettie's husband filed suit against members of the Sprague family, accusing them of defrauding the Hoyt family by denying them the full financial benefits owed them as part owners of a textile business. The case dragged on for ten years, going all the way to the Supreme Court. The Hoyts lost the case, and the sisters barely spoke to each other again.

Their relationship suffered yet another blow when the sisters fought over what to do with Salmon Chase's home, Edgewood. Kate wanted to live there and Nettie wanted it sold. Kate eventually paid Nettie $16,000 for her share of the property, but Nettie insisted that all the furniture be sold and the proceeds split between them. A date for a public auction of the furniture was set.

Kate could not bear the idea of strangers wandering around her beloved father's study, library and bedroom. She left for Europe before the auction took place. She hoped that she could educate and raise her children more economically while overseas. She also wanted to enroll her son Willie in a German school noted for its strictness. She felt that the negative influence of her husband's lifestyle was responsible for Willie's sloppy attire and unruly attitude.

***

William Sprague quickly lost interest in his businesses once he was forced to step down as president of his companies. One of the bank trustees now running Sprague's A&W Manufacturing thought William to be "of unbalanced intellect, and unfit for management of any business."

Sprague also lost interest in public service. He chose not to run for re-election to the Senate. In one of his last acts there, he was the only Republican to vote against a bill supported by President Grant that would return the country to the gold standard and remove greenbacks (printed under Chase's term as Treasury Secretary) from circulation.

***

Kate must have been mellowed by the distance that separated her from her unfaithful husband, for she began to write him letters of support and encouragement. When it appeared that the bank trustees were struggling to keep his old businesses solvent, she urged him to be aggressive in attempting to regain control of them. If he would do so, she promised she would "go home at once to help you bear it with heart and soul...You may make me General Inspector of the Factories, or head of a Corps to gather up the waste and fragments, that nothing be lost, everything to be of use." She even signed off "...Faithfully always, your wife." What caused her to write these surprising letters can only be speculated. Was it embers of love for him not yet fully extinguished, or fears for her children's future without his financial support?

William Sprague never replied to Kate's offer to come to his side and fight for his business. She remained in Europe with her children.

Kate's brief change of heart ended when a woman she had long suspected of being William's mistress self-published a book in 1876 entitled *The Merchant's Wife, or, He Blundered; A Political Romance of Our Own Day and Other Miscellanies*. Everyone saw it for what it was it was; a story of Mary Viall and William Sprague's long running intimate relationship thinly disguised as fiction. It contained descriptions of rooms at Canonchet, Kate and William's mansion, that were so detailed that Viall must have been in them. Of course Mary Viall did not refer to the house as Canonchet in her story. In her fiction work, Viall referred to the character that closely resembled Kate as "that more unfortunate blunder of his life, the statesman's daughter."

Kate finally returned to America in October of 1876.

***

William Sprague had been open about his infidelities, and they were, to the great embarrassment of his wife, widely reported in the press. For her part Kate had apparently remained monogamous. As long as her father lived she would risk no action that could blemish his name, even indirectly. But now her father was gone, her sister was estranged, her son in Europe, her husband cavorting with Mary Viall. She craved intimacy and a fitting partner with whom to share the rest of her life. Enter Senator Roscoe Conkling of New York.

Kate had known Roscoe Conkling since the Civil War. President Grant had tried to appoint him Chief Justice of the Supreme Court after Salmon Chase's death, but Conkling had refused. He preferred to keep his seat in the Senate and with it control of New York's powerful patronage machine. He was now acknowledged as the most powerful man in the Senate. His enemies saw him as arrogant and vain, a man who never forgot a slight or the enemy who issued it.

He came from a politically active family, was educated in the classics, and loved to quote Byron and Shakespeare in his Senate speeches. He stood six feet two inches tall, with sandy colored hair and an athletic, muscular build that bespoke his interest in boxing and physical fitness. He favored brightly colored clothing of the latest fashion. Women routinely crowded into the Senate gallery to watch him deliver his speeches.

Conkling was a married man. His wife Julia was the sister of Horatio Seymour, the 1868 Republican nominee for President. She was a quiet, shy woman who stoically tolerated the fawning crowds of female admirers that followed her husband wherever he went. By this time in their marriage, Julia was living apart from her husband. He stayed in Washington most of the time, while she and their daughter Bessie lived at the family home in Utica, New York. Even when Conkling came back to Utica he stayed separate from Julia in a nearby boarding house. Just as with Kate and William Sprague, Roscoe and Julia avoided divorce, which was considered unacceptable in the society of their day.

Exactly when their affair began is not clear. Friends of the couple believed that it probably started in secret sometime soon after Kate returned from Europe in 1876.

The Presidential election of that year brought them closer together. Democrat Samuel Tilden of New York ran against Republican Rutherford B. Hayes of Ohio. Tilden narrowly won the popular vote, but neither man had a majority of the Electoral College vote. There were 19 electoral votes, all in the South, that were being contested. If Hayes somehow got them all, he would win. If even one state's vote went to Tilden, he would win. As the nation convulsed with partisan rancor President Grant proposed a solution. He would send a bill to Congress calling for the creation of a bi-partisan, independent electoral commission to study the situation and award the disputed votes as their findings indicated. To ensure fairness, the commission would have 15 members: five Republican congressmen, five Democratic congressman and five Supreme Court Justices – two Republican appointees and two Democratic appointees who together would chose the fifth Justice. Public and insider political opinion believed that the crucial fifth Justice would probably be David Davis of Illinois, an independent who frequently sided with the Democrats. Grant's solution seemed to create a commission favorable to Samuel Tilden's chances.

Roscoe Conkling had a strong dislike for Rutherford Hayes. Hayes campaigned on a platform that called for creating a national Civil Service that would end the patronage system that Conkling was so carefully nurturing in New York. As a Republican, Conkling was expected to support Republican President Grant's bill, but as that bill appeared to favor the fortunes of Democrat Tilden, things were less certain. Further complicating the matter, Kate Sprague hated Samuel Tilden. She believed that Tilden had betrayed her father at the 1868 Democratic convention. When the Election Commission bill came to the floor of the Senate in June of 1877, Roscoe Conkling gave a thoughtful defense of the bill as the fairest way to settle the electoral impasse. Passage of the commission bill, he said, would "once again proclaim to the world that America is great enough, and wise enough, to do all things decently and in order." The bill passed in the Senate, and despite strong Republican opposition, passed in the House as well.

Before Republicans could raise too much of a fuss about their upcoming denial of the Presidency, Justice David Davis shocked everyone by resigning his seat on the Supreme Court to accept a position in the Senate that the State legislature of Illinois had just voted to offer him.

The four Justices on the electoral commission then chose the most independent Justice left on the Supreme Court, Joseph Bradley, to be the fifth court representative. Though generally an independent in his actions while sitting on the Court, Bradley was none the less a Republican.

In their deliberations, Bradley consistently voted with the Republicans on the commission. Rutherford B. Hayes was awarded all of the 19 disputed electoral votes, and was declared the winner of the election. Yet the struggle for the White House was still not over. Democrats in the House refused to accept the decision and began a filibuster. Their plan was to continue it until after inauguration day, when newly elected Representatives would take their seats, giving control of that chamber to the Democrats, who could then decide the election outcome. Tilden Democrats convinced Republican Roscoe Conkling, whose dislike of Rutherford Hayes was well known, to speak to the Senate in favor of the Democrats regarding a single state election result, in Louisiana. If he could rally enough Republicans votes to add to the Democratic ones and secure Louisiana's electoral votes for Tilden, the Democrat would defeat Hayes.

When the day for that vote arrived, Democrats were aghast to discover that Conkling was not on the floor of the Senate, or even in Washington. Without him actively urging fence sitting Republicans to support the Louisiana electoral vote reversal, it failed, and Rutherford Hayes was confirmed as President-elect.

Where was Conkling? He had taken a train to Baltimore to visit friends, and Kate Sprague, who happened to be visiting there. A reporter of the day, Billy Hudson, claimed in his memoirs that Kate had been convinced by other Republicans to ask Conkling to come to her there. It is doubtful that she would have needed much convincing. She hated Tilden for what he had done to her father in 1868. Another influential Washingtonian of the day, in a memoir penned years later, quoted Kate as saying "I got even with Mr. Tilden for defeating my father."

Another explanation of Conkling's absence from the Senate that day came from George Hoadly, a former law partner of Salmon Chase. He claimed that top Republicans, gathered at a meeting the evening before the Senate vote, told Roscoe Conkling that if he aided in any way the election of Democrat Samuel Tilden, his future in the party would be destroyed. Where the truth lies is unclear to this day.

∗∗∗

In February of 1877, Kate and her husband had yet another ugly confrontation at Canonchet, more frightening for her than any in the past. Kate claimed that he was so drunk and out of control that he tried to throw her out an upstairs window. She immediately left the mansion, taking her daughters with her back to Edgewood in Washington. That summer she, Ethel, Kitty and Portia left for Europe. Once again, distance from her husband was her way to ensure domestic calm for her children. The trip would also unite her with her son Willie, who was back at his school in Germany.

Roscoe Conkling also left for a trip to Europe at the same time, though he travelled separately from Kate. Whether they met up in Europe is not known. Both Kate and Conkling returned to the states, again separately, in August.

From America, Kate continued her correspondence with her son Willie. She was concerned that he was manifesting the same bad habits she saw in her husband. Willie dressed and groomed himself carelessly. He was not focusing enough on attaining good grades. Her letters began to sound very much like her father's to her. They contained little praise and much correction. "I shall send you a list of words that you misspell," she wrote, "which I want you to return to me with the correct spelling written opposite my list." Ironically, she also chastised him for his spending habits, writing that he should not "throw away money on useless things."

Willie was being fought over by his estranged parents. While Kate was sending him letters that scolded and corrected him, her husband praised Willie, saying "Indeed, at your age I could not write and express myself as well as you do now by a good deal." William Sprague had made no great effort to halt Kate's control over their daughters, but he would not let Willie go as easily.

Kate and Roscoe Conkling continued their relationship in a more public way upon their return from Europe. They were frequently seen together at parties in Washington. Rumors began to spread among Washington socialites that Kate was Conkling's mistress, while they continued to live separate lives from their spouses. Don Piatt, a Washington D.C. columnist, wrote of their relationship as being "the most open and defiant social transaction."

Willie came back from Germany in the summer of 1878 and stayed with his father at Canonchet. Kate, at the urging of Sprague's mother, came to Canonchet to see her son, and possibly attempt some level of reconciliation with her husband. The attempt failed quickly when William Sprague was arrested for what Kate described as "a disgusting orgy" with Mary Viall on a beach in Narraganset, Rhode Island. Kate retreated to Edgewood and her daughters. Willie stayed on with his father.

Roscoe Conkling now had his eye on the White House. There was an election coming up in 1880, and he was a leading contender, along with Secretary of State James G. Blaine. He knew that Kate's charm, intelligence and political instincts could be invaluable to him. Others thought they were a perfect match. A society writer of the day noted "Mrs. Sprague is a born diplomat" who could do for Conkling what "in his vanity and arrogance he would overlook or thrust haughtily aside." His great ambition deepened their mutual attraction.

In Congress, Conkling pushed for a piece of legislation that was called "Mrs. Sprague's bill." It called for Salmon Chase's Edgewood property, where Kate now lived, to be exempted from all past and future taxation. Conkling called it a tribute to the former Chief Justice, but most members of Congress saw it as an unjust favor to Kate. It did pass, but was amended later only to cover taxes up to 1880.

Conkling's marriage was being strained to the breaking point. When his daughter Bessie was married, Conkling was not present. He claimed he was detained by business matters. More probably the absence was caused by a fight between Conkling and his wife. He wanted Kate to be invited to the wedding and his wife and daughter both refused. Rumors began to circulate in the local papers that Mrs. Conkling was about to file for divorce.

***

In August of 1879 an incident occurred that would change the futures of the Spragues and the Conklings. William and Kate were spending some time together at Canonchet that summer. Kate was helping him to sort out the many legal and financial messes that were putting a strain on their income. Roscoe Conkling had travelled to the area after hearing from Kate that her husband would be leaving for a business trip of several days. Once Conkling heard from Kate that William Sprague had departed on his trip, not to return until August 9th, he joined Kate at her home. She was there with her three daughters and a couple of friends from New York. Though they were not technically alone, Canonchet was so large that Kate and Conkling could easily find places in the mansion to rendezvous in private.

The couple enjoyed each other's company in carriage rides around Narragansett and probably did what most tourists coming to the area did; boat excursions, riding, hiking, seeing a play at the local theatre or perhaps even taking in a local baseball game.

On August 8th, William Sprague returned to Canonchet late in the evening from his business trip. He was back a day earlier than he had planned. Everyone had already retired for the evening, so Sprague chose to sleep in a usually unoccupied bedroom in the huge mansion. Too restless to sleep, he left the mansion early in the morning and headed into town to visit his favorite restaurant and billiards parlor. There, while having several drinks, he overheard townspeople talking about Roscoe Conkling being at Canonchet for the past several days. Sprague immediately left and raced back to the mansion. According to the coachman who took him there, Sprague met Conkling outside on the piazza and angrily told him he had twenty minutes to pack up and leave. Once he had delivered this ultimatum Sprague ran upstairs to get a shotgun. Conkling kept his composure and departed the mansion, not even bothering to gather his luggage. He headed to a café in town where he waited to catch the 5:30pm train out of the area.

Sprague followed Conkling into town and found him standing in front of a café. According to the café owner, they exchanged heated words, with Sprague threatening to kill Conkling if he ever saw him again. With that Sprague left, and Conkling re-entered the café to await the train.

Not long after this confrontation Kate showed up at the café and spoke with Conkling. She explained that she and the girls were leaving Canochet that day and would spend the night in a neighboring village. Conkling then departed on the 5:30pm train.

Kate and her daughters spent the following week living secretly in a hotel in Providence, Rhode Island. She met with lawyers there and declared that she "would never sleep under the same roof with Mr. Sprague again."

On August 14[th,] Kate and her children met with William Sprague at the pier just down the hill from Canonchet. Her only reason for this meeting was to gather her own and her children's belongings before heading back to Washington, D.C. Fearing an incident, she brought her lawyers along with her.

Sprague addressed her as soon as she arrived, saying "This is your work, madam." The conversation went downhill from there. He accused Kate of lying to the newspapers about what had happened between him and Conkling. She accused him of mistreating her when he was drunk. Sprague finally asked if she was returning with him to Canonchet. "I fear for my life if I do", she replied, reminding him that he had once pointed a gun at her head. While not denying this accusation Sprague replied "I never harmed anyone, and you are safe."

It was clear neither of them would give ground. Sprague then insisted that Kate surrender the children to him. Horrified, Kate consulted the lawyers she had brought with her. They explained that Sprague was on solid legal grounds with his demand, and counseled Kate to yield the children to him, which she did. Sprague then left with the children and returned up the hill to Canonchet. The evening grew darker as Kate sat and contemplated what might be happening to her daughters up at the mansion. Finally, she grew so fearful for their safety that she and the lawyers headed up to Canonchet together. At the mansion door Sprague heatedly refused to let the lawyers enter, but told Kate she was welcome. She decided to enter and remain there until the legal issues of custody were worked out. She would not abandon her daughters to a man who barely knew them.

Newspapers around the country ran countless stories about what had occurred at Canonchet. At first the public sentiment favored Sprague as the wronged man, cuckolded by his fellow Senator. When more stories appeared describing Sprague's affair with Mary Viall and his cruelty to his wife, opinion began to swing back in favor of Kate. Holed up in her rooms at Canochet with her daughters, she invited members of the press to come and hear her side of the story. Sprague did not object. He wanted to counter rumors in the press that Kate was being held prisoner against her wishes.

The New York Sun dispatched a reporter to get the inside story of the ongoing drama at Canonchet. The editors knew that this kind of exclusive could sell a lot of newspapers. Once on the property, the reporter sat with William Sprague, who told him that Kate was in no way being held prisoner. Sprague said that Kate could come and go as she pleased as long as she did not take the children with her. The reporter spoke next with Kate, who had an entirely different agenda. In her day being perceived as an unfaithful wife was socially inexcusable, and if proved, could lead to loss of custody of her children to her husband. Her strategy was to disprove any affair ever took place with Roscoe Conkling. She began telling her version of events by explaining to the reporter that "for thirteen long years my life has been a constant burden and drag on me." She told him of her husband's strange letter to her in 1866 asking for permission to see other women.

"For years I have had this thing weighing upon me, and have striven with all my might to stand between my husband's wrong doing and the public. I have done it for the sake of my children, not for any affection that existed between us; for there has been none for years."

Then she pivoted to her real reason for asking him to come, the rumors of her infidelity with Conkling.

There is not a word of truth in all these atrocious reports. Conkling has never paid me any attention a wife could not honorably receive from her husband's friend, and it is false to say otherwise. Mr. Sprague was simply worked upon by his business troubles, which have been culminating for years, and by his indulgence in strong drink. He regarded everyone, no matter how honorable, who was a friend of mine, as an interloper and an intriguer against him.

The reporter pressed her further, asking what brought Conkling to Sprague's estate in the first place. Kate explained that Roscoe Conkling came to Canonchet to offer business advice to her husband and that during his stay Conkling occupied a room distant from the one where she slept.

Kate concluded her interview claiming that all rumors of an affair between her and Roscoe Conkling were "outrageous slanders."

After the interviews Kate began moving all her things from Canochet while devising a way of leaving with the children. She started shipping jewelry, personal papers, favorite furniture and rare artifacts from the mansion to Edgewood in Washington D.C. Sprague was aware that she was doing this but chose not to interfere as long as she and his children remained with him.

When she could no longer safely ship away any more of her belongings, Kate began to form a plan of escape from Canonchet. She sent a letter to her lawyers asking for advice and received their blessing to leave Canonchet immediately and begin legal proceedings to gain custody of her children. She waited for a time when Sprague would leave the house for an extended period of time, so she could execute her plan. By August 29th their marital discord turned into real physical danger for Kate. William Sprague came home drunk and climbed the stairs up to the room where maids were dressing the Sprague's children; it appeared to him, for some kind of trip. "I'll show you who is master here!" he shouted to Kate as she stepped into the room. With that he grabbed her and began tossing her about the room, finally trying to throw her out of the window. Sprague never agreed to this version of the events of that day, but others present that day supported it.

Kate's opportunity to leave finally came on the afternoon of August 30th, when Sprague came home from an outing on a nearby beach and fell sound asleep in a room at the front of the mansion. Household staff and local townspeople sympathetic to Kate's situation helped her leave the area with her daughters before Sprague woke up. Her little party travelled eleven miles by carriage to the town of Wickford, where they would catch a boat to Massachusetts, then travel overland to the home of friends.

William Sprague woke up from his nap and was informed by one of the servants whose job it was to keep an eye on Kate and the children that they were seen leaving Canonchet in a carriage some time earlier.

Sprague immediately led a search of all the likely locations Kate might head to, such as the railway station and boat docks, but she was nowhere to be found. She had made good her escape.

Sprague contacted the newspapers to grant interviews so that he could put out his version of what had transpired that afternoon. He told reporters that he did not plan on chasing Kate around the country, but would commence legal action to regain custody of his daughters.

Kate and her children spent two weeks at the home of a distant relation in Babylon, New York, recovering from the stresses of their escape and flight. Once fully rested they went on to Kate's home, Edgewood, in Washington, D.C.

Kate grew dispirited reading the many newspaper reports of what had gone on between her, her husband and Roscoe Conkling. None of them received any sympathy. An article in a paper printed in Hillsboro, Ohio, near where many of Kate's relatives lived, was typical. It accused Kate and Conkling of "attentions such as no honorable man ought to have paid to another man's wife, and such as no prudent married woman, with a proper respect for her own and her husband's honor, would have permitted herself to receive from any other man."

A reporter who interviewed her at Edgewood observed that she looked pale and tired. She told him

The bitterest part of my recent troubles has been that I should be thought a silly, vain woman… To be so misrepresented, so misunderstood, has given me my greatest pain. I have been charged with all sorts of misdoings, of which I am totally innocent.

She began from that time forward to call herself Kate Chase, never using her married name again.

Roscoe Conkling was silent about the whole Canonchet incident. He did not defend Kate or himself publicly. His bitter enemy President Rutherford Hayes wrote "…exposure of Conkling's rottenness will do good in one direction. It will weaken his political power, which is bad and only bad." Once Conkling's affair with Kate Chase Sprague became fodder for the newspapers, he ceased any thoughts of running for President.

Kate resumed hosting parties at Edgewood, trying to appear as if nothing had happened to alter her status as the reigning queen of Washington society. She and Conkling also resumed their affair, though with much more discretion than before. In January of 1880 she held a dinner party for Senator Conkling and his wife. Much to everyone's surprise, Julia Conkling attended. No doubt her husband had persuaded her to help create the illusion that everything was fine between them. If that was the case, then the plan failed. A reporter at the party observed "Mrs. Conkling does not appear to have the slightest reconciliation with her husband, but went through the performance at his request."

The 1880 Republican convention opened with Roscoe Conkling leading the effort to nominate Ulysses S. Grant to head the GOP ticket and claim a third term as President. Kate watched him from the gallery as he roused the hall with a dramatic speech placing the ex-President's name in nomination. The convention deadlocked between Grant, Senator John Sherman of Ohio and James G. Blaine for 35 ballots. Conkling was able to keep 306 loyal Grant supporters together as a voting block throughout the chaos, but that effort was not enough. On the 36th ballot a dark horse candidate was put forward and the weary and frustrated convention delegates rallied to James A. Garfield as the compromise candidate of the G.O.P. As a thank you for her constant support at the convention Conkling gave Kate a beautiful brooch containing jewels forming the number 306, with an arrow through it.

James Garfield was no friend of Conkling's, and he knew that he needed the powerful Senator's support in New York state to win in the fall election campaign. To secure his help Garfield, despite his oft-stated support for civil service reform, agreed to give Conkling free reign in New York State dispensing patronage jobs if and when he was elected. To further bind Conkling's Stalwart wing of the party to him, Garfield asked Conkling's protégé Chester Arthur to be his Vice-Presidential running mate. Arthur, surprised and flattered by the offer, accepted despite Roscoe Conkling's advice to decline it.

Conkling campaigned hard for Garfield, crisscrossing the east by train. Reporters took note of the fact that Kate Sprague was often seen riding on the same train, in the same car as Conkling. One wrote "Mrs. Sprague has been travelling with the Republican Party this fall. Roscoe Conkling is in the same palace car. Comment unnecessary." William Sprague read these stories and called them "positive proof of criminality extending over many years."

Kate no longer cared what her husband thought. On November 5th, 1880, three days after James Garfield was elected President, she filed for divorce. When Kate's lawyer tried to retrieve some of her belongings from Canonchet and serve her husband William with the divorce papers, their fifteen year old son Willie fired a pistol at him. The lawyer accused Willie of attempted murder and the boy was taken to court for a preliminary hearing. After the judge heard conflicting statements about whether or not Willie's pistol was loaded with powder but no bullet, and whether he aimed at the lawyer or only in his general direction, he dismissed the charges for lack of evidence. The fact that his mother's lawyers were trying to convict him of attempted murder while his father defended him was not lost on Willie. His relationship with his mother, rocky in the best of times, was now nearly over.

Once James Garfield was inaugurated and took office as President, he began almost immediately to clash with Roscoe Conkling over the issue of patronage, despite their arrangement at the convention. Garfield ignored Conkling's recommendation for who was to become collector for the port of New York Customs House, a very lucrative position, instead appointing a man of his own choosing. Conkling resigned his position in the Senate in protest and began a campaign to be reappointed to the seat by the state legislature. Once that was done he could then rejoin the Senate as an even more powerful opponent of the President. His plan backfired when the legislature, tired of his bullying and bad press, denied him the office. Conkling was, for now, out of office.

Two years after it began, the divorce proceeding between William and Kate Chase Sprague was over. Kate would have custody of her three daughters and Sprague would maintain custody of their son, Willie. There was no alimony granted, but the right for Kate to ask for it in the future was approved. Kate was also allowed to resume use of her maiden name, Kate Chase.

During the years the divorce proceeding made its way through the courts Kate and William Sprague's lives had been a headline topic in newspapers all across the nation. Conkling's name was mentioned as frequently as the two principles, and all of their reputations suffered greatly. Throughout this difficult time Kate never wavered in her support of Roscoe Conkling.

Four months after taking office, President James A. Garfield was killed by an assassin who favored Conkling's Stalwart wing of the G.O.P., thereby elevating Conkling's protégé, Chester Arthur to the Presidency. Kate immediately began to lobby President Arthur to appoint Conkling as his Secretary of the Treasury. Eventually Arthur gave in to Kate's charm offensive by offering Conkling a seat on the Supreme Court, but Conkling surprised both of them by refusing the position offered to him by the man he called "His Accidency."

Kate waited several months to see what would become of Conkling's marriage. He left Washington and moved to Manhattan to begin a law practice. His wife Julia remained at their home in Utica, New York. They continued to live separately but did not divorce. Sometime in the late spring of 1883 Kate and Conkling must have decided to end their intimate relationship, for Kate announced that she and her daughters were moving to Europe and would remain there for several years. Without her husband's wealth to support her lavish lifestyle Kate felt she could live more frugally in Europe than in America. With her future plans made clear Kate and Roscoe Conkling parted amicably.

Kate and her daughters reached Europe in July, 1883, and stayed for the next four years. They lived for a time in the fashionable Boise De Boulogne district of Paris, where Kate resumed her usual lifestyle by hosting weekly receptions which were heavily attended by Americans living in or travelling through the area. Her shrinking income may have been the cause of their moving from Paris to a small village just north of the city. There her life was tranquil and secluded. Kate was probably the only American living in the town at the time. She enrolled her daughters Ethel and Portia in a boarding school for girls, trying to give them something like the fine education she had received. She told a local newspaper reporter

France is superlatively the best place to educate girls in all practical ways. My little girls are in a village, not learning about dress and the frivolities of fashion, but living a perfect home life, learning the truths of nature...And I have advantages in France that with my limited means I could not enjoy elsewhere.

She kept her mentally handicapped daughter Kitty with her at her apartment, along with a maid and an instructor of German language that she had hired.

Kate returned to America briefly in 1884, not co-incidentally a Presidential election year. President Chester Arthur was planning to seek re-election, but first he would have to convince his party to re-nominate him. This would not be easy. Even though Arthur had conducted himself well as President following James Garfield's assassination, Garfield had plucked Chet Arthur from the obscurity of a state level patronage job in New York City to make him his running mate in 1880. No one then thought Chet Arthur was of Presidential material, and many Republicans still remained unconvinced of it. Arthur visited Edgewood to seek advice from his friend Kate. She told him not to trust James G. Blaine, the late President Garfield's Secretary of State, who had promised Arthur that he would not seek the nomination. Arthur assured her that Blaine was not going to oppose him, but Kate predicted that Blaine would seek and get the nomination, though she believed that he would lose in the general election. Unfortunately for Arthur, Kate's prediction was accurate.

Kate rejoined her family in France and continued a quiet life, not mixing with her fellow expatriates in nearby Paris. Her dwindling income forced her to begin selling some of her fine gowns, jewelry and furniture to pay expenses. Whether out of necessity or by choice she was simplifying her life. She told an acquaintance "The glitter and transient pleasures of social life are but vanishing joys. They soon pass and leave nothing."

In August, 1886, Kate and her daughters returned to the United States for good. Her father's remains were being moved from Washington, D.C. for reburial in the Spring Grove Cemetery in Cincinnati, Ohio. As she travelled the across the country, Kate found clear evidence of her continuing unpopularity amongst the women of high society. President Grover Cleveland greeted her at the White House while she was in Washington, but Cleveland's wife failed to attend the meeting, claiming illness. When Kate passed through Columbus Ohio, former First Lady Lucy Hayes was not available to greet her. Mrs. Hayes also wrote to the then current First Lady of Ohio, Julia Foraker, advising her not to meet with Kate. "Why should it be you? We must not judge her – let the Lord do that – but I think – in your position – to countenance even the appearance is a mistake."

While she was in the states, her son Willie wrote to her, hinting that he might be open to meeting her, despite his "shabby and dilapidated condition." After Willie had moved in with his father, his life had taken a bad turn. At first all seemed well. In 1883 William Sprague had married again. The new Mrs. Sprague, Inez Weed, was an aspiring opera singer, young, beautiful and free living. In 1885 Willie, at age 22, married his step mother Inez's 17 year old sister Avice. A little more than a year passed when Avice gave birth to a daughter. Rumors were rife that Willie was not the baby's father. Speculation centered around two people as the child's real father; a rich 48 year old former suitor of Avice and Willie's own father William Sprague. Willie, convinced that he was not the child's father, deserted his wife and left the Sprague family estate and his father.

By 1888 Kate's father had been dead for fifteen years, and only one man since then had come close to filling the void that had been created in her life. Roscoe Conkling had given her hope that she once again might scale the heights of society, and even achieve residence in the White House. Now he was seriously ill. He had refused a ride from a cabbie who Conkling felt was asking too high a fee for his services, and chose instead to walk three hours in a blizzard to attend a meeting. When he returned home he fell into a coma. Kate rushed to New York to see him, but Conkling's wife, who had left Utica to tend to her husband, refused to let Kate enter the room where he lay. Conkling died the next day.

Kate renewed her relationship with Willie that year, helping him get a job, and seeing him through his divorce from Avice, who promptly married the man who may have fathered her child, her former suitor Gerritt Wheaton, a rich officer of the Standard Oil Company.

Despite his mother's attempts to help him, and her many letters of encouragement, Willie's life continued to unravel. He swore to his mother that he had stopped his drinking and general dissipations, but that was not the truth. In October, 1890 he wrote a bitter letter to his father referring to William Sprague's "diversions" in his marriages, accusing him of being "cold and chilling." He rambled on.

With my very sensitive and highly considerate nature I cannot conceive how a man can so ruthlessly knock a man down, gouge his eye and otherwise figuratively abuse him with so little, or, in fact, no cause.

The letter remained unfinished. It was found next to Willie's dead body. He had slit his wrists, then apparently changed his mind, binding his bleeding wrists with a shirt, then changed his mind again and wrapped his head in a chloroform soaked bedsheet and died. He was 25 years old. The darkness that had always followed the father had gotten the better of the son.

Kate blamed her ex-husband for Willie's death. She attended the funeral service with her daughters, and never looked across the church aisle that separated her from the entire Sprague clan seated there. She also went to the burial site to watch Willie's coffin as it was lowered into the ground. William Sprague did not attend, but sent a representative instead.

Kate returned to Edgewood to live a much simpler life than she had before. Her daughter Ethel made her stage debut in New York's Madison Square Garden Theatre. Kate had encouraged her in acting, hoping that Ethel's income would help the family. Ethel went on to marry a physician/playwright and lived in Brooklyn, New York. Kate's daughter Portia, must have caused her much disappointment and heartache. After spending most of her life living with her mother, Portia wrote to her father, reconciling with him in 1897. She moved back to Canonchet and lived with William Sprague and his second wife, Inez. Eventually she married twice, settling down in Narragansett, Rhode Island, near her father.

Kate stayed on at Edgewood with Kitty, trying to make ends meet. The estate had once glowed with the light of the many luminaries that had partied there. Now it was mostly dark and empty. Many pieces of furniture and objects of art had been sold to pay the bills, and what remained was cheap and functional at best. Kate and Kitty occupied little of the great space the mansion boasted. The few neighbors who got to know Kate in these years said she had become "soberer, less spirited, more kindly," than the younger Kate.

Income remained her daily concern. By now there was little left of the inheritance from her father's estate and the money given her by her mother-in-law years earlier. She mortgaged and remortgaged the property to gain the means to keep the estate up and running, but by doing so she incurred debts that could not be repaid. The banks foreclosed her mortgage and began auctioning off her personal property. Kate travelled to New York to appeal to old friends for help, and they gathered up $80,000 to provide a trust fund for her to live on. The wife of one supporter who saw her in New York was shocked at the changes age had wrought in the former Queen of Washington society. She remarked after meeting Kate

The glorious eyes were dull and inflamed as though scalded by salt tears; she apologized for her looks, saying that she had been on the coast of Maine and the air did not agree with her – a subterfuge, I felt sure. Poor broken woman! She elicited my pity but not my admiration.

By 1897, as the trust fund her friends were setting up for her was taking shape, she began to sell produce that she was growing at Edgewood to local neighbors. This small income was all that kept mother and daughter from want. Her lifestyle is described in a letter she sent to a neighbor that year.

I was sorry not to be able to send you the asparagus and rhubarb for your dinner

today. Kindly give your order for the next day and we will be glad to fill it if we have what you wish…What we have is good and I am pleased to send it to one so appreciative as you always are. We now have milk – two fresh cows and a good deal of milk and cream. Are there any of your neighbors who would care to have our milk and cream? My work this year is largely field work. My men go to work early and are constantly busy until 6pm and we run no wagon so can only serve after working hours.

Kate could not go to her sister for any financial help. Nettie and her husband had for a time prospered, but the severe financial downturns of 1873 and 1893 destroyed their fortune. Nettie's husband died from alcoholism and she, like her sister, struggled to make ends meet. Also, Nettie and Kate were no longer close. After her sister's death Nettie explained why.

What grieved me beyond everything, more than any injustice to me, was the way Kate (although she did not realize the harm she was doing) injured our father's memory. The unjust and grossly exaggerated criticisms of his great desire for "the Presidency" came all through her intrigues with second rate politicians during the latter part of his life. And since his death it was very hard for me to have her beg money in his name.

Neighbors in the late 1890's often saw the familiar sight of Kate, rounder than in her youth and quite matronly, driving her one horse carriage filled with produce up and down the street of northern Washington, D.C., delivering her goods to customers. They must have felt some pity for her and how far she had fallen, but Kate herself remained unbowed.

Bank trustees decided in 1899 that they would put Edgewood up for sale. It was in great disrepair and Kate no longer had the means to keep it up. They felt that money from the sale would be sufficient to pay off Kate's debts to them and give her and Kitty an annuity to live on in some other less expensive housing.

Before that sale could take place, Kate's health took a turn for the worse. She had not been well for some time, but had refused to go to the doctors to be examined. Now they came to her and determined that she was in the late stages of Bright's disease, which was what kidney and liver failure was called in those days. Portia and Ethel travelled to Washington to be with her. Surrounded by her three daughters, she died on July 31, 1899, at age 58. She was eventually reunited wither father, when both were both reburied in Spring Grove Cemetry, in Cincinnati, Ohio.

When the daughters looked through her meager belongings they found the "306" pin that Conkling had given her hidden away in a drawer. Kate had sold all of her jewelry but this one piece.

Portia, Ethel, Kitty, a few servants and friends were all that attended her funeral. Nettie did not come. All her life she had been fawned over, admired, even lusted after by Senators, heads of foreign governments, ambassadors and wealthy businessmen. None were there for her at the end.

Years before her death, Kate had stopped using her married name, so it is not clear if she or one of her remaining family members chose the name to appear on her tombstone. It read

Kate Chase Sprague 1840-1899

***

The phrase "power couple" is a recently coined one, but were it in use in the 1800's it would definitely have applied to the father/daughter team of Salmon Chase and Kate Chase Sprague. Their effect on the course of the nation was certainly greater as a pair than it would have been if either was without the other.

Salmon Chase attained much in his lifetime, but not the one thing he really wanted – the Presidency. He died revered, never the less, by a nation that honored his valuable contributions to preserving the Union and freeing slaves from bondage.

Kate Chase rose along with her father, using him as her means of attaining high social standing and a marriage into great wealth. When her father died, her life began a slow descent into eventual poverty and obscurity. There was an element of tragedy in her loss of wealth and position, but to her credit it never seemed to embitter her.

Both have remained popular subjects of historians, with recent biographies and articles written about them. They have also received frequent if secondary treatments in many movies.

Brains and beauty still prove an irresistible combination to this day.

THE ORIGINAL PRIVATE EYE

Allan Pinkerton

THE LATE ALLAN PINKERTON

At 5:45pm, February 23rd, 1861, a short, stocky Scotsman with broad shoulders, muscular arms, thick reddish beard and bright, penetrating blue eyes strode into the lobby of the Continental Hotel in Philadelphia, Pennsylvania. He suspiciously surveyed the large crowd of people there, as he pushed through them and headed up to the second floor room of Norman Judd, the nervous, red faced confidante of the President-elect of the United States. Together they walked down the hall and knocked on the door of the adjoining suite. When the door opened, the Scotsman came face to face with Abraham Lincoln, who smiled wearily and reached out to shake his hand. They were not strangers to each other, having worked together over past years on business for the Illinois Central Railroad.

Allan Pinkerton spent the next several minutes explaining to the

President-elect that he and his agency had uncovered evidence of a plot to assassinate him when he changed trains in Baltimore, Maryland, enroute to his inauguration in Washington, D.C.

Lincoln found the plot Pinkerton detailed for him hard to believe, but he knew firsthand the thoroughness and efficiency of Pinkerton and his men. He considered if he should heed the warning or not. Even if he believed it, how could he change his publicly known schedule at this late date and get safely to Washington, D.C.? And what damage would be done to the confidence of the nation in its new President if he had to sneak into the Capitol in the dead of night?

***

Allan Pinkerton was born on July 21, 1819, the third of four children born to William and his second wife Isabella Pinkerton. William's first wife, also named Isabella, died giving birth to the seventh child of their marriage. The family lived in a two room tenement flat on Muirhead Street in an area of Glasgow, Scotland called the Gorbels, a poor working class district on the south bank of the River Clyde. William was a former trustee at the city jail, who had lost his position due to an injury received while on the job. The three daughters from his first marriage, Love, Mary and Janet, were in their teens when William lost his job, and to his embarrassment, they became the breadwinners of the family, earning badly needed money working thirteen hours a day at the local mill.

Allan's father died when he was about ten years old, in circumstances that are not clear. He was either killed during a political riot, or he may have been badly injured in a riot and died later from his wounds. Whatever the case, Allan was without a father at a young age. He received an education typical of the time, being taught to read and write and cipher by two neighbors who operated a school in the Gorbels. That formal education ended with his father's death. Any further education would be up to Allan to glean from life lessons.

His first job, at age 10, was as an errand boy for a friend of his father who operated a business as a pattern maker for nearby loom businesses. Allan graduated from running errands to making patterns, but soon tired of the repetitious, boring work. At age twelve he decided to learn a new trade and found himself an apprenticeship with a businessman named William McAulay, as a cooper, or maker of barrels. Six years later, in 1837 he earned his card as a journeyman cooper and began what he expected would be his life's work.

***

Scotland in Pinkerton's youth was a country in political turmoil. Only the landed class could vote for candidates to the national Parliament, and working men were organizing and protesting to gain that right for themselves. A new Poor Law was enacted, forcing the unemployed into workhouses where they slaved for long hours to earn wages too meager to buy enough food to feed their families. Desperation led to violence in the streets and the formation of a new movement called the Chartists, and they organized as a group named the Universal Suffrage Association. They supported a People's Charter, which called for annual parliaments, universal suffrage, vote by secret ballot, abolition of the property qualification for members of Parliament, payment of MP's and equal constituencies. Working people believed this Charter to be their best hope for a decent life, while the establishment saw implementation of the Charter as dangerous and revolutionary.

While the country struggled over the Chartist controversy, Allan Pinkerton remained oblivious to the chaos. He was without steady employment after losing his position at McAulay's workshop, where he had been working for the past seven years. The owner's son had finished his own apprenticeship, and McAulay could not afford to employ two journeymen. For the next four years Allan drifted around Scotland and northern England, moving to wherever he could find work.

Allan returned to Glasgow occasionally when he could find work there, and stayed with his mother. Perhaps his long struggle to secure work made him more sympathetic to the worker's cause, for this is when he became more committed to the Chartist movement. He attended meetings regularly and was soon recognized as a local leader. In 1839 he participated in a violent demonstration in South Wales intended to protest the imprisonment of a top Chartist leader, and was lucky to escape from it unharmed when British soldiers fired into the crowd, killing 22 people and wounding many more.

Pinkerton escaped back to Glasgow more determined than ever to see Chartist principles made law, but he no longer believed the Universal Suffrage Association was the group to get the job done. He started his own organization, the Northern Democratic Association, stating "We are determined to carry the People's Charter peaceably if possible, forcibly if we must."

For the next several months, Pinkerton, Treasurer of his new group, worked hard to raise the funds necessary to make it viable. He staged concerts as a means of attracting potential new members and raising much needed cash. In the summer of 1841 he arranged for a concert to be held at the Unitarian Church in Glasgow. Dr. Harris, the church's choir master, played the piano accompanying his choir as they sang traditional Scottish folk songs for the crowd. Pinkerton and his mother sat in the front row taking in the evening's entertainment. When a young 14-year-old girl named Joan Carfrae stepped on stage to sing solo, Pinkerton could not take his eyes off her. She was slim and pretty, with a beautiful, clear soprano voice.

Allan began to attend other choir concerts where he knew Joan would perform. He later explained "I got to sort of hanging around her, clinging to her, so to speak, and I knew I couldn't live without her." Within months they were together constantly.

Food shortages plagued Scotland after a poor harvest in 1841, and the winter that followed was very severe, creating much hardship and discontent in the working classes. The economy suffered and many working men lost their jobs. Talk of emigrating to Canada or the United States became widespread. Allan's best friend Robbie Fergus, fearing arrest by the police for his participation in Chartist activities, left Glasgow for America.

Pinkerton was growing frustrated. The Chartist movement had achieved none of its goals so far, and worse, the working people of Scotland seemed to be losing interest in it. He feared his own possible arrest and went into hiding. For months his friends hid him from the authorities. He finally decided it was time to leave Scotland for a brighter future. There was only one thing holding him back – Joan Carfrae.

When Pinkerton disappeared from the streets of Glasgow, Joan begged his friends to tell her where he was hiding. They took her to him. He explained years later what happened next.

When I had the price set on my head, she found me where I was hiding and when I told her I was all set up to making American barrels for the rest of my life and ventured it would be a pretty lonesome business without my bonnie singing bird around the shop, she just sang me a Scottish song that meant she'd go too, and, God bless her, she did.

On March 13th, 1842 they were secretly married, and on April 8th they set sail for the new world on a barque called the "Kirk," planning to end their travels in Montreal, Canada.

***

Ocean voyages in those days were nothing to be taken lightly. The Atlantic could be treacherous, regardless of how good the ship or crew might be. Their trip proved to be a severe test for the newlyweds. Accommodations were crude and basic, and it was necessary for Allan and Joan to be in separate quarters. Joan stayed in a small cabin with the other women on the ship, while Allan bunked with the crew.

Their first challenges came quickly as the ship hit rough weather, bobbing about on the high waves of the storm tossed Atlantic. The interior of the ship soon stunk with the sour odors of seasickness. In rare moments of relative calm, many passengers ran topside to suck in what fresh air they could before bending over the rail of the ship to relieve themselves of their last meal. Then they found themselves stuck in a hurricane that pushed their ship far off course, finally running them aground 250 miles south of their intended port.

Their trials were not yet over. Once the crew had safely shuttled them from the foundering ship to the shores of the Sable Islands, they were set upon by native Indians and robbed of all their valuables. Joan's wedding ring was lost to the thieves. She never wanted a replacement, saying none could mean as much to her as the one that Allan had first given her.

Luckily, if that could fairly be said of them at this point, the Sable Islands were on a major shipping route, and within days, Allan, Joan and the other bedraggled passengers of their now sunken ship were rescued. In May the Pinkerton's reached Montrea,l Canada, and Allan found seasonal work as a cooper at a meat packing plant. They did not stay long. By winter the season for meat packing had ended, and with it Allan's job. It was time again to move.

Allan had heard that Chicago, Illinois, was a growing town of 1,200 people with a bright future. The Pinkerton's packed their meager belongings and headed for the frontier town on Lake Michigan. Allan never left an explanation why, but when they reached Chicago they did not settle there. Instead, they continued west to the small borough of Warsaw, on the Illinois shore of the Mississippi River. The town itself had little to recommend it as a place to set up a shop except its nearby neighboring city, Nauvoo. Nauvoo was the new home of the Latter Day Saints (Mormons). and as such it had rapidly grown to become the largest city in Illinois, boasting a population of 20,000. Pinkerton must have decided that the demand for good coopers would grow as fast as Nauvoo had.

Joan and Allan had barely begun to settle into the little town when disaster struck them yet again. Thieves broke into their homestead and stole nearly everything they owned but the clothes they were wearing. Allan considered what to do and quickly chose to leave Warsaw and head for Chicago, and his friend Robbie Fergus from Glasgow, who had emigrated there just before the Pinkertons came to America. They walked the miles from Warsaw to Chicago, intent on finding Fergus and asking for his help. Chicago was not a large town in 1842, and Pinkerton knew that Robbie was a skilled printer. There could not be many in a town that small. In a few days Allan located his friend, who insisted that the Pinkerton's move in with him until they could earn enough money to arrange for a place of their own. Fergus introduced Allan to a friend who worked as a foreman at the nearby Lill Brewery, and Allan was able to hire on there as a barrel maker. His work day started at 4:30am and ended at 6pm, for which he received $.50, a decent wage at the time. The young couple enjoyed their first few months of normal married life, free of natural and man- made disasters. Alan, however, was restless to establish himself in his own business. After only a few months at Lill's Brewery he told Joan that he was going to give his notice. He had heard of a string of towns 30 or so miles northwest of Chicago that had been settled by earlier groups of Scottish immigrants. Named after cities in the old country,

Dundee, Elgin, and Inverness, they stretched along the Fox River surrounded by rich farm land. He would visit this area and see for himself if it was the right place for them to forge their future. If it looked promising, he would send for her.

Joan walked with him from Fergus's house, reluctant to say good-bye. When they reached the edge of town, just past Fort Dearborn, they hugged and kissed. Joan watched him as Allan walked into the tall prairie grasses, quickly disappearing from sight. She knew he was still near, as she could hear him whistling one of her favorite Scottish ballads. Soon the whistling faded and she sadly returned to the Fergus home.

***

After 3 days of walking, Allan reached the village of Dundee. He began to question townspeople about other coopers that might be in the area. He knew he had made the right choice when he was told that there were no coopers close by and that neighboring farmers would eagerly buy any barrels he could produce. With that encouragement, Allan walked the area, looking for the best place to build his new cooper's shop. He found it on a small rise just a few hundred yards from the main road that crossed the wooden bridge into town. Everyone coming to Dundee would have to pass it by. He commenced building his shop and within a week he was hammering into place a large sign that looked down onto the main road. It read "Only and Original Cooper of Dundee." He sent for Joan and when she saw the little house/workshop, she knew she was home.

For the first time in their marriage, they had a place of their own, and Joan began to make it a place fit for the family they hoped would soon fill it. She later recalled

In the little shop at Dundee, with the blue river purling down the valley, the auld Scotch farmers trundling past with the grist for the mill, or their loads for the market, and Allan, with his rat- tat -tat on the barrels whistling and keeping tune with my singing, were the bonniest days the Good father gave me in all my life.

The little cooper shop prospered, and by 1846 Allan employed eight men at his business. Townspeople criticized Pinkerton for hiring them because they were not Scots, but recent German immigrants from east of the Fox River. Pinkerton ignored his neighbor's comments, accepting the men as hard workers who needed a job, just as he once had.

Allan had developed a routine of searching the nearby forests for trees that would yield lumber suitable for building his barrels. He was not afraid of the hard work involved in felling and preparing the lumber for use in his shop. It was much cheaper than buying wood already cut and trimmed. In June of 1846, while on such a mission to gather wood for his barrel making Allan rowed out to a small island just north of Dundee, near the town of Algonquin. While searching for a suitable copse of trees to fell he noticed the remains of a recent campfire. It puzzled him that anyone would spend time at night on this little island. There was no game to hunt, no promising spot to fish. Allan's curiosity was piqued, and several days later he visited the island again. He headed to the same spot where he had found signs of previous use and found evidence of yet another campfire having been built. He decided that he needed to visit the island again, at night. On the evening of the night surveillance, Allan sat, concealed in the tall weeds near the campsite. Soon he heard sounds of a boat running aground on the shore, and men climbing out onto the island. The men headed for the mysterious campsite and started a fire. Allan was convinced they were involved in some illegal activity.

The next day Allan convinced the Sheriff of Kane County, Luther Dearborn, to come with him to observe the strange night gathering. Allan, the sheriff and a small posse returned to the island a few days later, found the men gathered there and arrested them. They were counterfeiters who were using the fire to heat base metal and shape it into fake dimes.

Word of the incident spread quickly in the area, and Allan became a local celebrity. Customers who came to his shop began asking him to tell the story of the arrest of the criminals on what they now called Bogus Island. Soon Allan was approached by the owner of the general store in Dundee and asked to do some detective work for him. Allan protested that he was a barrel maker, not a detective, but the neighbor insisted, and Allan reluctantly agreed to do the job.

Allan grew suspicious of a man who had recently appeared in the town.

He followed him, made his acquaintance and convinced him that he was down on his luck and needed desperately to earn some easy money. John Craig, his target, agreed to sell him fifty fake $10 bills for $125. The handoff was to take place in Chicago. When Allan met Craig and received the fake money, Craig was arrested by the Deputy Sheriff of Cook County, who Allan had tipped off about the transaction.

When Allan got back to Dundee, he discovered that word of his actions had already reached the town. Luther Dearborn, the Sheriff of Kane County, who had worked with Allan to arrest the counterfeiters on Bogus Island, offered him a job as Deputy Sheriff of Kane County. Allan agreed, since the job would only be part time and would allow him to continue his main occupation as cooper for the town.

In 1847 the Pinkerton family grew by one. Joan gave birth to a healthy baby boy, named William, as Scot's tradition called for, after both his grandfathers.

Holding two jobs kept Pinkerton busy, but not so much so that he did not have time to pursue a cause close to his heart. The abolition movement in 1840's America was growing in strength, and it drew the former Chartist Pinkerton to it. He had always supported universal suffrage, and slavery in the British Isles had already been outlawed. Allan became active in the Underground Railway, a group of citizens who provided hiding places for escaped slaves who were trying to make their way out of the South to Canada and freedom. Slave owners were relentless in pursuing their lost property and the local officials of the law were expected to assist them in recovery of their goods. People like Allan, who hid runaways and gave them food and lodging, were taking a great risk. That did not deter the stubborn Scotsman, for whom the principle of freedom was so dear. While they stayed with the Pinkerton's in their cooperage in Dundee, Allen often taught the runaways the basics of carpentry and barrel making, so they might have a skill to help them earn enough to feed themselves when they reached Canada.

His clandestine activities soon brought him to the attention of M.L. Wisner, the conservative pastor of the Dundee Baptist Church, where he and his family attended Sunday services. When Allan announced he was a candidate for county sheriff, Wisner sent a letter to the local paper accusing Pinkerton of being unfit for public office. They

244

published it, and it created a schism in the church and the town. Rallying to his support were most of the younger Scottish immigrants in the neighborhood, while pastor Wisner received backing from the older members of the community, most relocated from New England. The Dundee Baptist Church "tried" Allan in its own court and found him guilty, not of harboring runaways, but of "selling ardent spirits." The absurdity of the charge and conviction (Allan did not drink and would not allow liquor in his home) drove Allan and many of its young members from the church.

Allan failed to be elected sheriff of Kane County. The dispute with the church had done its damage to Allan and the community. People who were once his friends crossed over to the other side of the street now when they saw him coming. Allan saw the beautiful little town of Dundee as small minded and intolerant. He decided it was time to move again. William L. Church, the Sheriff of Cook County, had sent word that he wanted Allan to join him in Chicago and become his deputy. He loaded the wagon with their personal and household goods, helped Joan and Willie onboard, and brought the family to the city on Lake Michigan.

***

The Pinkertons reached Chicago in the early fall of 1847, and spent two weeks lodged with Allan's friend Robbie Fergus while their own home was completed. The two room single story clapboard house on Adams Street was located in a semi-rural area of the city not far from the stretch of Lake Michigan that would later become Grant Park. When it was finished they moved in and Joan began to make it livable.

Soon the family grew, with Joan giving birth to twins, Joan and Robert, in December, 1848. Mary was born in 1849, but died at age two, followed by Joan at age seven in 1855. Another baby was born in 1855, named after the recently deceased seven year old Joan. Two years later the Pinkerton's last child was born. She was called Belle, and was sickly from birth, never really attaining full health.

Pinkerton worked hard at his duties and was rewarded for his efforts in 1849 by being named the first detective ever in the ranks of the Chicago Police Department. The city had grown to over 30,000 citizens, so it's one detective was quite busy. By 1850 politics began to interfere with Allan's future as a detective. The new mayor of Chicago, Levi Boom, was a Democrat who disliked Abolitionists, and made it his job to rid his administration of anyone who espoused that philosophy. Allan, a proud and active Abolitionist, resigned when pressured to support the Democratic anti-abolitionist administration.

***

When the officers of the U.S. Post Office heard he was available, they appointed Pinkerton Special U.S. Mail Agent. He worked for the Post Office until 1852, when he made a decision that changed his life. Allan had recently made the acquaintance of a young, up and coming lawyer, Edward A. Rucker. Rucker realized that the Chicago Police force was barely able to contain criminal activities in the rapidly growing city, and proposed to Pinkerton that together they form a detective agency. Rucker believed that his legal knowledge and business connections combined with Pinkerton's skill at tracking down criminals would make a great crime fighting team. Pinkerton agreed. Together they rented a small office at 89 Washington Street and advertised their new business.

Allan Pinkerton and Edward A. Rucker, under the style of Pinkerton and Company, have established an agency at Chicago, Illinois for the purpose of transacting a General Detective Police Business in Illinois, Wisconsin, Michigan and Indiana; and will attend to the investigation and depredation, frauds and criminal offenses; the detection of offenders, procuring arrests and convictions, apprehension and return of fugitives from justice, or bail; recovering lost or stolen property, obtaining information, etc.

Rucker and Pinkerton knew that the great limitation of the day in law enforcement was that it was directed locally, within county jurisdictions. All a criminal needed to do was to travel across county lines to evade detection. They would not be limited by such boundaries. They became the first regional law enforcement organization in the country.

Within a year the agency was busy signing up a growing list of clients. Rucker and Pinkerton were frequently at odds about how to grow their business. Allan, the more stubborn and relentless of the two, usually got his way. Rucker, upset with his steadily declining influence, withdrew from the partnership after a little more than a year. Allan did not lose a step in pressing ahead to make the changes he believed necessary to improve the efficiency of his agency. He started by creating an emblem for his agency, what might now be called branding. He adopted the wide open eye, with the slogan "We Never Sleep." This eventually gave rise to the popular expression "private eye" as a reference to a hired detective.

The first man Pinkerton hired, George Bangs, was a descendent of Mayflower pilgrims. Unlike Pinkerton, he was tall, and always elegantly dressed. But, like Pinkerton, he was intuitive, quick thinking, and a master at unravelling complicated evidence trails. He would become Allan's trusted lieutenant, and eventually his general superintendent. Next Pinkerton hired a New York police officer named Timothy Webster, then two other promising young men. By 1856 he added three more new hires, and then broke with tradition and hired the first female detective in the United States, Kate Warne. Kate marched into his office one day and announced that she wanted to become a detective. She was a pleasant looking young widow of twenty three, mature beyond her years, who had the rare ability to put people at ease and gain their trust easily. Pinkerton thought about her request for a few days, then realizing her potential as an undercover agent, offered her a job. He was so far ahead of his time in this that it was not until 1891 that other police forces hired women in a similar capacity.

With branding done and new hires in training, Pinkerton began to perfect investigative techniques as yet unpracticed in his new profession. Each case worked was meticulously documented and added to their files. Pinkerton began to build a detailed file on criminals his detectives had encountered, including their physical description, favorite hangouts, unique physical and mental characteristics and criminal specialties. Pinkerton compiled a Rogues Gallery of mugshots using the new daguerreotype process (photos fixed by sunlight) developed in the 1840's, copies of which he could easily send anywhere in the country to aid in tracking down subjects of his investigations.

***

A case brought to Allan Pinkerton in 1854 by Edward S. Sanford, Vice President of the Adams Express Company, a rival of Wells Fargo and American Express, serves as an excellent example of how Pinkerton's agency went about solving crimes. $40,000 had disappeared from a locked pouch while it was being shipped by Adams Express from one of its branch offices to another. Sanford sent a letter to Pinkerton in which he detailed the events surrounding the movement of the pouch and asked him if he could identify the thief based on the information provided in the letter.

Allan was surprised by Sanford's blunt question and unrealistic expectation of what Pinkerton could deduce from a simple letter, but he decided to accept the challenge, if not the case. He carefully studied all the details contained in the letter, spent a weekend pondering the matter and sent Sanford a detailed nine page letter explaining that the culprit had to be Nathan Maroney, Sanford's office manager in Montgomery, Alabama, where the locked pouch had started its journey.

Pinkerton did not hear back from Sanford, and assumed the matter was concluded. Then, a few weeks later he got a request from Sanford. Could Pinkerton please send a man to follow up? Allan knew that the Adams Express was headquartered on the east coast, and that he could gain more clients there if his agency's work impressed Sanford, so he acceded to Sanford's request and decided to go himself to Montgomery, Alabama to size things up and begin work on the case.

Sanford met Pinkerton in Montgomery and nervously explained that he had taken his advice and Nathan Maroney had been arrested, but the evidence had been slim. At the preliminary hearing the judge, citing the flimsy evidence, lowered Maroney's bail and set a court date. Maroney then made bail and was released. That, Sanford explained, had prompted him to call in Pinkerton. More solid evidence of guilt needed to be found before the case came to trial.

Pinkerton decided to call in his entire team to help. They gathered together, developed a strategy and split up to work the case. One operative, John Roche, was to be in disguise as a dim-witted Dutchman, complete with shabby pants and a battered old cap. He would shadow Mrs. Maroney, the suspect's wife. Another Pinkerton man, Adam Fox, would go undercover as a watchmaker in a little shop

Pinkerton rented in a town where Mrs. Maroney was known to visit relatives. Kate Warne, Pinkerton's female detective, was dispatched to the same town as soon as Fox reported that Mrs. Maroney had come there. Kate, dressed in the latest fashions, was to pose as the wife of a wealthy businessman, and meet Mrs. Maroney. Soon she was able to arrange an introduction, and the two began a casual friendship. Eventually Kate let it slip that her husband had made his money from forging bank bills.

The court date was rapidly approaching and the extensive surveillance had not yet yielded any solid new evidence. Pinkerton decided it was time to turn up the heat on Nathan Maroney. He believed that Maroney probably could not easily access the monies he had stolen. They were hidden away somewhere. He therefore probably had little loose cash. Pinkerton convinced Sanford to have Maroney re-arrested on vague charges of conspiracy. Soon Maroney was locked up in a prison in New York, awaiting a preliminary hearing and setting of bail.

Pinkerton then had arranged for another of his men, John White, to be locked up in the same cell as Maroney, posing as a forger, with John Bangs, Allan's right hand man, posing as White's attorney. To make things really uncomfortable for Maroney, Pinkerton began sending anonymous letters to Maroney that stated Mrs. Maroney was having an affair while he was stuck in jail. She actually was having a fling, but unbeknownst to her the suitor was another undercover Pinkerton man. Maroney was miserable and desperate, fearing he was losing his pretty young wife to another man. His cellmate, John White was sympathetic, agreeing with him that Maroney was in a desperate and unfortunate situation. Within days the cellmate's attorney (Pinkerton's lieutenant) came to the jail cell with news that he had bribed the judge and White was soon to be set free. Maroney, at wits end, begged White, once he was released, to use his connections to arrange a bribe so that he too could be set free. White explained that that would cost a lot of money.

Maroney managed to get a note sent to his wife telling her to get the stolen money and meet with John White to pass it to him. When she got the note Mrs. Maroney was uncertain of what she should do. Perhaps she was having too much fun with her new suitor, perhaps she feared getting caught. She went to her good new friend, Kate Warne, for advice. Kate assured her that saving her husband was the right and best course. Mrs. Maroney then dug up the buried Adams Express money and delivered it to John White, as her husband had instructed. Pinkerton informed all of his operatives to maintain their covers until the day of Nathan Maroney's trial on Sanford's original charges.

As the trial unfolded on the first day Maroney felt sure the bribe had worked and that he was on the way to gaining his freedom. His beautiful wife was in the courtroom, as were many old friends and supporters. No solid evidence had been presented. The second day was quite different. The first witness the prosecution called was his old cellmate, John White, now identified as an agent of the Pinkerton Agency. Maroney nearly fainted, then regained his composure and requested that his attorney change his plea to guilty. He received a sentence of 10 years at hard labor in the state penitentiary, and his wife collapsed in hysterics. Her sentence was suspended.

***

The Pinkerton agency's success in closing this case, along with their work on kidnapping, counterfeiting and railroad robbery cases, resulted in their signing four of the nation's largest railroad companies as clients. On February 1, 1855, Allan Pinkerton signed a contract with the Illinois Central Railroad to provide security for their passengers and cargo. The corporate attorney who drafted that agreement for the railroad was an Illinois lawyer named Abraham Lincoln. He and Pinkerton would meet many times in the next few years, and that acquaintance would prove crucial to Allan Pinkerton's future.

In 1857 Allan met the chief engineer for the Illinois Central Railroad while both were riding in the same rail car. George Brinton McLellan was a graduate of West Point who had fought in the Mexican War, built several military fortifications around the country, and was sent by the US Army to study the tactics and organization of European nations. Eventually he resigned his commission and began a career as a civil engineer for the Illinois Central Railroad. The two men became friends, sharing much in common. Both were short in stature, offset by towering egos. Both had tremendous power of concentration, and were able to absorb, recall and properly apply large amounts of detail to the task at hand. Both men were quick to dismiss those they felt lacked seriousness, and both felt they were destined for greater things. In a few short years both would assist each other in defending the nation from its greatest threat to survival.

The abolition issue was causing more and more dissension throughout the country as the 1850's neared an end. The Pinkerton's new home at 5th and Franklin Street was often crowded with runaway slaves seeking a safe haven on their way to Canada. Once this kind of activity was frowned upon and could cause bad feelings between neighbors. Now, in 1858, with Congress's passage of the Fugitive Slave Law, it was illegal. Pinkerton was living a double life, upholding the laws through his agency's work, and breaking the law at home by following his political convictions. If this philosophical conundrum caused him any distress he did not leave any record of it.

A man named John Brown was the prophet of the abolitionist movement in the late 1850's. Brown was over six feet tall, rail thin, and possessed piercing, steel blue eyes that seemed to glow with an inner fire when he was aroused. He had gained national attention by leading a raid on the town of Pottawatomie, Kansas, in 1856; killing five innocent civilians there as retaliation for the earlier murder of five Free State (abolitionist) men. He went on to lead other raids, generally terrorizing pro-slavery settlers. With authorities hot on his trail, Brown left Kansas with a dozen runaway slaves and fled to Chicago, Illinois. On the evening of March 11, 1859 he showed up at the door of Allan Pinkerton's home, looking for a place to rest and have his runaway slaves fed and sheltered. Allan answered the door and, seeing Brown standing there in the darkness, embraced him and brought his party inside. Pinkerton took it upon himself to gather funds for Brown and his party by asking his fellow abolitionists in Chicago for donations. After a few days he managed to round up $600 and the promise of a railroad car stocked with provisions to carry the runaways secretly to Detroit. Allan, his wife and son rode in their carriage to the Chicago train station and met with John Brown, who was there to take an early train to Detroit to complete plans for the runaway slaves to escape to Windsor, Canada. As Brown climbed aboard the train Allan said to his son "Look well upon that man. He is greater than Napoleon and just as great as George Washington."

One the runaways crossed safely into Canada Brown turned his attention to a new plan, armed evolution against the United States. On Sunday, October 16, 1859, Brown and twenty-one other men captured a federal armory in Harpers Ferry, Virginia, hoping to steal rifles and ammunition to arm slaves in the South, who they believed would rise up in rebellion against their masters when they heard news of the approach of Brown's little army. The U.S. cavalry responded quicker than Brown anticipated, surrounded his men in the armory and forced their surrender.

During Brown's incarceration and trial, Allan Pinkerton did whatever he could to aid him. He raised money for Brown's defense, wrote letters to influential men asking them to petition the judge for a stay of execution and wrote prominent politicians asking them to plead with the judge for mercy in sentencing.

John Brown was convicted of attempting an armed insurrection against the United States of America and was sentenced to be hung. On December 2, 1859, in Charlestown Virginia, the sentence was carried out. Robert E. Lee was in attendance, along with T.J. Jackson (later known by the nickname Stonewall), a Professor at the nearby Virginia Military Institute, Jefferson Davis, the Secretary of War, and a popular actor named John Wilkes Booth. When the trapdoor was sprung and Brown's neck broken in the downward fall, the local troop commander pronounced the words "So perish all such enemies of Virginia, all such foes of the Union." Allan Pinkerton and millions of others did not agree with that sentiment.

***

In November, 1860 Abraham Lincoln, the corporate attorney for the Illinois Central Railroad, was elected President. Lincoln was not an abolitionist. He repeatedly stated that it was his position that the U.S. government had no constitutional authority to meddle with slavery in the states where it already existed, andbut that under no circumstances should it be allowed to spread into any U.S. territories. Slavery would be contained, and, Lincoln believed, would then die a slow but certain death. This was close enough to Pinkerton's views to make Lincoln his preferred candidate in the election. Lincoln was in Springfield with his family and campaign managers, busily planning a circuitous railroad trip to Washington, D.C. for the inauguration, which was to take place in March, 1861. The election campaign had stirred the coals of the slavery debate white hot, and the President-elect was receiving bundles of death threat letters daily. As a routine, he filed them away and discounted their seriousness. He believed, just as a New York newspaper had recently stated, that "assassination is not congenial to the American character."

***

When Lincoln and his entourage reached Philadelphia, they rested at the Continental Hotel. That night Allan Pinkerton travelled to Philadelphia in secret, and explained to the President-elect that if he kept to his planned itinerary, he would be killed in Baltimore, Maryland. The Pinkerton Agency had been working on a security case for Samuel Felton, now President of an east coast railroad, when his operatives stumbled upon the plot.

In January of 1861, the state legislature of Maryland was debating whether or not it should join South Carolina in seceding from the Union. The vote was going to be very close. Samuel Felton, a past client of the Pinkerton Agency who was now president of an east coast railroad company, had received numerous anonymous letters from Southern sympathizers in Baltimore, Maryland, threatening to blow up railroad bridges, tunnels and locomotives if the North made any moves that threatened the South. Felton asked Pinkerton to investigate the threats and advise him as to a proper course of action to avoid damage to company property.

Pinkerton considered the information Felton had sent him, and replied that Felton should order several of his most trusted railroad workers to infiltrate local Maryland militia units to determine whether they were loyal to the Union or the secessionists. Pinkerton's future actions would be guided by what they reported back to Felton. The information those infiltrators gathered convinced Pinkerton to travel to Baltimore, and with the help of his operatives, try to flush out the people behind the threats to railroad property.

In late January two of Pinkerton's operatives, Timothy Webster and

Hattie Lawton (yet another female detective) were dispatched to northern Maryland, to work undercover as a married couple. Webster had heard rumors of a secessionist organization forming there.

Pinkerton set out for Baltimore. He rented an office there as J. H. Hutchison, a businessman from Charleston, Virginia. The office was across the hall from a man named Luckett, one of the leading secessionists in the city. Pinkerton began to frequent bars where he knew Luckett had been seen recently. Soon Luckett and Pinkerton met and were exchanging stories about their mutual hatred for Lincoln and the Union.

One evening Luckett introduced Hutchison (Pinkerton) to Cypriano Ferrandini, a charismatic former revolutionary who had fled from Italy to escape execution for his treasonous activity there. Ferrandini, now earning his way in America as a barber, was the Captain of a Maryland militia unit that was suspected of secessionist sympathies. He was also a member of a private para-military group called the Constitutional Guards, who later were suspected of promoting riots and committing acts of murder and sabotage.

Pinkerton later described him as he appeared when they first met.

As he spoke his eyes fairly glared and glistened, and his whole frame quivered, but he was fully conscious of all he was doing.

Pinkerton quickly realized that this barber could exercise a certain power over his audience, and that he was

a man well calculated for controlling and directing the ardent minded. Even I myself, felt the influence of this man's strange power, and wrong though I knew him to be, I felt strangely unable to keep my mind balanced against him.

Ferrandini was hesitant at first to speak openly to Hutchison/Pinkerton, but soon warmed to the task of savaging the Union and its President-elect.

Murder of any kind is justifiable and right to save the rights of the Southern people. If I alone must do it, I shall. Lincoln shall die in this city.

Harry Davies, another one of Pinkerton's operatives, was also in Baltimore working undercover. He managed to make the acquaintance of a young southerner named Otis K. Hilliard, who was fond of making open statements about his "willingness to die to rid his country of a tyrant such as he considered Lincoln to be." After several nights of drinking and carousing together, Hilliard finally felt like he could trust Davies. He mentioned a good friend named Ferrandini, and confided to Davies that he was involved with the man in a plot to murder the President-elect while he was switching trains in Baltimore. Davies asked if Hilliard could introduce him to this brave, bold fellow, and Hilliard agreed to do so.

Pinkerton also heard from Timothy Webster in northern Maryland. Webster and his beautiful young "wife" had been fully accepted into their little northern Maryland community, and Webster had managed to join a Confederate militia unit there. He soon learned from some of their officers that when they received word of the President-elect's assassination in Baltimore they were going to cut the telegraph lines to Washington D.C. and blow up railroad bridges to prevent Federal troops from coming into their state.

All of this information that Pinkerton and his operatives had gathered led him to the conclusion that a lot more was being planned in Baltimore than just the destruction of railroad property. The President-elect had to be warned of the threat to his life that existed in Maryland. Pinkerton sent a note to Norman Judd, a mutual friend of his and Lincoln's, who was in charge of the President-elect's inaugural entourage. "I have a message of importance for you. Where can it reach you by special messenger?" Judd replied that the messenger should try to meet them in either Columbus, Ohio on February 13th, or Pittsburg, Pennsylvania, on the 14th. Pinkerton was too worried to wait that long and immediately dispatched an operative to meet the Lincoln party in Cincinnati, Ohio. Judd received Pinkerton's warning there. He read Pinkerton's note detailing what he had heard and told the messenger that Pinkerton would have to come up with more hard evidence before he would speak to Lincoln about changing the itinerary of the trip. Lincoln's inaugural train continued east the next morning, despite the warning from Pinkerton.

In New York, Judd received additional information on the Baltimore plot from Kate Warne, whom Pinkerton had sent to urge Judd to convince Lincoln to alter his travel plans. Judd made no such promise, but did agree to let Allan Pinkerton meet with the President-elect in two days, when he would be in Philadelphia, Pennsylvania. Lincoln had been invited to appear there to raise a flag in front of Independence Hall that bore an additional star representing the recent admission to the Union of Kansas as a free state.

On February 21st Lincoln met with Allan Pinkerton at the Continental Hotel in Philadelphia and heard firsthand about the plots being hatched in Baltimore to kill him. Judd urged Lincoln to heed Pinkerton's warning. Lincoln was not yet convinced that the plot was real or as serious as was being reported. It took a visit from Fred Seward, son of Lincoln's future Secretary of State William Seward, to finally convince him. Fred carried a message from his father, endorsed by Commander in Chief of the U.S. Army, Winfield Scott, detailing the same Baltimore plot, which Scott's spies had discovered in an investigation completely separate from Pinkerton's. Together, these reports were enough to convince the President-elect to approve Pinkerton's plan to secretly move him through Baltimore. The President-elect knew that Democratic newspapers would ridicule him for sneaking into the capital, but he decided he could stand the heat if that guaranteed his being able to take the oath of office in March. Above all, the nation needed the continuity and calm of an uneventful inauguration.

In the early morning hours of February 23, 1861, Allan Pinkerton, Elihu Washburne, Illinois Congressman and old friend of President–elect Lincoln and William Seward, Lincoln's choice to be his Secretary of State, stood staring into the misty gloom at a train that had just pulled into the station. They believed that Abraham Lincoln would be on the train, having passed though Baltimore in the dead of night, far earlier than his official itinerary had said he would. Only a few passengers had disembarked and it seemed that no one else was on board. Just then they spotted a familiar, tall figure emerging from the last car. Lincoln was wearing a soft felt hat instead of his usual stovepipe, and was wrapped in a thick shawl, looking more like "a well-to-do farmer" than President-elect of the United States.

Pinkerton had done his duty, seeing the President safely to Washington D.C. Cipriano Ferrandini, Otis Hilliard and other leaders of the Baltimore plot were never arrested. They disappeared quickly after President Lincoln failed to appear at the Baltimore train station as expected. Ferrandini eventually reappeared in Baltimore and resumed his work as a barber, dying there in 1910 at age 88.

***

In May of 1861 Pinkerton was called to Washington, where he met with the President and the cabinet. They questioned him about how the Union government could go about gathering information about the many Confederate sympathizers in Washington D.C., and throughout the North. He outlined some possible strategies for them, and left expecting to receive a call back. When he did not hear from them the next day, he left for Chicago, realizing that with all the confusion caused by the early days of fighting Southern forces, there would be no call back.

Three days after his meeting with Lincoln and his cabinet, Pinkerton received a letter from an old friend, George McLellan. The former chief engineer of the Illinois Central Railroad, now a Major General in charge of the Department of the Ohio, asked Pinkerton to join him in Cincinnati, Ohio, and to come secretly, undercover.

McLellan asked Pinkerton to form a Secret Service Department for his army. After receiving permission from the Commander in Chief of the U.S. Army, Winfield Scott, Allan agreed, gathering all his senior operatives to the city.

Pinkerton's work for McLellan included a great many intelligence gathering activities. His detailed reports to McLellan included locations and descriptions of rebel fortifications, troop strength and movements; specific listings of the type of weapons in enemy positions and their capabilities; names of Union sympathizers living in areas held by the rebels who might provide additional information and assistance to Union troops; and analysis of enemy morale.

In July of 1861, Union forces suffered a crushing defeat at the battle of Bull Run, near Manassas, Virginia, just 30 miles south of Washington. The army retreated, then disintegrated into a mob and fled the battlefield, steaming into the streets of the capital. Citizens were in a state of panic, fearing Rebel cavalry would soon be entering the city on the heels of their defeated troops. President Lincoln sent for George McLellan and made him commander of the Army of the Potomac, responsible for the defense of Washington D.C. One of McLellan's very first acts was to send for Allan Pinkerton, asking him to come to the capital and set up an intelligence service for the nation's largest army. Pinkerton explained what McLellan expected of him.

I was to have as much strength of force as I required. I was to go whenever the army moved…All spies, counter brands, deserters, refugees and prisoners of war coming into our lines from the front were to be carefully examined by me, and their statements taken in writing.

Once in Washington, Pinkerton was nearly drowned by the flood of paperwork that he encountered. Major General George McLellan was a commander noted for his concern for the welfare of his troops. He believed that the Commissary Department, responsible for acquiring and distributing all the clothing, food, weapons and ammunition the army needed to wage war, was rife with corruption and inefficiency. He instructed Pinkerton and his men to add investigation of that department's workings to their list of responsibilities.

***

Washington D.C. was located right along the Mason-Dixon Line, and many of its longtime residents harbored secessionist sympathies. Pinkerton and his secret service spent a good deal of time observing the comings and goings of citizens suspected of spying for the Confederacy. It was while doing this type of routine surveillance that Pinkerton entered into one of his most famous cases.

Rose O'Neal Greenhow was an attractive widow, with dark eyes and a clear olive complexion. Her husband had died in a freak accident in San Francisco, after which she and her four children had moved back to Washington D.C., where she had been raised. She became friends with Harriet Buchanan, niece of then President James Buchanan, and occasionally helped host parties for them at the White House. Witty, charming, beautiful and available, Rose was irresistible to the powerful and influential men of the capital.

By 1861 Rose was a good friend of William Seward, Lincoln's Secretary of State, and was rumored to be carrying on an affair with Senator Henry Wilson, a married man and chairman of the powerful Military Affairs Committee. She was also a spy for the Confederacy. In July she had managed to smuggle a message to General Pierre Beauregard, commander of rebel forces in Virginia, containing detailed information about a planned Union advance toward Manassas, Virginia, (information possibly gathered from pillow talk with Senator Wilson). With that early warning, Beauregard's army had been able to soundly defeat attacking Union forces at Bull Run, and drive them back to the outskirts of Washington D.C.

Rose felt quite safe, with all her powerful friends and social activities serving as cover for her espionage. She continued gathering information and passing it through the lines to Confederate contacts in the South.

Months after the Union debacle at Manassas, Allan Pinkerton received a report from one of his operatives working undercover in Baltimore, Maryland. It contained a list of the names of several Confederate agents active in the U.S. capital. It also contained the name of Rose Greenhow, a person whose name had been brought up repeatedly in conversation by southern sympathizers. As a result of this report, Pinkerton assigned five men to tail Mrs. Greenhow as she travelled about Washington.

In August of 1861, Allan was informed that a young War Department officer named Captain Ellison was suspected of copying and stealing confidential files. As he had frequently in the past, Allan decided to work this case in the field with his men, so that he could keep his detective skills honed sharply. Pinkerton and two of his operatives were following their target one rainy evening when Ellison suddenly ducked into the doorway of a house. They thought he might be sheltering from the rain, but then a light in the house came on and the door opened. It was Rose O'Neal Greenhow. She pulled him into the house and closed the door. Pinkerton snuck up to the window and peeked inside. He saw the two embrace and head upstairs. An hour later, Pinkerton and his men, thoroughly soaked by the evening downpour, saw Rose and Ellison come back downstairs. The couple exchanged a few words, kissed, and Ellison departed. Pinkerton raced down the streets to the War Department and informed the Secretary of War of what he had seen. Ellison was apprehended coming home from Mrs. Greenhow's home and his quarters were searched. Evidence was recovered that proved Ellison had been stealing secret documents. He was immediately placed under arrest and taken to jail. In the morning Ellison was found hanging in his cell. He had killed himself before he could be questioned.

Pinkerton's agents kept Rose Greenhow under surveillance for the next few days while a civil warrant for her arrest was prepared by authority of the War Department. On August 23rd Pinkerton and a group of his agents knocked on the front door of Rose O'Neal Greenhow's home. When she opened the door and realized who was confronting her she tried to swallow a note she was carrying. Pinkerton managed to get it from her and unraveled it. It was a coded message. A search of the premises yielded many incriminating notes she had compiled about army munitions, armaments, and regimental troop strengths. Then they discovered her diary. It contained the names of Southern couriers and agents working in the capital. Also named were lawyers, bankers, politicians, railroad men and businessmen from whom Rose had gathered information.

Rose and her young daughter, were confined in Old Capitol Prison. Her friendship with so many prominent Washingtonians assured her of good treatment there. In any event, her stay was brief. By July of 1862 she was released on parole and sent to the South. After being feted there as a heroine, she travelled to England where she arranged for the publication of her prison diary. "My Imprisonment and The First Year of Abolition Rule at Washington" was published in November and became a best seller. She became engaged to a Duke, and agreed to deliver English diplomatic correspondence to Jefferson Davis in the U.S. before the wedding. Her ship foundered off the east coast in a storm. Most passengers were rescued, but Rose Greenhow drowned, having been pulled under the waves by the weight of gold sovereigns she had sown into her corset for use if she had been captured by Union forces.

***

Allan Pinkerton grew to admire George McLellan as the early months of the war months passed. It was an odd pairing, they being as different as they were similar. McClellan was a cultured man who mingled in the highest strata of society. Pinkerton was a rough edged child of the Scottish tenements, who was not above using his fists when necessary to apprehend a criminal. McLellan had a West Point education in engineering, while Pinkerton had barely any formal education. Yet both were ambitious men who could master voluminous details and focus with unshakeable intensity on their chosen goal. McLellan was a Democrat, and as such, a man who did not support interfering with the institution of slavery in the South. Pinkerton was an ardent abolitionist, though not a supporter of Lincoln.

Historians have long debated the accuracy of the intelligence that the Pinkerton-led Secret Service supplied George McLellan during his time as commander of Union forces. President Lincoln, frustrated by McLellan's frequent calls for more reinforcements before moving against enemy forces, described him as having a case of "the slows." McLellan may have been reacting to reports from Pinkerton that set the number of the enemy facing him at a much higher number than later proved to be true. Searches of the records seem to show that while some estimates were too high, others were accurate. It is more likely that McLellan was influenced by his political philosophy than by Pinkerton's troop estimates. McLellan wanted a negotiated peace with the South, which would see them returned to the Union with their institution of slavery intact. He did not want to inflict a crushing defeat on the South that might humiliate them so much that they would not be willing to come to the peace table to discuss terms of reunion.

After two years of stalemate between McLellan's Army of the Potomac and Confederate General Robert E. Lee's Army of Northern Virginia, President Lincoln finally removed McLellan from command. Pinkerton saw McLellan as a man "struck down at the peak of his career by secret enemies who endeavored to prejudice the mind of the President against his chosen commander...wily politicians...jealous minded officers." Upset by what he saw as an unfair dismissal of his friend, Pinkerton resigned his commission as a

Major in the U.S. Army, though he and his Agency continued to do work for the government.

In 1864, George B. McLellan was nominated by the Democratic Party as their candidate for President of the United States. "Little Mac," as he was known affectionately by his men, expected strong support from his soldiers in the election. He failed to get it, with President Lincoln earning the lion's share of the enlisted men's vote and thereby gaining a crushing re-election victory. McLellan resigned from the army on the day of the election.

Allan spent the closing months of the war investigating reports of massive frauds in cotton sales in New Orleans. He successfully uncovered a vast web of corrupt officials and businessmen who had defrauded the government out of huge sums of money, much of which was recovered and returned.

***

By its end, the Civil War had resulted in great losses and surprising gains for the country. The North spent twelve billion dollars and the South four billion to wage the conflict. Over a million American lives had been lost. Yet the need for swift transportation of troops had forced expansion of the railroad systems, and the need to be able to communicate between far flung forces had encouraged the spread of telegraph lines all across the country. Foundries and factories had been built to supply the vast quantity of war material needed, medical advances had been made in wound treatment, and hospital sanitation procedures had improved greatly. America after the war was a different nation than the one that existed in 1861.

The Pinkerton Agency had changed along with the nation. It was now called The National Detective Agency, and to reflect its new name, branches were opened in New York and Philadelphia, in addition to the home office in Chicago. Despite its growth, Allan Pinkerton still insisted on micromanaging its affairs. He insisted on receiving detailed reports from his operatives about even the most trivial of cases. George Bangs, now his superintendent of the New York office, quickly learned to deflect his boss's angry complaints about the slowness or inadequacy of reports received. This need to control every detail would prove nearly fatal to Allan in years to come.

On January 6, 1866 the largest train robbery to date in the United States occurred near New Haven, Connecticut. Thieves broke into a railroad boxcar, opened two safes belonging to the Adams Express Company and made off with $700,000 in cash, bonds and jewelry. Edward Sanford, president of the Adams Express Company, once again called on Allan Pinkerton and his National Detective Agency to solve the crime.

Allan, along with a group of his detectives, travelled to the scene of the crime. After an intense search of the surrounding area they found the point on the tracks where the robbery had actually taken place. Focusing there, they soon discovered a bag containing $5,000 in gold coins, part of the missing shipment. It appeared that during their getaway the culprits had accidentally dropped the bag. The detectives then headed to the nearest town, asking questions of the store proprietors. They learned from a stable owner that a group of men had tried to rent a horse and buggy on the night of the robbery, but the owner refused them because they were not from the town. He told the detectives that he thought the strangers had stayed in a local hotel. Once they located the hotel, its proprietor gave the detectives a description of the men, and said he overheard them say they were heading to a nearby town, Norwalk. In Norwalk they found the suspects gone, but did get a couple of names, John Grady and an older man named Tristam. They tracked Tristam to New York City, where he had travelled to lay low with his married sister in a small East side apartment. When the Pinkerton detectives raided the apartment, they found Adams Express bags containing $113,000. They located Tristam at a nearby saloon and placed him under arrest. He soon gave up the rest of the gang and the whereabouts of the remaining stolen valuables. The case received wide press coverage, and the reputation of the National Detective Agency was greatly enhanced.

***

Several months after the conclusion of the Adams Express case, Pinkerton and his detectives were brought in on an even more challenging one. On October 6, 1866, three masked men boarded an Ohio and Mississippi Railroad train as it pulled out of Seymour, Indiana. They overpowered the Adams Express messenger in the company's special armored car, pushed two safes off the train, and then jumped off themselves. The thieves cracked open one safe and took out $15,000 in cash, but could not open the second one. Then they disappeared. Adams Express once again contacted Allan Pinkerton. Pinkerton travelled to Seymour, Indiana, where he determined, after some interviews with locals, that a gang was operating in the area. Headed by the Reno brothers, Frank, John, Simeon and William, they had robbed, pillaged, and intimidated citizens and businesses in the area for some time. Based on testimonies he had gathered, Allan believed that it was John and Simeon Reno, along with another gang member named Franklin Spark, who had held up the train.

Allan called in a group of his detectives, who, in his usual style, he had infiltrate the town of Seymour undercover. One detective, Dick Winscott, posing as a shady character who was escaping trouble out East, opened a dark and dingy saloon in the town. Soon it attracted the lesser elements of the local citizenry, including the Reno brothers. The Renos continued to stage robberies in the area, and Pinkerton was growing frustrated, unable to catch them in the act. After some serious drinking at his establishment one night, Dick Winscott talked John Reno and Franklin Sparks into posing for a photograph with him. Once developed and forwarded to the Chicago office, it went up on the Pinkerton Rogues Gallery Wall. Pinkerton was soon able to get confirmation that it was the Reno gang that had committed the latest series of robberies in the Seymour area. He wanted to arrest them, but feared that a shootout would erupt in town if he tried, and innocent civilians might be injured. It was decided that they would kidnap John Reno, the ringleader. Pinkerton dispatched a group of his toughest operatives to Seymour and told Dick Winscott to use some ruse to convince John Reno to visit the train station with him when Pinkerton's men were scheduled to arrive. The plan worked perfectly. John Reno was arrested, placed on the next train to depart town and taken to the Missouri State Penitentiary.

That was not the end of the case. The other gang members, despite the loss of their leader, were still on the loose, looting and terrorizing. The Pinkerton detectives set off on a chase to round them up. Simeon and William Reno were arrested in southern Indiana. Frank Reno and the few remaining members of the gang were reported to have fled to Windsor, Ontario, just across the river from Detroit. Allan headed there himself, and, together with a posse of local law enforcement officers, cornered and arrested Frank Reno and three other gang members in their hideout in a rundown section of the town.

Frank, Simeon and William Reno, along with another gang member named Charlie Anderson, were incarcerated in a prison in New Albany, Indiana, awaiting trial. Before that trial could be organized, a mob of enraged citizens, frustrated at justice delayed broke into the prison, dragged the four gang members out of their cells, and hung them from the beams of the jailhouse.

Ending the reign of the Reno Gang had taken two years of travel across six states and two Canadian Provinces, and painstaking detective work, some of it undercover in dangerous situations. Twice in Canada, friends of the Reno Gang had tried to have Allan Pinkerton killed. On both occasions the tough Scotsman had met the assassins head on, fought and disarmed them. The case exhausted Pinkerton, though he never complained or directly commented on that fact. It did, however, show in his treatment of subordinates. In late December 1868, he wrote a blistering, critical letter to his Superintendent of the New York office, George Bangs, in response to Bangs' statement that he was having some difficulty with the staff there. He instructed Bangs to give those "incompetents the boot. Show your fist, let them be kicked down the stairs as quickly as possible." Pinkerton needed to slow down and prioritize the use of his time, but he could not yet bring himself to do it.

Overwork was not the only cause of Pinkerton's exhaustion in late 1868. The year had begun on a sad note, with news of the early passing of his first female detective, Superintendent of the Female Detective Bureau, Kate Warne. After a long illness, Kate had died at the age of 35 years.

***

In early 1869, while working at his desk in Chicago, he felt a terrible pain in his head and saw nothing but bright, blinding light. He had suffered a stroke. For the next two years he was paralyzed down his right side and unable to speak. He travelled to New York, where specialists administered a series of treatments. After a year, they told Allan that he would spend the rest of his life in a wheelchair, and released him to go back home. He would not accept their judgment. He spent the next six months at a spa in Michigan, where the mineral baths were reputed to have healing powers. He devised his own exercise regimen to follow each bath, and tortured his body with continuous stretching and attempts to walk. By late 1870 he was boasting to his friends that he could walk twelve miles a day. With sheer force of will he had proved the doctors wrong.

During his recovery, Pinkerton made a decision that had been too long in coming. He turned over much of the responsibility for the running of the National Detective Agency to his sons, William and Robert. He used the spare time that gave him to build a new home for him and his wife on property he owned in Onarga, Illinois, eighty miles south of Chicago. He designed every detail of the home, including the extensive gardens that would surround it. He built "The Larches," like a fortress, with guardhouses at each entrance. The main building, known as "the Villa," was topped with a square tower that afforded a good view of the whole property for the sharpshooters stationed there. A racetrack, fish pond and wine pavilion were also built on the grounds. Here Allan and his wife began to entertain on a lavish scale, for the first time in their lives. The fabulously wealthy Commodore Vanderbilt dined with them, as did Chief Justice of the U.S. Supreme Court Salmon P. Chase and President Ulysses Grant.

On the evening of October 8, 1871, only three weeks after Pinkerton had decided he was strong enough to return to work, a fire started on the south side of Chicago. High winds caused the fire to spread rapidly, and the city, mostly built of wood, was nearly destroyed before the fire could be contained. Three and a half miles of the city center, containing over 17,000 buildings and property worth over $196,000,000 were destroyed. Pinkerton's extensive case files from the Civil War were burnt, and the Rogues Gallery of criminal photos he had amassed over the years was reduced to cinders. His losses from The Great Chicago Fire were great, but to balance them, his National Detective Agency got many contracts from businessmen in the city to guard their remaining goods, and from the city itself to protect burned districts from looters.

Pinkerton showed his resilience and toughness in a letter he sent George Bangs after his stroke and the Chicago fire. "I will never be beaten, never. Not all the Furies of Hell will stop me from rebuilding immediately."

1872 proved a real test to Pinkerton's resolve to never be beaten. The country's economy went into a tailspin after the collapse of New York financier Jay Cooke's Northern Pacific Railway. Railroad construction ceased, causing steel and iron manufacturers to fail. Many people lost their jobs, and those who kept them suffered wage cuts. Not surprisingly, crime rates climbed, keeping Pinkerton's Agency busy. But that piecemeal work was not as lucrative as the contracts he usually signed with the railways and other big companies.

Desperate to take any good paying assignment, Pinkerton agreed with the Spanish government to assign his operatives to investigate a wealthy Cuban sugar planter named Manuel de Cespedes. An insurrection against repressive Spanish policies on the island had been raging for months. Pinkerton's operatives reported to headquarters that Cespedes was guilty of nothing more than advocating the very principles that Allan Pinkerton, the Old Chartist, had fought for back in Scotland as a youth. When the Spanish government began a particularly brutal campaign against the rebels, committing atrocity after atrocity, Pinkerton recalled his operatives from Cuba and terminated the agreement with the Spanish government. Critics point to this decision by Pinkerton to aid a repressive regime in Cuba as a sign that he could overlook his principles for the right price. At least he finally came to his senses.

The National Detective Agency was in financial trouble. In August, 1872, Pinkerton wrote an anxious letter to his chief operative in the Chicago office.

...on every hand I am in debt. It is nearly Saturday and you and I know I have to pay everyone. I must have money for they must have money. I would not for anything allow them to go without their wages, but how am I going to get the money unless you and the others do your duty and bring in the money?

Somehow, Pinkerton found a way to pay his employees, and would continue to do so.

Beset by financial difficulties and still recovering from the effects of his stroke, Allan looked for diversions to ease his mind. He found writing was a way for him to escape the real world and relax. In 1873 he published his first book, "Bankers, their Vaults, and the Burglars." It mixed in reminiscences of old cases with practical suggestions for how to secure things of value. It sold well, and as a result in 1874 Pinkerton published a second book, entitled "The Expressman and the Detective," which dramatized some of his harrowing experiences in crime fighting. Eighteen books bearing his name as author were eventually published. It is believed that he actually wrote only five of them; the remainder were ghostwritten from outlines that he supplied to his publisher.

***

Pinkerton's late life was dominated by three major challenges, two of them professional and one very personal. The first challenge was presented by Jesse Woodson James, a former Confederate guerilla who turned to robbery and murder after the war.

Jesse James led a gang that included his older brother Frank; Cole, Jim and John Younger; Clell and Ed Miller; and Bob and Charlie Ford. At the peak of its fame, the public's opinion of the gang was split. Some thought them avengers of the poor and displaced, robbing from the rich and giving to the poor. President Theodore Roosevelt once called Jesse James America's Robin Hood. Most citizens saw the gang as criminals who stole the savings of hard-working people from local banks to satisfy their own greed.

The National Detective Agency began to track the gang in 1871, but Pinkerton's shaky finances soon halted the pursuit. In 1874 they resumed the chase. William Pinkerton dispatched an operative to travel undercover to Missouri to gain the trust of the gang and hopefully join it. Weeks after John Whicher arrived in Missouri, his body was found by the side of a road, shot multiple times in the head and body. Alan Pinkerton, angered over the loss of the young detective, dispatched two of his most senior and capable detectives to the state. They were joined there by a Deputy Sheriff, and the three, posing as cattle buyers, arranged to meet two of the James Gang, John and Jim Miller, to buy some stolen cattle. When the undercover detectives and sheriff rode up to the designated meeting spot the Youngers opened fire, killing one of the Pinkerton men. The Youngers fled while the fatally wounded detective was tended to by the other two "cattle buyers."

Pinkerton wrote to George Bangs in New York about the ambush.

I know that the James Youngers must be desperate men, and that if we meet it, it must be the death of one or both of us. They must repay…There is no use talking, they must die…I am going myself.

In 1875 a large group of men, including some Pinkerton operatives, surrounded a small log cabin in Clay County, Missouri, known to the locals as Castle James. They had received word that the James Gang was hiding out there. A firebomb was tossed into the window, with the intention of forcing the occupants outside. The second husband of Jesse James mother, Zerelda, hoping to protect those inside the cabin, kicked the firebomb into the fireplace, where it immediately exploded, hurtling shrapnel all around the little room. Zerelda's arm was ripped apart and Jesse's little half-brother was killed. The gang, having earlier received a warning that a posse was headed their way, was nowhere to be found. The public outcry over the incident caused the local sheriff to begin proceedings to indict the Pinkerton detectives involved with first degree murder charges. This was the first serious negative press ever garnered by The National Detective Agency, and it stung Allan badly.

Allan Pinkerton never caught the James Gang; they continued their criminal activities until 1882. The Fords eventually turned on Jesse, and Bob Ford killed him, shooting Jesse in the back of the head while visiting him on his farm. It was Allan Pinkerton's biggest failure.

***

While still involved with the case of the James gang, Allan Pinkerton took on his second great late life challenge when he agreed to investigate a group of Irishmen who were terrorizing workers in the coal fields of Pennsylvania. Franklin B. Gowen, president of the Philadelphia and Reading Coal and Iron Company, had been working with local law enforcement to stop a series of murders that he suspected had been orchestrated by a group called the Molly Maguires. Nothing seemed to work. In desperation he turned to Allan Pinkerton and his detectives.

The Molly Maguires of Pennsylvania took their name from a secret society in Ireland that had formed in the 1840's for the express purpose of hitting back at local officials and landowners who were oppressing them. The Pennsylvania version had less noble aims. They sought to intimidate English, Welsh and German immigrant miners and any police or mine officials who objected to members of their "order." If a member of the Molly Maguires had a grievance against someone, he reported it to his "body master," and that man would arrange for someone who lived a good distance away to come in and kill the offending party. For twenty years the killing continued, with local authorities unable to stop them, and the Molly Maguires continued to grow in numbers and power.

Though an undercover effort had failed with the James Gang, Allan still trusted this oft proven method, and decided to use it again.

It is no ordinary man that I need in this matter. He must be an Irishman and a Catholic, as only this class of person can find admission to the Mollie Maguires...He should be hardy, tough and capable of laboring, in season and out of season, to accomplish unknown to those about him, a single, absorbing subject.

Pinkerton found his man one day while travelling to work on a streetcar. The conductor was an undercover Pinkerton operative working on a pilferage case for the streetcar line. James McPartland was a young, healthy Irish lad who had received some police training before joining Pinkerton's Agency. Allan interviewed him, explained the dangerous nature of the work he would do and told McPartland he would think no less of him if he turned the job down. McPartland accepted his offer.

James McPartland left for the coal fields of Pennsylvania in late October, 1873, posing as Jim McKenna, a fugitive from a murder charge in Buffalo, New York. When he reached his destination, a coal company hired him and he began two plus years of backbreaking work in the mines.

McKenna became popular with fellow miners and the proprietor of the local saloon, where the tall red-head often entertained the crowds singing Irish ballads in his tenor voice. He made the acquaintance of Jack Kehoe, a leader of the Molly Maguires, and by 1874 was inducted into the order. Murders continued as the undercover man sought to gather as much information as he could while building his reputation with the miners. In June McKenna(McPartland) submitted a detailed report to Allan Pinkerton in which he stated that actions by Franklin Gowen and his coal company were responsible for the unrest in the coal fields. Pinkerton forwarded the report to Gowen, who received it and made no comment.

Allan became convinced that even if they could get the Molly Maguires to trial, they would be acquitted by a sympathetic jury of miners from the area. He argued that their best hope was to devise a plan like they did with the Reno Gang, kidnapping the leader and letting vigilantes finish the work on the rest of the order's leadership. His staff disagreed and the idea was shelved.

McKenna (McPartland), per instructions from headquarters, supplied Allan's office with a list of 374 persons he believed were involved with Molly Maguire murders. In late December, 1874, the list somehow was sent out and circulated a handbill in the coal towns without his knowledge. Soon after the handbills appeared someone broke into the home of a local Molly leader on the list, shot the man and his wife to death, and beat or shot and wounded his mother and other members of the family. When McKenna (McPartland) heard of the killings, he dispatched a letter to President Franklin Gowen stating that he was resigning. "I am not going to be accessory to the murder of women and children." Pinkerton was able to convince McPartland that the Agency had nothing to do with the murders, and McPartland decided to continue working undercover on the case.

By late February, 1876, things were getting very dangerous for Jim McKenna. He was told by a friend that leaders of the order suspected he was a traitor and had ordered his murder. He knew it was time to end his undercover work, and boarded a train headed out of the coal fields. A new district attorney was building a case to bring the Molly's to trial, and he needed James McPartland's testimony in order for the charges to stick. McPartland hesitated, knowing this would definitely put his life in even more danger. After receiving assurances from Allan Pinkerton that he would be protected, he agreed to testify. Eleven high ranking Molly Maguire leaders were rounded up and taken into custody. Two days later McPartland testified in court. As the trial progressed more Molly members were arrested. On April 16, 1877, Jack Kehoe was convicted of murder and sentenced to death by hanging. Later, nineteen other Mollies were also convicted and hung.

Some historians argue that the Pinkerton Agency was a tool used by the coal barons in their effort to further oppress starving miners, but it seems clear that this was not the situation that Allan Pinkerton and his men faced. The Molly Maguires were not a benevolent organization seeking to better the lives of working men; rather they were a vicious band of ethnic bigots looking to terrorize those not Irish, or not in sympathy with their cause.

***

Chicago had not only survived the great fire of 1871, it had grown and prospered. Once a city mainly built of wood, it now had many modern buildings built of stone soaring to "scrape the sky" (thus fostering the term skyscraper). When Allan and Joan Pinkerton built their first small home in the town, it numbered only 4,000 inhabitants. In 1876 it boasted a population over 420,000. The land that Allan had bought in the city in 1868 for $50 an acre was now worth $1,500 an acre.

The Agency was now international, and much of its day-to-day activities were being overseen by Pinkerton's two sons. When his health allowed him to, Allan travelled to various Agency offices throughout the country, inspecting their operations. He could not control everything anymore, but was still a force to be reckoned with when he stepped through the door at any one of his offices. Staff dreaded his visits and the critical letters they often received from him. Pinkerton concluded one such letter to his son Robert by reminding him that the National Detective Agency belonged to him, "and I mean to be the Principal of the whole and will continue to be until Death claims me as its own."

While he was often harsh and threatening in his dealings with administrative staff, he seemed to have sympathy for employees in lower positions. Late in 1876 he was made aware that uniformed guards in his security service were guilty of stealing from the businesses whose property they were hired to protect. Rather than fire the men, and thereby make it very difficult for them to find new employment, he reprimanded them and changed their training procedures and operating regulations.

***

Pinkerton's last challenge came from within his own family. Joan, his wife's namesake, and the only one of his four daughters to survive to adulthood, was a bright, attractive, headstrong girl. She had her father's passionate, fiery nature. One of young Joan's friends invited her to a party in the spring of 1876, where she met William Chalmers, the brother of one of her college classmates. He was handsome, well-mannered and college-educated. His father was a successful financier and industrialist and, like Allan Pinkerton, a Scottish émigré. William began to court Joan, with her mother's approval. Allan paid little attention to his daughter's budding romance until he realized that the couple was growing quite close. He had always pictured his daughter staying by his side, he being the sole recipient of her love. He immediately arranged for his daughter to take a tour of Britain and Europe. He hoped that time and distance would cool the young couple's romance. He was wrong. As soon as she returned from her trip, William Chambers came calling again and found Joan eager to resume the romance where they left off.

In November, Joan asked her father for his permission to marry William Chambers. He angrily refused, and a very hot argument ensued between the two quick tempered Pinkertons. With her mother serving as the intermediary, Allan and Joan calmed down, and young Joan very reluctantly agreed to back off on her plan to marry William Chalmers – for the time being. An uneasy peace prevailed between them through the parties of the Christmas season. In mid- January, after retiring to bed, Allan was awakened by some noise downstairs. On descending the stairs to his living room and turning up the gas lamp, he saw his daughter and William Chalmers sitting on the sofa. "What does this mean, Mr. Chalmers? You must leave this house at once and never enter this door." Chalmers left, making no comment, but Joan confronted her father. She was 21 years old, she said to him, and would not be brow beaten by a tyrant. She and William were in love and intended to be married. Allan said if she did, he and his wife would not attend the ceremony. Joan left the room in tears, packed her bags and announced that she was leaving home to live with her brother Robert in New York.

The separation continued for months, with Allan continually writing to Robert in New York, accusing Joan of betrayal and defiance. Slowly his letters reflected a softening tone. "Joan must know that the door is always open, all she has to do is walk in." The person suffering the most from this battle of wills between father and daughter was Allan's wife. In the spring of 1877 she grew ill, and was in bed much of each day. The doctors could find no sign of disease. She probably suffered from stress induced by her constant effort to reconcile her daughter and husband.

By late June young Joan was so concerned about her mother's health that she agreed to return home. She would help her mother regain her health and bide her time before marrying William Chalmers.

The Pinkerton's celebrated their 35th wedding anniversary in 1877, and to commemorate the occasion Allan dictated (after his stroke he had great difficulty doing any more than writing his name) a letter to his "bonnie wee lass."

I know, since you were eighteen years of age you have been battling with me side by side, willing to do anything, to bear our children and work hard, yet you never found fault, you never said a cross word but was always willing to make our home cheery and happy. ..Now Joan, on this day, I wish you to take things easy. When I can get home I will come and sit by you and talk to you and cheer you…this is a dark and gloomy day but wait, it will get to be brighter days and you will be able to go out again…Let us wish we may be spared a few more years …enjoying happiness and health ourselves….

The letter, written out by a secretary, was signed in the shaky, nearly illegible hand of Allan himself.

1879 saw Allan finally approve of Joan's marriage to William Chalmers. The couple had a long and happy marriage, with Joan, like her father, dominating the relationship. William Chalmers became a multi-millionaire industrialist, and together with his wife, became leaders of Chicago society in the early 1900's and chief organizers of the Chicago Opera Company.

Allan slowly but steadily turned over more and more of the responsibility for his Agency to his sons, and his visits to the Chicago office and other branches became very infrequent. He spent more and more time with his wife, sitting with her in their garden.

On October 31, 1883, Pinkerton dictated his last letter to a former slave named C.E. Chapman, who had written to him asking for his autograph, saying how much he admired Pinkerton's fight against slavery.

Your letter…asking me for my autograph has been received. I am not in the habit of giving my autograph to any person, for particular reasons to myself, but in this instance for the purpose you wish it, I forward it to you. I have always been a friend to the colored man and will do anything to secure him his rights.

The winter of 1883 found Pinkerton bedridden, but by the summer of 1884 he was up and feeling better. As he was out for a walk on a day in June, he accidentally tripped and fell, biting his tongue deeply. After three weeks in intense pain the wound grew infected and Pinkerton died from gangrene.

His Agency survives to this day (now publicly held after the death of his great grandson Robert II in 1967), a billion dollar worldwide organization with offices in twenty countries.

***

Allan Pinkerton and his Agency left this country a large legacy. They pioneered investigative techniques, and the expansion and co-ordination of law enforcement efforts to cover the entire nation. Before Pinkerton's detectives began their work, law enforcement was purely local and rarely worked with neighboring communities.

All of the alphabet intelligence agencies in the U.S. government (FBI, CIA, NSA, and DIA) can track their roots back to Allan Pinkerton and his Agency and their work with the U.S. government during the Civil War.

The detective novel found its beginnings in his writings.

The term and concept of the "Private Eye" began with Pinkerton.

Overly intrusive intelligence activities that sometimes stretch or break the law while attempting to enforce it can also be traced back to the National Detective Agency. Entrapment, legal in those days, was perfected by Pinkerton and his men. They were accused of using kidnapping and killings as tools to break enemies, not unlike our CIA today.

The short tempered, self-educated Scotsman, Allan Pinkerton, would probably feel quite at home with our intelligence community of today.

BIBLIOGRAPHY

Abbott, Karen, <u>Liar, Temptress, Soldier, Spy</u>, Harper Collins, 2014

Gallman, Matthew J., <u>America's Joan of Arc, The Life of Anna Elizabeth Dickinson</u>, Oxford University Press, 2006

Girardi, Robert J., <u>Civil War Generals</u>, Zenith Press, 2013

Goodwin, Doris Kearns, <u>A Team of Rivals</u>, Simon and Schuster, 2005

Jordan, David M., <u>Winfield Scott Hancock, A Soldier's Life</u> , Indiana University Press, 1996

Keneally, Thomas, <u>American Scoundrel, The Life of the Notorious Civil War General, Dan Sickles</u>, Anchor Books, 2002

Kunhardt, Dorothy and Phillip, <u>Twenty Days</u>, Castle Books, 1965

Longacre, Edward G., <u>Pickett, Leader of the Charge, A Biography of General George E. Pickett C.S.A.</u>, White Mane Publishing, 1995

MacKay, James, Allan <u>Pinkerton: The First Private Eye</u>, John Wiley and Sons, 1996

Oller, John, <u>American Queen</u>, De Capo Press, 2014

Pitch, Anthony, <u>They Have Killed Papa Dead</u>, Steerforth Press, 2008

Roberts, Cokie, <u>Capitol Dames</u>

Robertson, James, <u>After the Civil War</u>, National Geographic Society, 2015

Stashower, Daniel, <u>The Hour Of Peril</u>, St. Martin's Press, 2013

Swanson, James, <u>Bloody Crimes, The Chase for Jefferson Davis and the Death Pagent For Lincoln's Corpse</u>, Harper Collins, 2010

Stewart, David O., Impeached: <u>The Trial of President Andrew Johnson</u>, Simon and Schuster, 2009

WEB RESOURCES

http://Pabook.libraries.psu.ed Brief biography of Hancock

http://www.biography.com Brief biography of Boyd

http://www.civilwar.org Brief iography of Boyd

http://encyclopediavirginia.org Brief biography of Pickett

http://www.pickettsociety.com Reviews disagreement between Col. Mosby and Pickett over Robert E Lee's responsibility for the defeat at Gettysburg

http://findagrave.com Brief biography of LaSalle Corbell Pickett

http://opinionator.blogs.nytimes.com Follows Dickinson's rise as an orator during the Civil War

http://www.historyswomen.com Brief biography of Dickinson

http://www.pacivilwar150.com Brief biography of Dickinson

http://www.nytimes.com Synopsis of Dickinson's Cooper Institute speech

http://www.civilwar.org Brief biography of Sickles

http://sicklesatgettysburg.com A short but thorough biography of Sickles

http://womenshistory.about.com Brief biography of Kate Chase Sprague

http://www.biography.com Brief biography of Salmon P. Chase

http://www.thrillingdetective.com Brief but thorough biography of Allan Pinkerton

ABOUT THE AUTHOR

Bill Kolasinski began his first attempt at writing a book at the age of 16. High School and college interrupted the effort. Then, after college and a stint in the Army during the Vietnam era, he and two friends wrote two musicals, and saw one come very close to being staged. Life once again interrupted any further writing. 40 years later, retired from a career in sales, living with his wife in Elgin, Illinois near their two daughters, and enjoying his two grandchildren, he has finally found the time and peace of mind to take up the pen and contribute what he can to the field of history he loves so much.

Made in the USA
Columbia, SC
29 December 2019